My Story My Song

Jane Hanzel

My Story, My Song

Copyright © 2014

by Jane Hanzel

Author Consultant
Felice Gerwitz of MediaAngels.com

Cover Illustration
Melinda Martin of TheHelpyHelper.com

Printed in the United States of America

ISBN-13: 978-1505410990

My Story My Song

Dedication

I dedicate this book to John, my husband of nearly fifty-four years, for his love, faithfulness, and joy, during all those wonderful years that we shared, and, to the Holy Spirit, for His constant inspiration, guidance, and encouragement.

Acknowledgment

I want to thank all my children for their help and support, during the several years, in which I wrote this book. And thanks to Felice Gerwitz at Media Angels for the help in editing, and preparing this book for publication. I appreciate all of your help.

Contents

Prologue

I t was a lovely summer in mid-April, 2009. I settled myself in my prayer chair to seek the Lord. As usual, I began by thanking Him for His guidance and direction. I spoke to the Lord in prayer and listened for His answer. To some, this may seem strange, but from experience I learned this was indeed what our Lord wanted from me.

This time I came seeking His advice and discernment in regard to the summer ahead of me. I had my plans but was seeking His. I purchased a condo in Michigan the previous year and wanted to change the landscaping in the front. I asked the Lord for His consent, and I felt a silent nod of approval

Then the question I put before Him: "When do you want me to return to Michigan?"

I was quite surprised when He answered quite promptly. I didn't hear an audible voice, however I knew this instruction came from Him. *Go up in time for Mother's Day this year and attend to the landscaping project so that you can spend the rest of your time on a special project I have for you.*

I was humbled and thanked Him. Then I asked, "What is this special project? How should I prepare?"

I was surprised when I heard in my heart: *I want you to write a book about your life story,*

Many excuses ran through my mind, and I was ready to share them with the Lord.

"How could I possibly do that in one summer? That is a HUGE project! Where do I start? What do you want me to say? What will I do with it when I'm done? I don't know the first thing about publishing a book! Who would want to read such a thing? You can't mean it—that would take a

LOT of time! Will I have enough time to finish such a project? I'm already seventy-nine years old."

I found myself sputtering. Then I stopped, feeling embarrassed by my doubts and boldness in asking so many questions. I immediately apologized for my lack of trust. I spent the rest of the day agreeing to do all that He asked but pleading that I would need His help every step of the way. First I had to be sure that I understood His plan correctly. I humbly asked for confirmation and His direction.

I prayed, praised, listened, sought, and asked. Finally at the end of the day, I felt the Lord say, *Yes, it will all be revealed to you when you need it. Place your trust in Me. Just begin.*

From that day forward in my daily prayer time, I recalled bits and pieces of stories I should include. I started to write down short phrases to remind myself, and gradually it took the form of an outline.

I received confirmation about what I termed, "The Project" when I least expected and from surprising sources. Even when working about the house, not at all focused on the book, my subconscious would give me ideas that tumbled forth from various periods of my life. I soon discovered the title for the book.

One day I found myself humming a song, which I began to sing. I sang this hymn long ago in the little country church I attended. It goes like this, "This is my story, this is my song." I laughed with joy. That is the title for the book! It began to take shape in my mind. But I still had some lingering doubts.

In prayer, I asked Him, "I feel more comfortable about this project, but how can I write about it all? My memories are so disjointed! Where should I start?"

And the answer came: *Just begin at the very beginning. It will all be revealed to you at the proper time.*

So I did.

The Beginning

This is my story, this is my song,
praising my Savior all the day long;
this is my story, this is my song,
praising my Savior all the day long.

Blessed Assurance
Text: Fanny J. Crosby, 1820-1915
The United Methodist Hymnal # 369

When I was born, my arrival made the tenth member of the household. Neither my mother nor my father had ever been married before. I was their first child and tumbled into a busy household made up of members ranging in ages from five to seventy-some years of age. My mother told me that I was born on a wintry day in early April of 1930. The story went like this. She had made many plans for my entry into the family, but I arrived early, about fifteen days early, according to the doctor's estimate. The baking hadn't been done, nor the casserole dishes made. All the carefully thought out plans had to be scraped as I would not wait. My Dad was at work, leaving my grandfather to drive her to the hospital. This was not the way my mother had planned this event.

I was a skinny, red faced, five-pound baby with a mass of inky, black hair, and big, blue eyes like my father. When Mother first saw me she was surprised to see that I had bangs, trimmed neatly above my eyebrows. The nurses explained that my hair was covering my eyes, so when I was cleaned up they decided to cut bangs for me. I was surprised to hear that I had black hair, but my mother told me that all that black hair fell out in big clumps and the new hair came in blond as could be. (It remained blond all though grade school and high school and gradually turned to an ash blond when I became an adult.)

I was told that I adored my grandfather, who lived with us until he died suddenly of heart failure when I was nearly two. The year after he died, the family was at a picnic in the park. I darted away and ran to hug a tall, old man who resembled my grandfather. He was astonished that a little girl would be so excited to see him. Since I grew up in such a large family, I was passed from family member to family member so often that I hardly knew a stranger when there was one.

I have no real memories of the house on North Galena, but my earliest memories took place in the house that my dad built. There was always a lot of activity, as the neighborhood children gravitated to our house. There you could find someone: pounding on the piano, pumping the pump organ, playing in the sand box, or planning some game or event. One of the favorite things to do was plan shows and performances. Mother was quite musical and taught us all to sing and play, so we developed skills to perform skits or musical presentations. Everyone had some part or another as an actor, performer, or simply part of the audience. Sometimes the stage was the front porch and the audience gathered in the lawn. At other times, if the piano or organ was involved, the stage was in the living room and the audience crowded on the stairs and clustered in part of the living room or spilled out on the porch. I loved all the excitement but, as the youngest, was seldom asked to play an active part. Frequently I was part of the audience but occasionally served as a prop, being led about by the actors.

One of my earliest successes in these performances was in a skit that I planned all by myself when I was about four years old. I invited the family out to the front porch after dinner one night. I prepared the stage in advance with cans from cartons of canned milk that had been left on the front porch.

I announced in a loud voice, "Sally Rand and Her Can Dance." I then proceeded to dance my doll up and down the elaborate series of steps, built of the cans of milk that I had stacked around the porch, all while humming a little tune. I was amazed at the response of the audience and the enthusiastic applause that followed. My doll and I were called upon to perform often whenever company arrived. Perhaps my doll's success was due to the fact that at that time there was famous fan dancer that was wowing audiences in Chicago. Her act was billed as "Sally Rand and Her Fan Dance" that was purported to be performed nude behind two very large fans.

Another early memory of that house was waking up from my nap and hunting for my mother. That day I found her in the attic, sorting and cleaning on a bright spring day with a trap door open on the roof. What a mystery. I had no idea how she made the hole in the roof. And you could see the sky and clouds through that hole!

We lived there from 1932 to 1935. My sister was born in December of 1932, and my baby brother was born about a year later but sadly lived only about eight weeks. When the doctor came on one of his many visits to check on Baby George, I was shocked to see that they placed the baby on top of a blanket on the library table! The library table was always treated with great respect. We were never allowed to touch anything on that table or place any of our toys upon it. I was amazed that my mother would allow the baby to be place there and be undressed, no less!

I lived in a blended family, and it wasn't until years later that I would learn the story behind why my parents were raising my cousins. (They belonged to my mother's sister.) At the time, it seemed perfectly natural that the person my sister and I called "Mother or Mama" was called "Auntie" by the "big girls". My cousin Bill, called Daddy "Uncle G". We never questioned this as odd.

As time progressed, our family numbers grew and declined. The oldest cousin, Jerry, went off to the University of Illinois the fall that I was born. By 1934, Bill went to the University, too, and Mary entered nursing school. That left only Alice, Nicky, and Lura, so we were briefly downsized to a family of eight in that winter and then to a family of seven when Baby George died. The older cousins usually came back for summer vacations and summer jobs, so it was still a lively, active family life.

There were many changes in the wind that swept through our country. In 1929, the era of the "roaring twenties" came to an abrupt end with the crash on Wall Street. That event was destined to change and affect all the citizens eventually. Initially, it didn't seem to affect the lives of the people in our little town in Northern Illinois, but gradually this disaster was felt all across the entire country, as workers were laid off, banks failed, bread lines began, and the value of money changed.

For many years, my father was employed as foreman and head maintenance man at the local Borden's Milk Factory. It was there that they canned several different kinds of evaporated milk and made caramels, for distribution locally as well throughout the state. He repaired or built whatever was needed; whether it was a new conveyor line, new windows, steps, additions to the building, and he even installed elevators. One of my fondest memories was the excitement of my father's arrival from work. We hoped he would bring the left-over spill of the last of the caramels. When the line was shut down and cleaned at the end of the day, there was still candy in the mixer. It would arrive wrapped in waxed paper and was about the size of a dinner plate, carefully hidden in Daddy's lunch pail. We loved that candy!

But this came to an abrupt end when the sad day arrived. My father was laid off and the nephew of the plant manager was hired to replace Daddy. My father was disgusted and appalled when he learned the Plant Manager's nephew, a recent graduate from the University, knew absolutely nothing about carpentry. Jobs were almost impossible to find and building came to a standstill. No one wanted to spend or invest money if they could avoid it. Labor unions were not prevalent in most factories in our town, so nothing could be done about the situation. No matter your qualifications, no jobs were available.

With a large family depending upon him, it was a very difficult position for my father to be in. I can imagine that my mother and father talked long hours into the night, away from the children. Eventually they announced that we would soon be moving to a farm that my mother owned in the spring of 1935. My mother and father had worked it out that the large white frame house was to be sold (for a song, as it was later explained). The money that they received from the proceeds of that sale would be used to buy equipment and farm animals to start farming. The previous tenant farmer had moved out, leaving behind unpaid rent and little else.

It caused quite an up-roar from the girls that were in high school. They did not want to leave in the middle of the school year. It wasn't just the fact of leaving their friends but of changing their courses of studies from the larger school to a much smaller, and supposedly inferior high school, which was in the district where the farm was located.

Eventually it was decided that Alice and Nicky could remain in town and finish high school. Arrangements were made for them to live with friends or work as live-in baby sisters for families that my parents knew from the church or the lodge. Mary was working as a student nurse at the local hospital. She would be able to see them from time to time, since she lived in the student nurses' dorm. All the details were worked out, and we were on our way to a new lifestyle.

Life on the Farm

●————————————————————————————————●

Early in March of 1935 a huge moving van was loaded with all our furniture and belongings. We were on our way to begin our life on the farm. It was a much smaller family that made the move, consisting of Mother and Daddy, Lura who was ten, Anne who was two and a half, and myself, soon to be five. It was on the farm that my life really began.

Life was very different on the farm. There were no neighbors within even shouting distance. In fact, we could see only one house, but it was over a mile away. There was no telephone or electricity. We got our water from the well out front, instead of just turning the tap at the sink. Also, there was a cistern that became full of water from the spring rains that drained off the roof. It was covered with big boards, and we were never allowed to stand on it or go near it unless my mother or father was there. They would remove the boards and drop a pail, which was tied to a long rope, down the cistern. It was used to scoop up a pail of lovely soft water that mother loved to use for baths and laundry. They filled the large reservoir in the cook stove in the kitchen; this was used for warm water when we needed it. On wash days, the laundry tubs and the copper laundry tub was heated on the stove. There was an outdoor toilet with three holes. We girls would all go together. Anne, being the smallest sat on the low one, while Lura and I used the higher seats.

There were huge areas to be investigated. We could go anywhere around the house, barn, and orchard but could not go off in the woods unless Mother or Daddy went with us. The barn was huge. It was soon filled with horses, cows, kittens, and a big puppy that grew to be nearly as big as the Shetland pony that Daddy bought for us at a sale. We named the pony Beauty and loved her. She was old and gentle and seemed to know that we didn't know much about ponies. She was patient with us. We patted her and stroked her long nose. Daddy would boost us up on her back, one at a time, and he would lead us about. It was fun! Eventually we became use to her and enjoyed our new live toys.

There was so much to explore. Lura was the first to climb up in the haymow. I soon followed. We were so high above the floor of the barn, yet the roof was still much higher above us. It was a great place to play. We took our dolls up there and played house in corners, making walls of the hay. I was a little afraid of the big cows and horses. I watched with fascination as my mother and father milked them. Occasionally Daddy would squirt us with a spray of warm milk or squirt it to the kittens. They loved it and were always around at milking time.

Lura walked to school each day and carried her lunch pail and her books. The school was a mile and a half away. We saw it when Mother took us there when Lura was enrolled. It was only one big room with lots of desks and children of all ages.

The sky seemed much bigger to us than it did in town. You could see so much more without the other houses in the way. It seemed the stars were much brighter here. Mother got a book about the stars from the library and showed us the different clusters of stars and taught us their names.

Nearly every weekend, Daddy would go shopping at farm sales and bring home all kinds of things, like new animals and machinery. My sister, Anne, was allergic to cow's milk, so Daddy brought a couple of goats. The milk from them seemed to be better for her. Most of us drank the regular milk and saved the goat's milk for Anne. We had baby chickens in the hen house and sheep in the small building that they shared with the goats. However the goats had only a small pen, but the sheep had most of that building, because there were so many of them. There were huge pigs in another building. There were many other buildings, like the machine shed and the corn crib. From time to time it was announced that a baby lamb had been born or baby pigs or a new calf. It was amazing to see them. We named all the calves, because they had different colors and had markings on them, but the lambs and baby pigs all looked alike so we didn't name them. Of course the horses and cows all had names.

In a few short weeks, Daddy was out plowing the fields with the team of horses. He worked long hours in the fields. He came back for dinner at noon and supper at night, but the cows had to be milked and bedded down before we were done and everyone went to bed. It was so quiet on the farm, especially at night. Things settled into a pattern, but it was still very different from being in town. We missed all the people that would pop in and out from the neighborhood.

That sums up our first few months on the farm. There were many other events that I remember, all very fond memories of the good times we had, but there were also troubles. While memories often fade, these remain vivid.

The spring and summers were the best of times. Our big garden was plowed; afterwards the oats and corn were planted. Daddy would hitch up one of the horses and a small plow and dig up the garden. Then we girls and Mama would rake it smooth and start the planting. We raised almost everything, it seemed. The radishes, lettuces, and onions were planted first. Then, when we went to town, Mama would buy about 50 to 75 tomato plants and two or three dozen cabbage plants. The seeds we had ordered from the seed catalogue included peas, green beans, lima beans, cucumbers, nasturtiums, zinnias, four o'clock, and petunias. They were planted next. The rhubarb and asparagus came up every year in an area that Daddy didn't plow. The sweet corn and melons were planted near the house in the corn fields near the big elm trees. By the time that school was out, there were things growing and often something to pick. The first tomatoes were a big event.

In the summer we had chores to do but lots of free time to play in the woods. As we got older, we knew the woods by heart. Then Mother let us go after the cows and bring them home from in the back pasture, because she knew we wouldn't get lost. We named all the various parts of the woods. There was Locust Grove, Strawberry Hill, Violet Hill, Gooseberry Hill, and Niagara Falls, which seemed very tall to us, but it was only about eighteen feet in height. It was dry in the summer, but in the early spring, water flowed down from the sheep pasture above, so it was only then that it was a water fall.

I thought the spring, that covered an area of a least twelve feet across and fifteen feet long was the best part of all the woods. It flowed from the big steep rocks that rose very high above into the creek below. The spring water ran clear until it reached the muddy creek below, twenty or thirty feet from the rocks to the creek. There were several large flat rocks at the edge of the spring and one in the middle of the spring. This was the site of many family picnics. Early in the day, we would be sent to carry the watermelon and put it into the deepest part of the spring to chill. We propped stones around it so that it would not float away. When the rest of the family came down with the picnic baskets, a table cloth would be spread on one of the flat rocks. When Daddy came, he would light the fire in the pit, which we had filled with sticks and leaves. It was there that we roasted wieners and marshmallows. This was really the best place to have a picnic.

The most remarkable thing about the spring was that the water was the same temperature winter and summer. In cold weather, if the cows insisted on going down to the spring for a drink before going to the barn from the back pasture, we would sometimes wade in the spring with our boots on. We could feel the warm water through our rubber boots. In the summer, the water seemed too cold to wade in, and we would see who could stand in it the longest. It really was about 50 degrees winter and summer. It never dried up and flowed about the same amount year after year. We found that there were seven places in which the water bubbled out. Mother said that the Indians called it the Seven Sisters, but I never knew if she just made that up or if she really read it in a book. But we knew that the Indians lived in the area long before we did, and I am sure they loved it as much as we did. Daddy found many arrowheads and, once in the corn field, he found the head of a stone tomahawk. I still have it and keep it by my fireplace.

I started first grade in the fall of the first year we lived on the farm. I was five, and my mother thought I was ready for school, so off I went with my new lunch box. Lura and I walked to school every day. Even when it snowed, we didn't mind the walk. I really liked school. It was fun to be with other children and get to know them. I listened in on their lessons sometimes when I had finished my work. There was always something interesting happening. And recess was always fun.

When summer came and it was warm enough, we were allowed to go swimming in the creek. Our favorite place to swim was by Sunday's Bridge. (That sounds like a funny name for a bridge, but it was because a nearby family's name was Sunday.) At first, Mother would go with us, but later in the summer my mother was convinced that Lura and I could swim just fine, and Anne was learning, so we were safe enough to go without Mother. Sometimes the older girls, like Alice and Nicky, would come out from town for few days, so there was always someone who wanted to go swimming. We would walk down the hill and past the spring a little ways, and there was Sunday's Bridge. On the way back we would pick flowers or berries to bring home, and usually Mother would have a freshly baked cake waiting for us.

We usually went to town once a week. Sometimes it would be Franklin Grove, which was three miles way. Mother sold the eggs at the Royal Blue Grocery store, and we would buy a few groceries or go to the bank. But we liked it best when we went to Dixon, as there were more stores and larger ones, and the library was there. We were each allowed to check out three books apiece. We only went to the library once every two weeks, so I would choose my books carefully. I usually read mine right away and then had to wait until the next time to get a new book.

On Sundays we would usually go to Dixon to attend the Lutheran Church and Sunday school. But it was nearly twelve miles to Dixon. We couldn't go if it had rained, as the roads would be too muddy. We lived about a mile from the paved highway. Our road was not even graveled. Our car could get stuck if the road was muddy. Then Daddy would have to hitch up the team and pull the car out of the mud. What a mess! If it started to rain when we were in town shopping or at church, we would have to quickly leave for home before the roads got too bad. Daddy never worked in the fields on Sunday, but of course we had to take care of the animals and milk the cows. It was always a rush to get everything done and everybody dressed in time to go to church, so sometimes we just didn't go at all.

Mother wanted to visit some of the churches in Franklin Grove, but there wasn't a Lutheran Church there. We tried a few, but Daddy was very unhappy about it. He only wanted to go to the Lutheran Church, but it was hard as Dixon was farther away, and sometimes we had car trouble. Then, when it snowed it was difficult to get out because of the roads. After a year or two, we stopped going at all. Mother would read a passage from the Bible, and we would listen to a church service on the radio.

In the summer there would be picnics and family reunions, always on Sunday afternoon, and there would be the thrasher picnic, which was the high-light of the summer for us.

Thrashing was done by a huge machine that separated the oats from the stalks. The oats flowed out of a huge pipe that funneled the oats into the bins in the crib, and at the same time, the stalks were blown out of another funnel into the loft in the barn. One side of the loft was for straw that we used to bed down the animals, and the other side of the barn loft was for hay. When the oats were ripe, they were cut and tied into bundles by one machine. The bundles were then placed standing up-right in shocks to dry. When it was time, the thrashing would begin. The farmers that raised oats would plan whose farm would be thrashed first and then progress around all the farms until the job was completed. At the end there would be the thrashers picnic at the park.

Mother always looked forward to thrashing time. It was great for Daddy to be together with the other men in the neighborhood. It took everybody to do the job. Wagons were loaded to gather up the oats from the fields and then fed into the thrashing machine. Everyone worked together to get the job done. At noon, the hosting family fed the whole crew, which might be about twenty men. Each housewife served her best meals, so only a light supper was needed at night. Mother would ask Daddy what they had eaten for dinner each day and try to plan what to have when it would be our turn to have the thrasher at our house.

It took a lot of planning. The housewives would help each other out when the thrashers were there, because it took a lot of cooking and dishwashing to serve that many people. We looked forward to our turn with a little fear and dread, hoping that everything would turn out well and go smoothly, but it was exciting and fun. We would set up a bench under the trees with wash basins, pails of water, soap and towels, so that the men could wash up before dinner. When twelve men were ready, we would serve that bunch and then set up for the second seating. In the meantime, the men would sit under the trees or on the porch, rest, joke around, and laugh. It was a wonderful social time for everyone. The young boys would serve as water boys. It was their job to bring cold, fresh water out to the men that were working, and the girls would help out at the house by setting up and preparing for the meals. Everyone had a job to do.

When our turn to host the thrashers was over, Mother would enjoy a little free time knowing that Daddy was enjoying the company of the others and getting a wonderful meal each day. She could use that time to read, relax, and do other projects like sewing or cleaning closets. We looked forward to the picnic at the end. There was always lots of great food, and the owner of the thrashing machine would provide a couple of large five gallon cans of ice cream. It was held at Lowell Park, which had a place to swim in the river and a bath house for changing into our swim suits. We looked forward to swimming there, as the water was clear and much deeper and wider than our little swimming hole.

In the summer, Mother was busy canning the vegetables from our garden. We feasted upon the fresh vegetables, but when they were ready, there were so many, that there was plenty left over to can. We had an orchard with pears, apples, and cherries, so we canned some of those, also. In August the peaches would come in from Georgia. We always brought a bushel or two of peaches, feasted, and canned the rest. While there was always plenty to do, I remember that time of year as being a slower pace. School was out, and there was lots of free time to swim in the creek, read, help around the house, or do as you pleased.

We were isolated from people. Occasionally someone stopped by to see us, and it was a great event. They couldn't call first as we didn't have a telephone, so it was always a surprise, and usually we would be in the middle of one project or other, but we were glad to see someone else and hear updates.

One of my jobs as I grew old enough to do it was to walk the mile out to the highway and bring home the mail. During the school year, we always stopped by our mail box on the way home and picked up the mail. In the summer time, I would walk to the highway and back to get the mail and newspaper. Sometimes there would be a letter from friends or one of the cousins.

If it rained, Daddy would come in from the fields. We made a big occasion out of it. Mother would make popcorn, and we sat around and played cards. What fun that was! We all learned to play pinochle at a young age. We played four-handed, so it was Mother and Daddy, Lura and I, with Anne watching. Later it was just the four of us.

When Lura was finishing seventh grade, I was finishing second grade. By that time, Mary was a registered nurse and working in the Dixon Hospital. Jerry had graduated from the University and was teaching French. She had a small apartment in Dixon. Mary and Jerry thought Lura should come and start eighth grade in Dixon, so that she could get re-acquainted. It would make it easier for her to enter high school the next year. Mother hated to see her go, but it did seem like a good idea, so from then on our family was only the four of us. It was quite a change. That fall

I walked to school alone for third grade, but by fourth grade, Anne would start first grade, so then, it would be two of us walking to school.

It was about then that I started to take an interest in cooking. Mother taught me how to make coffee and oatmeal. My parents told me that if I would get up every morning and have it ready for them when they came in from milking the cows, I would be paid two cents a day. Ah, my first job! It seemed like a fortune at the time. I remember the first thing I bought with my newly earned money was an alarm clock so that I would be sure and wake up in time to do it. That would provide job security.

It seemed different going off to school alone, but I soon got use to it and spent the time walking back and forth from school, reviewing in my mind my school work or going over the arithmetic that I was learning, so the time passed quickly. Soon, I was at the mail box and back home. Some of the time, in snowy weather, the neighbor that lived at the end of our road would be there to pick up her daughter and give me a ride, too. Then there was only a mile left to get to our house.

The next year Anne and I went together, but she was not used to the long walk. She walked more slowly than I, so it took us longer. Indeed, Anne found the transition from home to school very difficult. She missed being home alone with Mother, where she could do as she pleased much of the time. She was the baby of a very large family and had been sick a lot, too. It wasn't that she found the school work too hard. She could read a little and knew her numbers and letters. There were two others in first grade that year, but they had to start at the beginning, so Anne found it boring. She complained a lot about school and didn't want to go. We had quite a bit of snow that winter, so Anne stayed home a lot of those days. By spring, Anne was really sick, and the doctor said she had TB. Mother taught her at home through most of her first grade.

By the next year, several families had moved way, and two graduated from eighth grade at the end of the previous school year, so by fall there would be only three coming to school: the girl that lived at the end of our road, and Anne and me. It was then that I learned that we were not really in that school district. Our farm was listed as being in the Hillside School District. That school was two and a quarter miles away, in the other direction. Since there was really only one pupil legally living in the Hausen District, the board rightly decided that they would bus her to town school and close Hausen School. We had to make other arrangements.

Mother and Daddy had known all along that we belonged in the Hillside District, but it had long been an established custom that the children on our farm would go to Hausen School, as it was closer. Now we had to decide what we could do about it.

Anne was still not well. Mother decided she would just teach us at home until we could attempt to have our farm re-districted from Hillside School to Hausen School. Mother knew the Superintendent of Schools from when she had taught, and she was well qualified, so he gave his permission for us to be home schooled, before it was fashionable to do this. I was home for the fifth and sixth grades, and Anne for her second and third grades. We became more and more isolated.

I really missed going out to school. When the weather was nice in the fall or an exceptionally nice day in winter, I would walk over and visit Hillside School to see where they were in the books and satisfy myself that I was keeping up with them. Actually, I usually was ahead, so that was reassuring, but I missed the fun of knowing others my age and being with them socially.

Mother loved having us home and assigned regular homework or desk work. We had workbooks that went along with our studies, so we did those, too. She told us all about history and geography, and we learned many extra stories about it all. She had us read aloud, recite, answer questions, and learn poems by heart, just as we would have done if we had been in a real school.

That winter was very snowy and extremely cold. In fact, in one spell, we were snowed in for six weeks! The snow was so high and drifted that we could not get a car or horse and wagon out to the highway. Once or twice during that time, Daddy did walk through all that snow, to the highway to pick up our mail and newspapers. The neighbors had taken in our mail and were keeping it for us, but they were very glad to hear that we were all okay. It was more than six weeks before we were plowed out and could drive a car to town to refill the pantry and go to the library. What a joy that was! We had plenty of food but were running out of some of the staples like flour, coffee, and sugar. Maybe it was meant to be that we were taught at home that year.

One memory that I have of those winters that we were taught at home was cutting up meat to be cold packed and canned. Daddy would butcher a calf, which he could do all by himself, but cutting up all that beef or veal was a huge task. There was no hurry about it, as the big sides of beef would wait for us in the cold summer kitchen, which was like a big, walk-in freezer during the cold winter months. It was good fun, all of us gathered around the dining room table, cutting the beef in small chunks and stuffing them into the glass jars, while talking about our history lessons or telling stories of things that happened long ago. When enough glass jars were filled to make a batch, Mother would process them in the large cooker or canner. Of course, we used some of the meat every day and cooked it fresh. Later the canned beef was delicious, and it provided easy, quick fix meals in the summertime.

Mother sent away to a publishing house in Elgin for some materials for teaching Bible lessons. I was very interested and poured over the catalogue to select some booklets that I wanted to buy. I had a little spending money now. I read them with great interest. That year, for my birthday, I was given my very first Bible with my name in gold print on the front of it. I was so pleased and read the text in the Bible and compared it with the stories I read in the pamphlets about David and Ruth and all the many stories about people whose lives were described in the Bible. The next summer I tried to read the entire Bible from beginning to end, but I got bogged down in the Old Testament, so Mother suggested that I start with the New Testament, which seemed easier to understand. I read that part all the way through and went back to some of the more interesting parts, like the Psalms, Daniel, and Job. The winter had been so severe that we stopped trying to go to church at all.

Sometime in that long, lonely winter, when we hardly ever saw anyone, except the four of us, Daddy came down with "the blues". Mother told us that he was really missing the life he had before we came to the farm. The adjustment of being separated from his friends, the work that he loved, and the contact with friends in his lodge, and the Lutheran church was very difficult for him. Mother had lived on the farm as a little girl until she was in the fifth grade. Her family moved to Dixon but continued to visit the farm, so for her, it was like coming home again. I remember my dad saying "I never liked farming" and "I'd rather dance than eat." We were very impressed with those statements, as we really liked to eat. We already knew that he really liked to play pinochle, so it was easy to understand that he missed playing cards at the lodge, too.

One evening Mother suggested that he get out his violin and play us a little tune. I had forgotten that he played. With us all urging him, he finally got out his violin and after a great deal of adjusting and tuning, he started to play. What fun that was. His favorite was "Turkey in the Straw." He really could play. He didn't need any music, as he "played by ear." Mother told us that he called for Square Dances a long time ago, and he still remembered how to do it. He told us he learned when he lived in Texas and worked on the railroad. He called a few dances and explained what the dancers would do. It was all quite fascinating.

Sometimes during those evenings, he would tell us stories about living in Texas, but he always ended with, "I didn't like living in Texas because I missed the winters, and I never want to live there again." He explained that there were only two seasons there, warm to hot and hotter. It sounded pretty good to us, as we cuddled close to the stove, all wrapped up in warm sweaters and wishing spring would come. But when he told us about the huge snakes that he saw and killed, I decided I would never like to live there either. We did enjoy the story telling, but later, when we were tucked in bed, we would bemoan the fact that nothing interesting ever happened to us and what stories would we have to tell our children.

It was during that snowy winter when we were snowed in for long periods of time that Mother told us more about her life. She told interesting stories about how things were when she was a girl on the farm. Eventually she got around to tell us about how it was that she raised her sister's six children.

In 1925, my mother, with her mother and father, lived a quiet life in the huge three story, white frame house in the north part of town. She was regarded as an old maid school teacher by day and a dutifully, attentive daughter to her aging mother and father in the evening. She prepared meals and helped out at home at night but found time to grade papers and to make lesson plans for the students in her one room country school. This left little time for social activities, except the necessary school events and meetings with the school board during the school year.

My mother's father was well known in the area as a gentleman farmer, who raised and trained Morgan horses, a popular carriage horse at that time. He had moved to town when their two daughters were ready for upper grades and high school, so that they could attend town school. A tenant farmer farmed the family farm, which he supervised, leaving him time to attend to his favorite tasks of breeding and training horses, socializing with the surrounding residents, and preparing his well-known sausage during butchering season. His sausage was prominently displayed in the local grocery stores with his name on the label, and it sold out quickly. He was a gregarious man, who loved to talk and socialize. He liked nothing better than a good laugh or a fair horse race on the back dirt roads, but he was always there to help out friends and neighbors when it was needed.

My mother's mother had arranged things exactly to her liking, keeping her daughters under strict control. After they had moved to town, she enjoyed long days by herself at home, happy that her husband enjoyed going out, and she could have the house to herself. She ran a very organized home and had delegated certain tasks to each daughter. She was determined to control their every plan and movement. Her oldest daughter, Laura, had rebelled at all the rules and supervision and took up with a man she met at the local college. Her mother disliked him at their first meeting. Against her approval, Laura continued to see him and was determined to marry him. When things came to a head, her father intervened. He realized the only solution was to make the best of it, so he agreed to provide a small, family wedding in their large home on the north side of town.

The ceremony took place in the living room with my mother playing the organ. The local Lutheran Pastor presided, and a group of about twelve to fifteen guests attended the simple affair. The room was decked with an abundance of fall dahlias, which her father loved to grow. But at the end of the day, because of the obviously, distressed mother of the bride, the occasion was flat and unpleasant. When her mother embraced her daughter goodbye, she whispered in her ear, "You will never be welcome in my house again."

Her father, never again grew dahlias in his garden.

Then and there my grandmother determined to never allow her remaining daughter to marry. She quickly found fault with every young man that Mother brought home. She did not hesitate to remind her family about her accurate assessment of Laura's husband, which qualified her as a great judge of character. She was the final authority on the suitability of any future spouse for Mother. She frequently complained of various aches and pains, which left many of the household chores to her remaining daughter. She planned to have her daughter with her always, to care for herself and her husband in their old age.

After high school, my mother attended a state teacher's college and soon became employed at a one room country school nearby. She traveled by horse and carriage to school at first. Eventually, she bought a car which she enjoyed very much. It was a more convenient way to go back and forth to school. She saved her money and attended summer sessions at a nearby college in order to complete her degree. She enjoyed the children in her classroom and found great joy in teaching. She found a certain level of happiness in her work and continued to write letters to her sister.

From time to time, letters arrived from Laura telling news of the birth or death of one of their children and the family news. Mother kept the correspondence going over the years. Laura's growing family moved about in order to find employment, mostly in states far away from the family home in Illinois. They lived in Kansas, Nebraska, and finally in Oklahoma. But Laura and her family all seemed like a distant memory and not a happy subject to discuss in the family. Indeed, nearly fourteen years had passed when the fateful telegram arrived in late summer of 1925. It was addressed to my grandfather, and it read "Come now if you want to see your daughter alive. A Neighbor". Telephones were rarely used for long distance calls, and urgent messages arrived by telegram, hopefully limited to ten words or less.

The three of them discussed what to do about this new development. It was decided that my Grandfather should be the one to go. My mother was scheduled to begin teaching soon, and Grandmother was clearly not able or willing to go, so Grandpa went out on the train. A few days later he wired my mother saying, "Send thousand dollars Stop Bringing Laura and children home Friday ten pm train Dad." My mother wired the money as soon as possible, and then started to make plans for their arrival. Grandmother was furious and took to her bed. Mother freshened all the bedrooms, satisfied that there would be plenty of room for all. Then she began planning meals for their homecoming.

When they all arrived, they were an exhausted group. Grandpa was in fine spirits and cheerfully herded the children into the family car. Laura and the baby were placed in the back seat of the car, surrounded by pillows and children, with the rest crammed into the front seat. Fortunately it was only a few miles from the train station to their home.

They were all so tired that they were happy to go to bed. The very ill Laura and the baby were settled in first, then the others. There were six children, five girls and one boy. Things sorted themselves out in the morning.

My Grandfather and Mother were the first to arise. Over coffee they had a quiet time to talk. He explained that when he arrived he found their living conditions deplorable. The husband was unemployed, very sad and upset. Laura was indeed very ill. It was decided that Laura and the children return with her father. The plan was that her husband would get in touch with them later.

The children ranged in age from twelve-years old to nine-months old. There was Lura, nine-months old, Nickie three, Alice five, Bill eight, Mary ten, and Jerry twelve. Mother began making plans for the older three to be enrolled in the local grade school. They would have the rest of the weekend to get acquainted and settle in.

My Mother never knew what her father said to his wife, but it was certainly effective. The next morning Grandmother rose to the occasion as well as she could and tried to make the best of things. It really did make a huge change in the household with the addition of seven people. But there is a certain kind of exuberance and excitement with children in the house that lifts the spirits in even very difficult situations. Mother was used to handling children, so the adjustment was easier for her. The large rambling home, large garden, and yard seemed to welcome the addition of children. Grandfather was joyful to be around the children and made up games and projects and planned little trips to the farm to introduce the children to the horses. Soon things fell into place, and the children thrived.

As time went on, Laura's spirits brightened, but her health declined. There was no word from Oklahoma. Healing of relationships between Laura and her mother gradually took place. Grandmother tried to cope with things, but her world had permanently changed. The children were noisy, and she was used to large stretches of peace and quiet. Doctors were called in to check the children, their mother, and grandmother. During that time my mother and her sister came to an understanding. Mother happily promised to raise all of Laura's children, if Laura didn't get well. If she recovered, the two girls planned to make a home together and share the responsibility for all the children. At last peace arrived and a regular pattern was beginning to take place.

Just as suddenly as the events of the last few months began, Laura died peacefully in the night, unexpectedly, in early November of 1925. Before funeral arrangements could be made, a telegram was sent to Laura's husband. After several hours, a telegram arrived from him which said, "Awfully sorry cannot come." That cleared the way to make plans for the funeral and the final goodbyes. It was a difficult time for all of them.

When spring arrived that next year, a newness and happiness came to all the members of the household that now resided in the large white house, which had seen so many changes during the past fall and winter. By fall, the quiet family of three adults had become a bustling family with six children; two were still at home, three were in grade school and one was a high school student. The children's father remained distant and appeared incapable and unwilling to assume responsibility for his six children. Letters from him were infrequent, and over the next years dwindled to none.

The grandfather of the children enjoyed the experience of young children in the large family home and planned excursions to the farm, riding lessons for those that were interested in the horses, and thought up games and projects for them in the summers that followed. There were picnics in the park and outings to visit the relatives that resided in the area. But the Grandmother found it all devastating and traumatic. After several years of the stress of coping with the children, she became ill and was diagnosed with cancer. In that era there was little that anyone could do. Sadly she died in the early spring of 1929.

The experience of being responsible for the children's well-being caused my mother's social life to expand dramatically. She took them to social occasions at the Lutheran Church and the Odd Fellows Lodge. It was there that my mother and father met. They discovered that they each were members of both the church and the lodge, so the unlikely courtship began.

When it became evident that her mother was terminally ill, they decided to postpone any wedding plans to await the outcome. School was out at the end of May, so the quiet wedding took place in the rectory of the Lutheran Church on June 21, 1929.

This event caused a huge stir of excitement among their friends. What a surprise to learn that a confirmed bachelor of nearly fifty years old would suddenly marry an old maid school teacher of 30 some years of age. (Actually my father was 18 years older than my mother.) When the shock wore off, there was an out-pouring of love and affection for both of them. Their friends showered them with good wishes and planned an elaborate surprise party.

Although it seemed that they had a lot in common, their backgrounds were very different. My mother's family came from England, Scotland, and Wales and could trace their ancestors living in America to before the Revolutionary War. My father's parents had come over from Germany more recently. They met on the ship traveling from Germany to the United States. They were both young at the time, but they stayed in touch with each other and eventually married. My mother grew up in a family of two children, while my father was one of eight brothers and sisters. While my mother's family was well settled in America, my father's family was in the process of becoming American and spoke German at home.

My father had struggled to learn the language and was encouraged to leave school after eighth grade. The family was living as a tenant farmer and help was always needed to work with the family on the farm. They were having trouble scratching out a living for their growing family, and there was an ever present need for money. When my father was eighteen, he went out on his own, picking up odd jobs, worked for a time on the railroad, and eventually discovered he liked and had a natural aptitude for carpentry. He apprenticed and became a skilled carpenter. He was able to build a house from the foundation up, cutting the rafters, installing the roof and the windows, plastering the walls and completing the finishing work of cabinets and moldings.

He had built several houses in the area, selling some, residing in some, and saving some as rental investments. He did the construction work on the houses on the weekends but worked at a full time job during the week. At the time that my mother and father were married, he was living in a large frame house with six bedrooms which he had built. He was living there as he completed the work of painting and finishing the woodwork. He hoped to move the family into this house after they were married, but Mother's father did not want to be up-rooted, so this home was rented, and my father moved in with his father in-law and mother's five nieces and one nephew.

Anne and I had heard parts of the story, but at last we had it all talked through, and there were no hidden questions about the past. It was a wonderful time of story-telling, during that snowy winter. Now we understood who our cousins were, although they seemed like our sisters and brother. We remained close to them for the rest of our lives.

End of Isolation

●————————————————————————————●

With the arrival of spring 1940, there seemed to be a feeling of change in the air, as well as spring cleaning, with work in the fields and a new garden. It was wonderful to be outdoors again. I remember my mother singing hymns at the top of her voice when she hung the first load of washing out on the line. She said over and over "How fortunate we are!" I think she was very happy that the winter was over, that nobody had gotten sick, and there was hope that the terrible depression was nearly over. She talked about the fact that many people had many more difficulties than we did.

I thought, *I don't think we are so fortunate. We don't get to go anywhere or do anything FUN.* I felt poor and lonely for friends and the big girls. Their letters were few and far between, but maybe it was because we did not get our mail very regularly. Our car was old, and I wished for some new clothes. We had plenty of clothes, but they were all hand-me downs. I wanted something new and different. I started praying, secretly, that something wonderful would happen, like our school would be redistricted and I could go to town school in the fall for sixth grade.

Well, that didn't happen, but something else happened that really changed things for me. A new family, the Reynolds, moved in the neighborhood. Their farm joined ours along the back pasture and the west fields. They were very nice and had two sons, one my age and one just a year or two older. Our families got acquainted, and before long the boys would ride their ponies over to deliver some message or other and stay and play for a while. They invited us all over for dinner one night. What fun that was. When they found out that we didn't attend church regularly, they invited us to go to their church. It never seemed to work out that we could get ready in time, so eventually, they said they would stop by when the road was okay and take me with them to Sunday school and church, at the Church of the Brethren in Franklin Grove. Anne was invited to go, too, but Mother thought it best not to send her, yet. Anne was still not completely well. But I was glad to go and loved it. That summer and fall I went regularly, and if the roads were muddy, I would walk out to the highway, and they would stop and pick me up. I rarely missed a Sunday. Daddy didn't really approve of it, but thought it was better than not going at all.

Our financial situation seemed to be improving. Maybe the depression was finally over, as there were definite signs of improvements in our country. I began to read the local newspaper, and questioned Mother about the war in Europe, but she said, "Don't worry about that. There are always wars going on somewhere in the world, and this is far away from us. It won't affect us."

I found that the newspaper was really interesting. Partly for lack of something else to read, I read it every day. One day, when Mother came in from the barn, I said, "Mother! We have to clean up this house!" (We always cleaned the house every Saturday morning, but in between times things got pretty messy. We really lived in our house! We cut-out paper dolls whenever we wanted to, and things were piled up all over.)

"Well, that is an admirable ambition, but what brought that on," she asked.

"It says in the Dixon paper, that right there in town, a family was fined a hundred dollars for keeping a disorderly house," I said.

Mother just laughed, and said, "Don't worry about that. They will never find us way out in the country like this."

I was amazed! How could she be so relaxed about it? I knew that a hundred dollars was a lot of money. I thought it was taking an awful risk. From then on, I was much neater about my things and was always cleaning up whenever I could.

I asked about going to town school in the fall, and she said she would look into it again, but she seemed in no hurry to do anything about it. I thought she liked things the way they were. I knew she worked hard and was out in the fields working with Daddy nearly every day, so I decided not to press it. They had bought a tractor at a farm sale that spring, so things were going along quite well, and we were busy as ever, with the garden and everything else. But I did wish that she would take my concerns more seriously.

That summer there were many changes with the cousins. Jerry and Gerry were the first to get married. They had been married for several years and living in St. Louis, before Mary and Ray were married and bought a little house in Dixon. Then Alice and Bob, and Bill and Dorothy were married, so by 1940, all were married except for Nicky and Lura, who were students at the university. We had some great family picnics and "get togethers" that summer. Mother said, "Getting married was like the measles. When one gets it, they all get it." But it would be some time before the younger two would marry.

Quite unexpectedly, Mother and Daddy decided to buy a new car. Well, it was not really a new car, but it was new to us. It was a 1936 Pontiac, but it was wonderful. It had a starter so Daddy didn't have to crank it like the model T Ford. Now we were much freer, and we went to town more often unafraid of car trouble. When it was a cool day and Daddy didn't need Mother to help in the fields, we could go to Dixon and shop. Sometimes she would take us to the movies. What a treat that was. We always stopped in to see Mary and Lura. If it was Saturday, they would not be working, but Ray would be. Our social life was expanding.

When school started in the fall, I decided to walk to Hillside School every day until the weather got really bad. At least I was going to school every day and to church every Sunday, which was the highlight of my week. This next winter was surprisingly mild, so it was nearly Christmas before we had the first really big, snow storm. Then I had to start my lessons again around the dining room table.

That year the weather was really mild for Christmas, so Mary and Ray and Alice and Bob came out for the day. What a jolly Christmas that was! Alice and Bob announced that they were planning a trip to Chicago and asked if they could take Anne and me to see the Marshall Field's window displays. Mother said yes.

We went for the day that next week. We got up very early and returned very late the same day, but what an experience that was. We had never been to Chicago before and had no idea it was so large and the stores so huge. My world was beginning to expand. Things seemed bright and new again, so I had hopes that things were really going to work out well after all.

I really enjoyed going to The Church of the Brethren. I became very familiar with their ways of doing things, which was quite different from the Lutheran church. There was not a fixed order of service, as there was in the Lutheran church. We always started with a hymn or two and a prayer, but it was not the same prayers as in the Dixon church. It seemed more informal, like the Pastor prayed from his heart and made it up as he went along, while in the Dixon church it was just as it was written in the book. I liked his sermons. He talked longer than in the other church, but it was very real and he spoke from his heart. The church was smaller and everyone knew each other. They welcomed me with open arms.

I liked the Sunday school part, too. It all made sense to me, as I had read quite a lot from the Bible before I started going there. It was great to meet some people my age. The class was being prepared to be baptized. I said I was already baptized when I was a baby and didn't even remember it. It seemed that the Brethren thought it was better to baptize their children when they were old enough to know what they were doing and make that decision for themselves. I asked my mother about it, and she said she knew that they differed in that way. I really wanted to be baptized and join the church with the class. We talked about it at home.

One Sunday Daddy decided to go to church with us. He saw how kind they were and welcoming, so after much discussion, my parents decided to let me join the church. Mother said it was similar to the Lutheran Church, when they had the children confirm their baptism when they join the church at about twelve or so years old.

The day came in early spring of the year I was finishing sixth grade. I was all ready for this, as all the details had been explained to us in Sunday school. Mother, Dad, and Anne all agreed to come and be there for this great event. There was a special place built in the church for this. It was like a large cupboard. From the back, there was a door to enter. From the front, visible to the main church, there was a sliding panel, about waist high that opened on cue. Behind the scene we all lined up to be baptized, one at a time. The girls all wore white dresses, and the boys were dressed in white shirts and dark pants.

When we entered one at a time, the pastor was already in the large tub of warm water. We stepped gingerly in, and after the panel was opened to the church, the appropriate prayers were said, and then we were totally immersed, three times, in the name of the Father, the Son, and the Holy

Ghost. It was a very moving experience. When we each exited, there was someone there to meet us, give us a big hug, and wrap us with a towel. Then we were led off to get dressed in dry clothes.

It was explained that this was the way baptism had taken place in the River Jordan, as it was described in the Bible. I felt so joyful and complete. It was wonderful to be a real member of the Brethren Church. I knew that I had made the right decision. I honestly felt transformed.

The next Sunday I went to communion for the first time. That was different, also. I had seen communion distributed during the regular church service in the Lutheran Church. Although I had not received, I was familiar with the procedure. In the Brethren Church the entire service was like the last supper in the Bible. The church was set up with pews facing each other with a table in between each set of pews. One side of the church was designated for women and girls, and the other side was for the men and boys.

When all were seated, passages from the Bible were read. Then the person on the end was given an apron and a basin of water. He, or she, knelt and reverently washed the feet of the next person. Then that person took the basin and towel-like apron and gently washed and dried the next and so forth around the circle. It was all done very lovingly and kindly. When, each in turn stood and received the basin and apron, she gave the person who had served her a loving hug. After this had taken place, communion was served, around the table, in memory of the last supper. It was all so special and reverent that I remember it as a wonderful, impressive event, which taught us that we were to be followers of Christ in everything that we do. Communion was celebrated four times each year.

One Sunday morning during the worship service in church, I happened to be seated near the Pastor's wife, Mrs. Cover. She overheard me singing one of the hymns at the top of my voice. After the service was over, she sought me out and said that I should be singing in the choir. I asked when they rehearsed and expressed doubt that I would be able to come. She indicated that she would talk to my mother about it.

It was about that time that we learned that our farm had been re-districted and now we would be bused to Franklin Grove School. We were now in the Hausen School District. Whoopee! I was so delighted. At last our little home school was over, and we would be going to a real school in the fall.

Doors were beginning to open. One day Pastor and Mrs. Cover dropped in to visit us. It had been a hectic day, as we were canning tomatoes, but that didn't seem to bother them. It was then that they invited me to go to Summer Church Camp at Naperville. It was about ninety miles away, but transportation would be included and there would be no cost to us, as there was a fund to pay all the expenses. My mother agreed that I could go.

It was there that I found the friendship and spirituality that I had always wanted. What a wonderful experience it was. There were boys and girls from all over northern Illinois, from both cities and farms, all about the same age. There was swimming every day, worship time, arts and crafts, and plenty of time for games and recreation. There was a dining hall where we were served three meals a day, family style. We all looked forward to that event as well. The best part of the day were the talks and singing around the campfire every night. It was there that I really gave myself totally to Christ and vowed to serve Him the best I could for the rest of my life.

That was a great summer, as everything seemed to grow and thrive. There was a large sandy hill near the back west field that previously had been deemed unproductive and useless. It had been left to go wild with brambles, so it was not plowed and left alone. That summer we realized that it was loaded with blackberry bushes. These bushes seemed to have crowed out all the other plants and taken over this acre of ground. We picked and so enjoyed them, but there were so many that we couldn't use them all, so we invited the neighbors to come and pick, too. It became very popular by word of mouth, and people came from the church and all over to pick. They insisted on paying us for the privilege to pick. Indeed the berries were large, as big as my thumb, because we had rain at just the right times. They came by cars up to the house and we took turns, but I was usually the one to go with them to show them the way. It became a custom to give us twenty-five cents for each picker. When I was at camp, Anne took my place, and by the end of the summer we had quite a large sum of money.

We couldn't decide at first how we would use this extra money. Mother named it the Blackberry Fund for Better Bed Blankets or the BBBBB Fund. It was true that our bedding was well worn, so that fall she used that money to buy wonderful new blankets and comforters for all our beds. What luxury that was.

That was a great summer to grow things in the garden. We had the biggest and best of everything in the garden, including wonderful watermelons and cantaloupe. We had much for which to be thankful. I eagerly looked forward to riding the bus to town school in the fall. Anne was a little doubtful, but she had a very, kind, skillful teacher that helped her get over her fears of school and being away from home. I was in seventh grade, and she was in fourth grade. I liked my teacher and was relieved that I could keep up with the rest in my class. In fact, I really learned very quickly, and in order to keep me busy, I was invited to join the band. They needed someone to play the drums and said they would teach me. Well, it was such fun. I picked it up quite quickly, as I could read music and could count out the beats etc. They practiced almost every day. I was excused from study time to go to rehearsals. The town school experience capped off a wonderful summer.

In the fall, the church choir started rehearsals, since they stopped during the summer, as everyone was busy with gardens and enjoying the lovely summer weather. Mrs. Cover invited me to join the choir, and it was arranged for me to stay overnight on Wednesday nights, as that was their choir night. I was so pleased that I could do this. The parsonage was a large white house with a wraparound porch, located several blocks from the church and a short distance from school. Every Wednesday night, instead of riding the bus home, I walked over to the parsonage and then walked back to school the next morning.

They were a lovely family. His mother lived with them and was quite elderly. It seemed she was always hooking rugs. They told me to guard my clothes, because if it was the right color, she might cut it up for one of her rugs. There was lots of laughing and fun. I was given a room upstairs, and it was dubbed my room for whenever I wanted to stay. Wonders never cease! It was such a wonderful experience, being with them and singing in the choir. I already knew a lot of the hymns, but we learned complicated songs to sing for special times in the Sunday service. It opened a whole new world for me.

Pastor Cover sang in the choir, also, so after supper, we went together to the church basement, where the choir room was. I was the youngest one in the choir. There were only two or three that were in high school. Most of them were adults with homes of their own, and some were really quite old, but could they ever sing. I loved it. I was taught to sing in harmony, but it was easy for me, as I had a strong, high voice and was a soprano. I sometimes took some of the music home to practice, since some of it was quite difficult. I could pick it out on our piano and learned to sing it by the next week.

The room where we practiced was the room that the women of the church used when they met several times a week to sew on the quilts. They were carefully covered with sheets at night. I was told that they worked on them and had a good time doing it and then sold them to make money for the church. They were really lovely hand pieced quilts. I was so impressed by how much all the members worked together for the church and had such fun doing everything.

Our choir director was an interesting man; he was a lineman for the electric company during the day. He had a wife and two little children. He really knew music and could look at it and sing all the different parts. Later we became friends. He brought his family to picnic with us at the spring once. He could listen to the birds and imitate their songs perfectly, and when he heard their song, he knew what kind of bird was nearby.

Pastor Cover was a great gardener as well as a great singer and preacher. He had a huge flower garden and a few vegetables. The members of the church were so generous in bringing in produce from their gardens that they didn't need a big garden like we had. I grew to know, love an appreciate him, as well as Mrs. Cover.

I was invited to come to the church scrambled dinners that they had once in a while. Sometimes I could persuade Mother and Anne to come, too. Mother liked it, but Anne didn't enjoy it. So it seemed like I either came with the neighbors, or Mother would drop me off in the daytime and I would stay all night with the Covers and then I would be there in plenty of time for Sunday services the next day, as the dinners were usually Saturday nights.

I remember thinking how wonderful it was, to be a part of such a loving, accepting group of people, of all ages, and backgrounds. Most were farmers, but some lived in Franklin Grove and worked in Dixon or had some business or other. But it didn't seem to matter what you did for a living or how much money you made; every one cared about the others just the same. It was truly a Christian group of people. There were young families, old families, and some just growing to be adults, but you could talk to all of them and be listened to like you were part of their family. I knew I didn't have clothes as nice as some of the others, but that didn't matter, either. You were accepted as you were to be one of the members. They truly liked one another and were supportive of one another.

I enjoyed meeting the kids at school. I already knew the ones that went to the Brethren church, and I easily became acquainted with the ones in the band and the ones that rode the school bus, so I quite quickly knew nearly everyone by name. But becoming close friends is something entirely different. I had hurt feelings, as I knew I didn't exactly fit in, so I tried to make up for this lack by excelling in my school work. In some cases, this didn't work to my advantage, because they resented me for that. I had much to learn about making real friends, rather than making acquaintances.

There were huge lacks in my experiences, such as listening to the radio. We had a radio, but it was powered by batteries, and in order to prevent them from going dead completely, we used it very sparingly. We listened to the news, and occasionally we listened to one program for an hour in the evening, like Major Bowes, and that was it. In the summertime, when we could get to town more easily and could get the battery charged, Mother liked to listen to her favorite soap operas, like Stella Dallas, but that really didn't interest me. As a result, when they talked about listening to the Green Hornet or scary mysteries, I had no idea what they were talking about. Sometimes they talked about the movies they had seen, as they seemed to go every Saturday afternoon, so I was out of step with that, too.

One Monday morning in December, Anne and I got on the bus as usual, and all anyone could talk about was what they had heard on the radio about Pearl Harbor. I had no idea what had happened. I listened intently, and to my horror, I realized that our country would soon be at war! I didn't say one word, but did I ever listen to learn more. I could hardly wait until after school, when I got our newspaper and read all about it. Mother and Father had learned about it on the radio during the noon news. I had plenty of questions to ask my parents. The war was all anyone talked about and certainly was the main part of our focus as information came our way.

Fortunately this turned out to be a mild winter, so sometimes on a Saturday afternoon, we would all go to the movies, even Daddy. A hush would fall over the audience when the news reels played. We watched, with fascination as the latest news about the war with Japan was played. We soon learned that war would be declared on Germany, as well. On the way home, Mother said she was worried, that Bill and the new son-in-laws would be drafted into military service. I was afraid that they would start bombing us, but Mother assured us that it was highly unlikely, as they would bomb the big cities like New York and Chicago first. Well, I thought that would be awful, too! It was all so tragic, seeing the bombs and the huge German military armies goose stepping in parades to show how strong they were. It was truly a frightening time.

We soon learned that for now Mr. Gerry was deferred from military service, because he worked for a chemical company in St. Louis. They also had a child and were expecting another, so he was safe. Bill was deferred, as well, as he was a baker for a bakery in Champaign, Ill. But Bob was sure that he would soon be called up, so he was closing up his business affairs in Orion, Illinois, in preparation for this event. Ray volunteered immediately, but he was turned down, because of some medical reason, and was listed as 4 F. He had his own business repairing cars in Dixon, so he was safe, as well.

In our church on Sunday the sermon was about the evils of war and how wrong it was to kill other people in any situation. I learned that the Brethren Church taught that even in war, you could refuse to serve, because you believed it was wrong to kill anyone in any circumstance. If you were drafted, you declared yourself a conscientious objector, but could serve your country in the medical corps, helping the wounded. I heard many discussions about all this at the church meetings. There was a lot to think about now that our country was really at war on two fronts.

It was about that time that I decided to work more diligently to learn to sew. I had learned to use our treadle sewing machine. I had started out making dolls clothes for our dolls for Anne and me but made a couple of things for myself. I decided that I could improve my skills in this area and make clothes nice enough to wear to school and church. Mother and Mary helped me with patterns and selecting materials. I wanted to look more like the others and not feel like I was such a country bumpkin. My first attempts were not really great, but soon I got the hang of it and made many skirts and blouses, which were less expensive than buying things ready-made.

Now, I had more spending money because I was old enough to baby sit. Sometimes I was asked to stay with a neighbor's children who lived on a farm near us, and sometimes I was asked to stay with children of families I knew through the Church. I was glad to have the extra money and saved it carefully so I could buy material for my sewing projects.

There were other areas that I puzzled about. I saw and heard the kids at school writing or saying words I did not know. So I looked them up in the dictionary at home, but they weren't in there. Mother had taught us that if we came across words we didn't know, this was what we should do. I sensed that these four letter words weren't nice ones, so I asked around and found out the meaning of these words. Ugh! Such words! I didn't tell Mother. We never heard anything worse than "darn it" at home. My Dad was such a kind man and even though he had worked on the railroad and probably had heard these same ugly words, he never swore or used such language. In fact, he was so kind and gentle with the farm animals that he had a difficult time if any of them became sick or injured. I began to realize what a wonderful home I had come from and what a sheltered life I had before we went to town school and was exposed to such things.

As I was finishing up seventh grade, Lura was getting ready to graduate from Dixon High School. She had done very well in school, and got a scholarship to the University of Illinois, so she was planning to go there, too, as the others had gone. She had a good job for the summer, so we didn't see her very often that year. In fact, anyone who wanted a job could get a great one now that the war was going on. I deplored the fact that I was too young to get any kind of job other than babysitting.

Alice announced that she was expecting a baby, and it would be born the next summer. She invited me to stay with them and help her when she came home from the hospital. They were living in Omaha, Nebraska, as Bob was at training camp there. They would send me the bus fare. I was so excited about going. I always loved Alice and Bob and would do anything I could for them. I had hoped to go right after school was out, but before that could be arranged, Bob was informed that he would soon be sent overseas. We were so worried about him, and I was very disappointed. Alice decided to close their apartment and stay with Jerry and Gerry in St. Louis, so the baby would be born there.

There would be no summer camp that year, because of the war. Instead, after school was out, Mrs. Cover asked if I would like to help with the vacation Bible school. It was a joint effort by several churches that arranged this for children ages five to eleven. I loved it, and it was fun working with the little ones. I knew all the songs and was very familiar with the Bible and the stories, so it was easy for me to take part in that project. It helped me get over my disappointment of not being able to take the bus to Omaha and spend some time with Alice and Bob.

The blackberry patch was very productive that year. I was busy on the farm, as I was now old enough to really be of help with the haying time and the canning of vegetables. This was very important now that we were at war. Many things were now going to be rationed. In a short time it became known that sugar, canned goods, meat, shoes, and gasoline were all rationed. We were issued rationing books, which had blue stamps for canned goods, red stamps for meat, etc. We didn't need most of them, as we had our own chickens, eggs, milk, and meat and the usual big garden, so we were very fortunate. We wanted to help conserve food and do everything we could to help with the war effort. Although gas was rationed, farmers could have access to the needed gas for the tractors, but we were limited in driving just like everyone else. Also, tires were not available, so we were glad we had a pretty good car with good tires.

The summer flew by, and soon school started. I would be in eighth grade, and Anne was in fifth. I found I was much more comfortable at school this year, because I knew what to expect. After a few months, my eighth grade teacher took me aside and asked me if I would like to be the school editor of the paper that year. My job would be to write stories about the things that were happening at school and take them to the printing shop in Franklin Grove to be printed, bi-monthly. In addition I was to go about town and solicit ads from the stores and businesses. I would be excused from classes at certain times to do all this. It seemed to me that each teacher just made up things to keep me busy, since we never had a newspaper before this. But I agreed to do it.

It was quite a challenging assignment. Soon, I was busy with all the details. During my excused periods, I visited each of the classrooms to find the news for the paper. I prepared the little stories and told about the upcoming events, schedules of school holidays, and school events, band concerts, and the general happenings. Some of it I already knew. When

I got it in order, I carefully printed it out by hand, in columns and with headlines, like the newspapers I had carefully read. I submitted the draft to my teacher. She made some suggestions, and I added them with final touches. Then I delivered the paper to the printer. The next week, I spent my off periods going about town to get the ads. I stopped by the print shop first to find out what it would cost to have it printed and how much time I should allow for the printing to be done. I suggested that it should be about six small pages, about eight and one half by eleven, like a booklet, with the ads I hoped to get. Then I could plan on a budget and calculate how much to charge for the ads so we would break even on the project. The printer made some suggestions about the copy I should submit, and we agreed on the price. I found it was great fun and was proud of my first October addition.

But I had three more editions to do. My teacher suggested the schedule for the paper. It was arranged that it would come out at the end of October, December, February, and April, so I had one down and three to go. In addition to all this, I had my usual school work, band activities, and the once a week, stay at the parish house with the Covers for choir rehearsals, so I was really busy with all of these fun activities.

The year flew by for me, but not so for Anne. It was harder for her to make friends and fit in. She had another bout of what the doctors thought was TB, yet she never tested positive for this disease. She was absent quite often in the winter but kept up with her school work at home. It was a worry for all of us, as she seemed listless and lacked stamina, but there appeared to be nothing we could do.

When spring came, we all felt better to have the nicer weather. Even Anne didn't mind the walk out to the highway to catch the school bus as she had before the weather improved. On Saturday I talked to Mother about finding a place for me to be a live-in babysitter in Dixon, so I could go to the larger and better Dixon High School in the fall. I remembered that Lura had started in eighth grade. It had been a good experience for her, which prepared her to go to the University of Illinois, so it was time for me to go. Mother and Dad talked it over and the answer was a firm no. I was to stay with my parents and go to Franklin Grove High School, even though they did not teach a foreign language or have as many choices of subjects of study.

I was very concerned about this, as I wanted to be well qualified to go to a good university when I graduated from high school. I talked about it to Mrs. Cover. She didn't seem to be worried about it. She assured me that I would certainly qualify to go to the Church of the Brethren Colleges that were in Ohio and Indiana. I thought maybe it would all work out for the best. I remember praying about it and asking Him to guide me and direct me so that I would be able to go where He wanted me to go. I let go of that problem, finished up my school work, and prepared for our graduation from grade school.

Near the end of the year, the class was asked to vote for one person, boy or girl, whom we thought was the best student in regard to scholarship, citizenship, and service to others and the community. The winner would receive the American Legion Award. I was sure that Dorothy Hussey would win it, as she was the most popular girl in the class, and her family was prominent in Franklin Grove. Her father owned the lumber yard in town. That was who I voted for.

There was a lot of planning for our graduation. The band would play, but I couldn't play this time, as I would have to march in with the others. Mother and I went shopping in Dixon for a new dress for this event. I was so happy with my new dress. That night as I was getting ready to go, Dad gave me his present. It was a gold wrist watch, a really good one! I was overwhelmed and so pleased at his thoughtfulness. I had secretly wanted one for so long, but I never asked for one, as I was sure it would be out of the question. That was a night full of surprises. I couldn't believe it when they called my name as the winner of the American Legion Award. It was a large medal with engraving on it with my name and the date and the occasion. I was so honored and excited about it.

That summer I helped with Bible school as I had before, but now I was given a whole class of my own to teach. I had another student helper, and it went well, and I enjoyed it. Then, it was back to the farm and the usual routine of farm work, gardening, and canning, with time to swim in the creek and enjoy the woods and the beauty of the outdoors.

It was a desperate time for our country. The outcome of the war seemed very much in doubt. It was the summer of 1943. Our country was fighting wars on two fronts. There were terrible losses in both the Pacific and Germany fronts. Paris fell, which was unbelievable! In the Pacific, we were pushed back and lost so many soldiers in island after island that we could barely find on the map. On rainy days we would all go to town and shop and go to the movies. Mother and Dad both wanted to see the news reels and find out what was really happening.

Nickie and George had been married the day after Christmas, in 1942. He planned to volunteer for the Air Force, following his graduation from the University of Illinois in January. He was sent to Pensacola, Florida, where there was a training field for pilots. Nickie and George were now living on the base there. George became a pilot and spent the rest of the war training other young men to fly. Their first child was born there, and Mary went down to stay with her during the last weeks of her pregnancy and the birth of little Mary Catherine.

Alice and her baby girl, Diane, were in St. Louis, in an apartment, waiting to hear news about Bob. He was somewhere in Europe with a tank division. It was about this time that Bill was drafted into the army. He became what they called "ninety day wonders," as they spent that short time in the army for training and were immediately sent overseas. We knew that he was somewhere in Europe. We were anxious about all of them. It was an uncertain time, as nearly everyone we knew had family members in the military service.

We stopped by to see Mary and Ray when we could, and they came out to the farm to keep us up to date with news of the family. She assured us that everything was fine with Nickie and George, and we saw pictures of the baby. Diane and Mary Catherine were about the same age, as they were born about ten months apart but had never seen each other, since travel was restricted during the war. I wondered when Mary and Ray would have children, and if Dorothy and Bill would ever have children as he was now overseas.

We had the usual busy summer on the farm. Anne and I enjoyed going to the movies more often now. Before the war, we only went to a few movies, like the ones with Shirley Temple, the Walt Disney movies: Snow White, Pinocchio, and the Wizard of Oz, but now we all wanted to see the news reels and the wonderful musical that was coming out. The music and dancing was splendid, so it was a real treat for us. The beginning of the big band sound was evident, and the costumes and staging was a delight to see. Not all the movies were happy ones, as Mother and I cried all the way through the movie, Mrs. Miniaver, about the war in England, and how the local men used their own boats to rescue some of the Navy that had been trapped by the enemy. There were other war movies that really inspired great respect for the armed forces but also showed the horrors of war.

Soon it was time to get ready for the thrasher and go to the thrasher's picnic, the signal that the summer was almost over and soon school would start. I would be going to High School. I wasn't anxious about it, as I knew so many of the students and was familiar with the building. The grade school was the first floor, one room for each grade, and the high school was on the second floor. But I knew it would be different.

When the time came, I found that it was more different than I thought it would be. The students that graduated from the surrounding country schools were now freshmen in Franklin Grove High School, so our class was quite a bit bigger. There was a large room with a desk for each student in high school. We met there every morning for announcements, before the regular classes began. This was also our study hall, so if you didn't have a class during one of the periods, you returned to study hall to prepare for the next class or do homework. I had only one or two free periods. I signed up to sing in the chorus and for band, also. There were rehearsals for this, and I had a lab with science class.

We had a gym class, with girls and boys in separate classes. In the nice fall weather we played baseball, out of doors. But when the weather turned colder we were inside in the gym and played volleyball and basketball, which I enjoyed. We were assigned gym lockers where we kept our gym clothes and shoes. After gym class we took showers before we went back to class. It soon fell into a pattern, and it was fun meeting the new kids at school and getting acquainted with them

The boys were working hard, practicing basketball and hoping to make the team. The schedule for the basketball games with other schools, was already posted on the bulletin board. I learned that the band would play at all the home basketball games. They were usually on Friday or Saturday nights. I talked it over with Mrs. Cover, and she invited me to stay overnight with them, whenever there was a game. It was so wonderful of them to let me stay, so that solved the problem. If it was Friday night, Mother would come for me on Saturday, or sometimes I would just stay until after Sunday services and the neighbors would bring me home. I had a home-away-from-home whenever I needed it, truly a great blessing. I felt a part of most of the school activities, by being able to attend all the home basketball games, and going to the events when our band played, or the chorus sang.

It was during that fall and winter when we got the news about Bob and Bill, who were both serving overseas. The first news was that Bob had been injured on a battlefield somewhere in Europe and was sent to a hospital in England to recover. He had been serving in a tank division. Then, we heard that Bill was reported missing in action, and was last seen in the terrible "Battle of the Bulge". It was all frightening news. We wondered how extensive Bob's injuries were and really feared for Bill, as he was serving in the infantry. Unfortunately, we weren't the only ones that had family members who were killed or missing in action or injured. Gold stars were lovingly posted in the windows of those who lost a son in battle. When would this terrible war be over, we wondered, and what would be the outcome? We poured over all the information in the newspapers and the newsreels at the movies. The only thing we could do was pray, watch, and wait.

In the spring of 1944, things seemed to be improving in the European front, but there were still many losses in the Pacific. There seemed to be a feeling of new hope as the trees budded, and Locust Grove was again fragrant with blossoms and the sounds of bees buzzing overhead. While things seemed normal and peaceful on the farm where we lived, in reality terrible wars raged overseas. We still observed black outs. That is, we could not show lights at night, so we closed the shades tightly after dark. There were still shortages of certain food items, but, since we raised our own meat and vegetables, the only things that really affected us were the rationing of gas and shoes. We now knew that Bob was recovering very well and would soon be sent home. There was still no news about Bill. It was amazing at times that life went on, even though the world was in such terrible turmoil.

School resumed with the long bus rides for my sophomore year. Anne was in seventh grade now and seemed to be recovering from her health problems. She surprised me one day as we were walking home from school when she remarked, "I am beginning to think I will live to grow up." I was amazed that she had been worried about that. I felt a little guilty that I had been so caught up with my activities and had not observed how concerned she had been. I tried to reassure her that she was really improving. I talked about it with Mother. She didn't realize how discouraged Anne had been, either. We decided to do all that we could to rid her of her fears.

Things went along as usual. I continued to stay at least one night a week at the Covers and continued to be active at school and church. We had a mild winter that year, so we were able to go about more and didn't feel as isolated. A family from the Brethren Church asked me to baby sit their four children, ages six to twelve after school, as the mother had taken a job. I was needed to stay with them a couple of nights a week. I would stay overnight and go to school the next day from their house. Sometimes she asked me to stay on Saturdays and help her with the house work as well as amuse the children. I enjoyed the job and the extra money.

One Saturday a friend of the lady I was working for had stopped in for coffee. I heard them talking about their situations. It seemed that her friend was about to leave her teaching job at a country school, before the end of the year, as she and her husband had quarreled, and she wanted to get away from him and begin a new life. She was determined to do this immediately, even though she had signed a contract. I couldn't wait to tell Mother about it. I encouraged my mother to look into it. Maybe she could finish out the year for those students, as it would be difficult to find a replacement. Mother was doubtful, at first, but did go to see about it and got the job!

Now, in the early spring of 1945, it seemed clear that the war would soon be over in Europe. Daddy had begun to talk about retiring from farm work when the war was over. He was now nearly 65 and clearly worn out from all the work. I heard them talking about how nice it would be to live in Dixon again, and surely when the men came back from the war, there would be someone who would like to farm on shares. Mother had shared her worry, wondering how things would work out financially. Now, with Mother teaching again, it opened up a way for this plan to be viable. Mother loved to be teaching again and was offered that position for fall.

One Saturday after school was out, we went shopping in Dixon. I told Mother that I had some money of my own, and asked if I could shop by myself. I would meet Mother and Anne, later. We agreed to meet at the grocery store in an hour. As we drove home, I dropped my bomb shell. I told her that I had gotten a job at the Walgreens Drug store, as a waitress at their soda fountain.

It came as a complete surprise to Mother, and she had lots of questions and doubts about it. I explained that I had been thinking about it for a long time. I knew that I couldn't get a job clerking in a store until I was sixteen, but at fifteen I could work behind the soda fountain. I had worked out a plan to walk out to the highway and hail the Greyhound bus to Dixon and return by bus in the evening when they would stop and drop me at the end of our road. I had gone to the bus station to inquire about bus schedules. When I applied for the job, I explained my situation: I could only work certain hours, which would coincide with the bus schedule. Mother reluctantly agreed to let me try. I wanted to work to make enough money to buy new school clothes for fall.

Changes in the Wind

●————————————————————————————●

There were many changes happening all around us and in our family. Roosevelt died in April, and our new President was Harry S. Truman. Germany had surrendered in June, and a few days later the Potsdam Conference was completed, where plans were drafted for post war Europe, many of which had been decided at Yalta, just before Roosevelt's death.

The horrors of the war in Germany were now coming to light. It was very upsetting to my dad. We had heard rumors of the persecution of the Jews by the Nazis during the war, but my dad did not believe it. He kept saying it was just propaganda, to keep people supporting the war. He said that he knew the German people, and they would not do such horrible things, like putting people on box cars and transporting them to camps where they were starved and mistreated. But now the news reels were full of stories about the liberation of such concentration camps. The pictures were unbelievable and very upsetting to view. We had no idea that such horrible things had taken place.

When the war in Europe was finally over we felt relieved, however we did not feel like celebrating when our Armed forces were still fighting bitterly in the Pacific. Our men were still dying in faraway places, and we were helpless to do anything for them. Certainly a spirit of change was coming over the entire world. There was a new spirit of hope that things would soon be better again and that peace was just around the corner. What would all these changes mean to our family and the cousins, and would we ever know what had happened to Bill?

Mother and I had real jobs outside the home for the first time I could remember. Mother had agreed to continue teaching in the fall, and I had started my job at Walgreen's as soon as school was out. I worked five or six days a week (but never on Sunday), catching the bus at the highway at 9:00 and returning about 6:00 every evening. It was fun learning to make milk shakes, ice cream sundaes, and soda fountain drinks, but usually there was a cook that prepared all the sandwiches, hamburgers, and other things we served such as coleslaw, salads, and French fries. I did all the serving, order taking, and making change at the cash register. Sometimes there would be an extra waitress to help out, especially on Saturdays. My replacement came in just before I left, and she would work during the evening hours until closing. I really enjoyed the work and the pay envelopes every Saturday and the few tips I received were wonderful. I felt a sense of accomplishment. I could help out the family budget by buying some of my own clothes.

Mother and Anne were busy gardening, canning the vegetables and fruits, and doing the things around the house. It was great that Anne was feeling better and able to do things now. The new tractor was a big help for Dad, but he still needed help at haying time, so Mother and Anne filled in there. There was less and less time for swimming and walking in the woods, which I so enjoyed, but we all needed to help out where ever we could, and hope for the best, for our world and our family and for the future. Sometimes Mary and Ray would come out for a picnic at the spring or Sunday dinner and we would catch up on the family news.

As the summer progressed, it was evident that this dreadful war in the Pacific would soon be over. Certainly our lives would be different. It had been a long struggle and so many lives had been lost. Then tragedy! Suddenly, in August, the first atomic bomb was dropped, not once but twice, one on Hiroshima and one on Nagasaki. Finally the war was over! We were stunned by this horrible event and with the idea that this new monster, The Bomb, was now in our midst. It was the beginning of the Atomic Age. It was a relief that the war was over, but it was difficult to celebrate this event, either. It had been a hard fought battle to the end. Surely, there would never be another war, now that this Monster Bomb was available. Why, it could destroy the world!

At least now we could make plans to move off the farm, which had been our home for more than ten years. I regretted that I would have to leave the Church of the Brethren and my friends at school. Even though I tried, it was no use to continue to plead my case for buying a home in Franklin Grove. I was the only one with so many ties there. My parents' roots were in Dixon, where they had many lifelong friends. They also owned two houses in Dixon. The sensible thing was to plan now to move there in the fall, after the crops were harvested and a farm sale of machinery and farm animals could be arranged, perhaps as soon as Christmas.

It wasn't such a jolt for Anne, as she would be moving in the middle of eighth grade, but I would be starting my junior year in high school, so the adjustment would be much more difficult. If I entered Dixon High School in midyear, it would seriously limit my choices of study. I wanted to start taking a foreign language, but while Dixon had several choices, Franklin Grove had none. I knew that most large universities require at least two years of a foreign language. The other classes that I might take would likely make transferring in midyear very difficult.

After much discussion, it was finally decided that I could stay with Mary and Ray for a few months, until the actual move took place. Now, I could make plans to start the school year in Dixon, beginning in September. That was a great relief to me, but still, I was uneasy about the huge change. I knew none of the other high school students. Everything would be strange and very different from the much smaller Franklin Grove High School. The buildings of Dixon High School were huge in comparison. "Please, Lord," I prayed. "Help me find my way in such a huge place and help me find friends and fit in with the others."

One Friday afternoon, Mother and I went to see about my registration and obtain the list of choices of subjects with the transfer information from Franklin Grove. It gave us time to think about it and plan. Classes would start right after Labor Day, but final registration was due in late August. We decided that I would take English, Latin, Physics, Ancient History, Math, and Gym. Also, I signed up for chorus and band. There was a play day scheduled for late August for girls, when there would be events including soft ball, volley ball, and tennis. I knew nothing about the grounds and tennis, but I decide to go and check it out. Now that I knew my fall schedule, I had a talk with the manager at Walgreen's and told him of my plans. After school started, he wanted me to continue working part time, but after thinking it over, I decided to end my job at the end of August. I would have enough to think about, with a new living arrangement at Mary and Ray's and a new school.

The play day was a lot of fun. I enjoyed everything and met some very nice girls. I hoped that I would see them again in school. I especially enjoyed meeting Emma, who was a wonderful tennis player. I talked with her after she played and found out she would be a junior, also. She learned I never played tennis and offered to teach me. We arranged a date and I started to learn. It was great to start school knowing at least one person. On play day I learned the layout of the school, gym, and library, so I began to feel more comfortable about the first day of school. I decided to sign up for everything that was available and perhaps I would soon get acquainted. And it worked.

My classes were all very interesting to me. They didn't seem to be too difficult, once I found my way around to all the classrooms. It turned out that I was the only girl in my Physics class, so I felt a little odd, but I seemed to grasp the subject. The instructor was very kind to me. In a few weeks he arranged for our schedules to be adjusted so a girl in another Physics class was transferred to my class. Latin class was made up of mostly freshman and sophomores, and I was the only junior. I found it very interesting but a little difficult. My other classes were just as I expected, so I felt comfortable with the class work. Also, I was learning tennis with Emma. We played frequently on Saturday mornings and became friends

Band practice was another entry into life at Dixon High School. This was a marching band, and we played at all the home football games. I played drums, furnished by the school. I was given a school sweater and required to wear it with a pleated white skirt whenever we performed. Mary and Mother helped me make the skirt. I knew nothing about football, but I soon learned since I went to all the games. Learning to march and play at the same time was new to me. There were four of us in the percussion section. It was great fun, once I learned the drills, and I made friends with other band members

On Saturdays Mother and Anne would come to Mary's for a little visit, but I stayed in town for the most weekends, because I played in the band at the football games. On Sunday morning Mary and Ray liked to sleep in, so I got up early and walked to the Church of the Brethren in Dixon. It was across the bridge and only about two miles away. I started to get acquainted there but really missed the Franklin Grove Church. It didn't seem the same to me, as the Pastor was very different in his style of preaching. When Mother found out about that, she said when our family was all together again, I would go to church with them at the Lutheran Church and that was that. Sometimes they came in on Sunday and we all went to the Lutheran Church for services. I learned that the other girl in my Physics class was the daughter of the Pastor at the Lutheran Church, so I started to meet people there. I didn't want to offend Dad, so it seemed best to go along with them for the time being. It was a big change to begin attending another church. I still missed the Franklin Grove Brethren Church.

The farm sale of equipment and animals was held on a Saturday between Thanksgiving and Christmas. I couldn't go because there was a football game. Mother told me afterwards that it was a very sad and difficult day for all of them, as they saw all the animals we had named and loved being sold at auction, so I guess it was just as well that I couldn't be there.

By Christmas, the move from the farm was completed and it was great to be together as a family again. Mary and Ray lived only a few blocks from us, so we saw them often. It was a lovely Christmas. Nicky and George came from Chicago with their two children, Mary Catherine and Billy, only a year younger than Mary. George was discharged from the Air Force the previous month. They stayed a few days with Mary and Ray. Alice and Bob and Diane could not come, as Bob was still recovering from his injuries from the war. He had been discharged and was now living in Orion, Illinois.

We had much to be thankful for that Christmas, as we gathered in our new home. We had all come through the Great Depression, the War, and weathered the lean years on the farm. Dad was especially happy to be back in Dixon and picked up with his friends at the Lodge and the Church. Mother enjoyed teaching at a country school nearby. Jerry and Gerry were happy in St. Louis with their two sons, Doug and Jim. Lura and Cap had two little boys now, Bill and David. Cap had become a Medical Doctor and was fulfilling his responsibility to the Army for having put him through medical school. They were living at an Army base in California. Bill was still unaccounted for, and now it seemed certain that he had been killed in the Battle of the Bulge.

In 1946, we began the New Year, our first in Dixon since 1935. I was glad to be reunited with my family. We had a phone installed, and soon I received calls from school friends. We arranged tennis games or other events and compared notes about our school work. What fun to have a phone after so many years without one. I still remember the number, B-399.

The phone lines were much simpler then, no area codes, or long numbers or exchanges in our area. Occasionally a boy would call arranging for a date. That was new! Life was full of surprises.

At school the football season was over and the basketball season began. The band played at all the home basketball games, usually on Friday nights. One of the guys from our percussion section played basketball, so that left us with only three, so we doubled up. It was fun going to all the basketball games, as I was much more familiar with the rules of this game.

I had free time on Saturday, so I soon found a job in Klein's Department Store, in the children's department. I could use the extra spending money, and I learned that employees received a discount on the clothes. One of the boys from my class worked in the shoe department, which was adjacent to our department, so we became well acquainted. He had been sent to the United States from Germany during the early part of the war. He was Jewish and had been in great danger. It was very fortunate that he had been able to come to our country. Later, he learned that many of his immediate family had been killed. It was very interesting talking to him about his past. It brought the history of the war in brighter focus for me as the result of our many talks. We became very good friends, even though we came from very different backgrounds. It made me realize how tragic the war was for the many people in Europe. We thought life was difficult on the farm during the depression and war years, but in reality, we were very blessed to have plenty of food and the peace we felt out in the country.

Looking back over my junior year in Dixon, I realized that my plan to sign up for everything that interested me had paid off in a big way. I worked on the school newspaper as a reporter and several of my articles were used. There were two plays, one in the fall and one in the spring. I tried out for each one and made the cast every time. What fun that was, and it was a great way to really get to know other students. There were several Choral Concerts, most notably the Christmas Concert and the Spring Concert.

My favorite of all of these activities was acting in the plays. In both plays, I was one of the four or five leading characters. It involved after school play practice, four days a week for a month, as we prepared for the performances. It was amazing to see it all come together with props, sets, microphones, and lighting. I thought I might get stage fright, but I found that the footlights blocked out our view of the audience, so I soon forgot they were there and had no trouble following the script. It was fun to hear the audience's reaction, and the applause. The bonus was the new friends, the other members of the cast.

The drama facilities at Dixon High School were excellent. The principal had been the drama coach when Ronald Reagan had been a student there, about fifteen years earlier. (Reagan, a Hollywood favorite, credited his early experiences at Dixon High School as the source of his early interest in theatre. He would later go on to be elected President of the United States.) The principal was very supportive of the drama department. The fact that nearly two thousand students enrolled in the four year school added to the variety of talents available. Much time and effort is poured into each production, with many students helping in the background with the sets, lighting, and sounds. It was a wonderful experience for me, and I looked forward to my senior year and hoped to make the cast again.

I dated some that first year and was pleased to get a date for the Junior Prom. There was nothing very serious about the dates, and I certainly was not ready to go steady. It was just fun to have a date now and then for the dances and movies once in a while. All in all I was surprised that the year had gone as well as it had. I decided I had to seriously start saving for college. That summer, I continued clerking at Klein's full time and got a weekend job at the local hamburger hang-out, which had a menu similar to Walgreen's, so I found it to be an easy, enjoyable job.

In July I heard about an opening at the local music store and I applied. I got the job and it was by far my favorite job to date. I worked full time until school began, and then after school whenever I could and all day Saturday, unless there was a home football game, as I played in the band. What fun! I sold records, sheet music, and small items, leaving time for the owner to sell pianos and musical instruments. We carried a full line of band and string instruments. At that time we had listening booths, so customers could preview a record before purchasing. The store was a gathering place for young people, who loved to listen to records. I found I was quite successful in the sales department, because I was fond of music and became very knowledgeable about our stock. It was a great job!

During my senior year I took English Literature, Latin, USA History, Chemistry, and Economics. Economics turned out to be my favorite class and introduced me to the world of investments and the stock market. In addition to my usual commitment to Band, Chorus and Drama Department, I signed up for the Yearbook, so it was a very busy, wonderful year for me. To top it off, I received a leading role in the fall production. For the spring production, the drama teacher asked me to be the student director. I saw the entire production from a different view point, as I helped fit the play together.

I continued to attend the Lutheran Church. Occasionally, now that I could drive, I was allowed to borrow the family car and attend services in Franklin Grove. What a treat that was. I was confused about what would come next and prayed constantly for guidance. I wanted to attend college, but the way seemed blocked from a financial stand point. I sought to find a college I could afford and hoped I could work more the following summer. I considered taking a year off to earn money for college, so I was faced with a challenging decision.

At the music store, where I worked I continued to make more friends and dated much more often and with several different fellows, so my life was very full. Near the end of the school year, two things happened that change my direction.

One morning during class I received a message that I was wanted at the Principal's office immediately. With my heart racing, I went, all the while trying to recall anything that might be the cause. With fear and trembling, I entered his office. He was very kind, allying my fears. He had looked over my school records and wondered if I had any college plans. I told him my financial situation and about a small college in Wisconsin I was considering. I asked if he could suggest something.

He explained the scholarship opportunity to attend the University of Illinois. This required an all-day exam at the county seat's office, conducted on a Saturday in June after the close of school. He strongly encouraged me to apply and take the exam. So I filled out the necessary forms, but I was concerned about going to such a large University. It would not have been my first choice of colleges. I decided to wait and see the outcome.

Right after that, the owner of the music store called me aside and asked me what my plans were after graduation. When I expressed doubt about going to college for financial reasons, he told me he was thinking of retiring in a few years, and if I would work full time for him, he would give me music lessons, so that I could demonstrate pianos, and he would teach me the business from the ground up. In five years or so, he would begin retirement and gradually help me buy him out, so that I could become the new owner. I was overwhelmed with such a generous offer. I thanked him over and over again. I definitely wanted to work for him during the summer, and I would give him my answer soon. I needed time to think it over. I told no one about his offer, outside of my family.

I was only seventeen. Now, I was really overwhelmed. I had two very different choices. I didn't know what to do. I prayed and prayed. I talked it over with Mother and Dad, who thought it was a wonderful offer, and it would be great for me stay in Dixon. However, going to college was a good plan, too, if it was feasible.

Graduation was wonderful. I found out there would be two valedictorians, one girl and one boy, and that I was second in line for the girls. I couldn't believe it. In our class of over 400 students, I ranked in the top ten in the class. I went to several parties, and I had a date for the Senior Prom. I was on the decorating committee, so I was involved in a lot of the planning during the final months of school.

Graduation was exciting, but I had mixed feelings about ending this stage of my life. Dixon High School had been such a wonderful experience and a time for really growing up. I knew that I had many more advantages here than I would have had at Franklin Grove High School. The family attended but the only cousins who could come were Mary and Ray. My two aunts, Dad's sisters, came as well. Aunt Emma lived in Dixon now, and we saw her often, but I was very impressed that Aunt Annie and her husband, Uncle Floyd, came down from Rockford for the event.

There were graduation parties in the next few weeks after the main event. We all wanted to stay together as much as we could that summer, as our fall plans were so diverse. Some had wedding plans, some had firm college plans and some of us were still undecided. It was an important time in all of our lives. Four of us girls decided to learn to play bridge. We met each Wednesday evening with one of the mothers overseeing us and teaching us the basics, plus we studied a bridge book. Another good friend invited me to take a series of golf lessons with her. She reported there was a new golf pro at the club, and she thought it would be fun to check him out. So I bought a used set of clubs, and we went and had lots of fun. I really tried to learn and enjoyed it, but I think she was more interested in the golf pro. (Years later I found out she eventually married him, and they ended up owning their own golf course.) Looking back, these were great experiences to prepare us for our new adult life.

I had dates occasionally. I dated a friend who had his own band, whom I had met at the music store. He planned to go to the Julliard School of Music in New York City as soon as he could save up enough money. I also dated my date from the Senior Prom. He was busy with a summer job and was still undecided about where he would be going in the fall. Another fellow I started dating then was someone that was a few years older than I. He had started his own business right after high school. Now, he owned his own airplane. He flew his plane all around the state, delivering packages and repair parts to various businesses in the area. We became good friends, and he invited me to go along and fly with him while he made some delivers. I was very excited about it and really enjoyed it. I had never been up in a plane before. He thought I should take flying lessons, but I could not afford that at this time. I was saving everything I could, in case I managed to go off to college in the fall or sometime in the future

That summer I went to Chicago twice, once with my band leader friend to the matinée at the Chicago Symphony Orchestra. This was an unforgettable experience. The other time I went with my date from the Senior Prom and another couple to the Amusement park in Chicago and rode the roller coaster and many other rides. Both times we took an early morning bus in and returned on the evening bus, arriving back in Dixon about 11:30 or midnight. The fellows seemed to know their way about. It was a big thrill for me. I had only been to that city twice before this, once when Alice & Bob took us to see the Christmas lights and once with the Covers when they took me along for a conference there.

I had told no one about the possible scholarship. I had taken the exam at the court house in Dixon on the third Saturday in June. What an experience that was! It was conducted in a large room with about thirty candidates from all over the county. The teacher who presided instructed us to be seated with two empty seats between each other in all directions. Then she passed out the exam, a huge stack of papers, for each of us, and instructed us to write at our own speed, starting at the beginning, answering as many questions that we were sure of and skipping those that we had trouble with, moving to the end of the exam. Then, return to those sections that took more time to work out, so that we could cover the entire exam in the allotted time.

Some were short answers, and others were essay questions, covering many subjects including English Literature, Grammar, Math, Science, and History. I wrote and wrote. We had an hour for a lunch break at noon. I walked home for lunch and mother asked me how I was doing, but I had no idea. It was so comprehensive and detailed that it was impossible to gauge how I had done. We worked till 5:00 when we all handed in our papers. I walked home very tired from my days work but happy that it was over and hoped I would soon know the outcome.

I remember that summer as filled with the many mile long walks across the bridge, going back and forth to work in the music store. I cherished those walks as times for prayer, asking God to guide me and help me make the right decisions about my future. I had taken the exam in June, and kept hoping I would hear soon. Finally the letter arrived in mid-July. There were two scholarships awarded for our county, one for women and one for men. I won first place for women in our county! It was a four year scholarship, covering all tuitions and fees, to be used in the area of my choice. I was over-whelmed. I had to decide and respond in one week. If I declined, then it went to the next one on the list. What to do?

I prayed and prayed. What did God want me to do? What about the music store? I had saved enough money for my clothes and room and board, so now it was feasible. I talked it over at home, but it was clear to me that it was my decision to make this time. I woke up one morning certain of what I was to do. I was going to the University of Illinois! The hardest part was telling the owner of the music store. As soon as I knew, I told him everything and thanked him for his generous offer. He was gracious and kind, happy for my award, but I knew he was disappointed that I would not be coming to work there permanently.

I had tears in my eyes on the way home. I loved working at the music store and hated to disappoint him. He had no children and had come to look upon me as a daughter, but I felt sure that I had made the right decision. It was just too soon in my life to settle down in one career. I wanted to explore options, see what I really wanted to do, and what I could do, but most of all, I didn't want to throw away the opportunity that had come my way. I wanted to spread my wings and become better educated. I thought I might be a school teacher, like my mother, but I wanted to consider other careers, before I settled on final plans for my life.

There were so many things to take care of, in a very short length of time. Alice arranged to take me down to Champaign Urbana, where the University is located. She had received a similar scholarship there years ago, so she was very familiar with the University. She helped me find a place to live, showed me some of the major locations at the University, and the various buildings, such as the buildings where classes would be held, the library, the football arena, and Huff Gym. There were so many details to work out. I had to pack my clothes, fill out forms, receive schedules, and make all the necessary plans, while I wrapped up all the many details of my life in Dixon. I felt similar apprehensions, when, two years before, I had moved from the farm, and started Dixon High School. This time I would be starting an even larger school, nearly twenty thousand students, and I was filled with wonder.

Another New Beginning

●──●

School officially started around the 20th of September at the University of Illinois, but the freshmen were scheduled for orientation before that, so the time to leave for campus was fast approaching. In the middle of trying to decide what clothes to take, what I needed to buy, and planning a budget so that I would have enough money to last me until the next summer. The last days were filled with work, bridge games, parties, and last dates. Everyone was starting to go off in different directions, and my time was filled with hugs, goodbyes, promises to write, and exchanges of addresses. There was never enough time for it all. Yet, by the middle of September, I found myself on a Greyhound Bus with packed suitcases and packages, ready for another new beginning.

Mother would have liked to drive me to school, but she was teaching every day and really couldn't find the time on weekends, with papers to grade and housework to catch up on, so off I went, alone. It was similar to my starting Dixon High School two years ago. I knew no one at school, only an impression of where I would live, and a sketchy idea of the campus lay-out. It was about a five hour bus ride, which I used to put things into prospective. I used much of my time praying, asking for His help every step of the way. It was a time to separate myself from my life in Dixon, to plan and hope that "… in all things God works for the good for those who love him, who have been called according to his purpose," as it says in Romans 8:28.

When I arrived at the bus station in Urbana, I planned to take a taxi to my new address at The Mansion House where I would be staying. What an experience that was! After storing the luggage in the trunk, I settled in the back seat of the taxi. He proceeded to drive like crazy, flying around corners at break neck speeds, and arriving at the right address in nothing flat.

I arrived, sick as could be from motion sickness and a little homesickness. I attempted to gather myself together, pay him, and struggle up the steps with all my belongings. This is not a very good beginning, I thought. But these feelings soon passed as I stepped inside and was greeted by an upper classman who kindly took charge, introducing me to the house mother and showing me around the house and eventually to my room.

My luggage was already there, placed in my room by the bus boy, who was also a waiter in the dining room and a general all around helper for us at the house. It was peaceful to finally be alone in my room, to sort things out.

Our room was for three students to share. Here we lived, studied, dressed, and kept all of our things. The large dormitory at the rear of the building was reserved for sleeping only. It was furnished entirely with bunk beds, my first experience with such an arrangement. I had been told by the upper classman that showed me around that I could select any unclaimed bed and make it up with the sheets and blankets I had brought from home. There was no heat at all in the sleeping area, and, most of the time, we would be sleeping with the windows open. I quickly decided upon an upper bunk not too close to the windows and made up my bed. I could bring an alarm clock with me and put it under my pillows if I needed to wake up for an early class. Breakfast would be served from 7:00 to 8:30. Actually it wasn't hard to wake up. There were about thirty girls in our house, and when we started to stir about 6:30, in time to shower, dress and go down to breakfast, we all seemed to wake up about the same time.

With that accomplished, I headed back in my room to sort out and store my clothes. We each had a dresser, desk, and chair, but shared one closet, which looked very small to me. It was obvious that my roommates had arrived before me, as the other desks and dressers had been claimed. I folded most of my clothes and put them in the drawers, but the dresses, coats, jackets, and slacks had to be hung in the closet we shared. The room was surprisingly functional and adequate. Downstairs was a large living room, a library, with the dining room in the back of the house. I knew I could make it work.

Soon, I met my roommates, Carmen, who was a freshman, and Teddy, who was a girl from Dixon, but I had never met her before, as she was several years older than I. Before long I knew nearly all the girls by name, as we had regular house meetings in the living room to get acquainted, to establish the house rules, and to deal with any problems that might arise. Our house mother was usually present at all the meetings. It was chaired by the house president. All the officers had been elected at the end of the previous year. At our first meeting, the freshmen were introduced first and then in turn, all of the others, each telling a little bit about themselves. We were instructed to keep strict hours. During the week, Sunday through Thursday, the front door was locked at 10:00 p.m., and any visitors in the living room would be asked to leave. Friday and Saturday nights we all had to be in by midnight, and this was to be strictly enforced. Plans were made for up-coming events. We were given the assurance that the upper classmen would answer questions or problems we might have. It seemed to be a warm and friendly place to live.

Orientation started the day following my arrival. The university scheduled our time well. It included a campus tour, information sessions, and individual interviews to help us plan our own courses of study and to explain the registration process. I had enrolled in the College of Liberal Arts and Sciences. I thought I would probably like to be a school teacher but was open to other possibilities. There was a large variety of career choices, but the first two years were quite general, with mostly required courses and very few electives. We were informed that the required classes were English, the level to be determined by a placement exam, a Science class, a Foreign Language class, and Women's Hygiene. I was appalled that Women's Hygiene was a required course. What a waste of time! I thought they would teach us to bathe often, brush our teeth, use deodorant under our arms, and something about nutrition. My! I had a lot to learn. It was a sex education class! It included information about sexually transmitted diseases and went into detail about our bodies in this regard. Wow! For my elective courses I chose Music Appreciation and a beginning arts course. I chose Spanish for my foreign language and Biology for my science class. I went through all the steps and was finally properly matriculated.

Back at the house the girls were talking about getting season football tickets. The student rates were quite reasonable. One of the girls said she was in Block I. I found out that this was a large section in which the students held up cards of various letters or colors at certain times to spell out cheers etc. This sounded like something I would be interested in, so

I asked more about it and decided to sign up for it. It was really a lot of fun. We had to practice for it and arrive a little early to do this, but the advantage was we had seats near the fifty yard line. I was amazed at the planning that had been done to accomplish the desired results and was excited about attending my first football game held at the huge field house with the band playing and so many people in attendance. It was fun to have a small part in the student section of Block I. I knew instinctively that I certainly was not qualified to play in such a well-trained band so I didn't try out.

All the preliminary steps had been taken, and now I felt quite at home and ready to start my classes. I quickly realized that any real studying was best accomplished in the library on campus. There were just too many distractions at the house. I loved the library. It was huge, with so much information so easily accessed. It was quiet there. Soon I found a favorite corner to which I usually gravitated and quickly developed a plan for study time.

The social aspects of University life were many and varied. Freshmen Mixers at the Student Union were Wednesdays at 4:00 pm, which were tea dances in the ballroom. It was great fun to dance to the records of the Big Band Sounds of Glenn Miller, Tommy Dorsey and others, all music very familiar to me. I met several interesting fellows but no one special. It was just fun to have a movie date or a date to the Big Huff Gym Dances with the real live performances of these bands, which made the route around the country. I soon had a fairly busy social life.

Life back at the Mansion House was a little troubling. It seemed I had very little in common with either of my two roommates. Carman had lived a very sheltered life and had never been allowed to date before coming to the University. She proceeded to make up for lost time and was soon frequenting the beer halls nearly every night. Several times in the last month I had to let her in after hours from the fire escape, and she was really drunk. I tried to talk to her and straighten out her priorities. I talked to an upper classman I had come to know and she tried also but to no avail. Eventually the house mother found out, and she put her on probation. I felt badly about it but stayed out of that matter.

Teddy had many problems, as well. She seemed mildly depressed. She was twenty-two-years old and had completed only four college semesters because she had to take a semester off at least once a year to earn enough to pay her own college expenses. I felt very sorry for her. She was trying so hard to make it. I noticed that she had bitten down her fingernails to the quick and was a chain smoker. When she wasn't in class, she spent most of the time back in our room studying or reading books and smoking. I was so thankful that I slept in the dorm in all that lovely, fresh, cool air, instead of in our smoke filled room.

I became friends with some of the girls in our house with which I had more in common. About that time, I heard about mid-term rushing. I had been thinking how nice it would be to live in a house in which all the girls shared similar values and goals. That seemed to be what sorority life was all about. One of my friends from the house and I decided to sign up for informal rush and see if we found what we were looking for in a college rooming house.

In regard to finding a church home, I realized that there was not a Church of the Brethren on or near campus. The nearest one was on the other side a town and would require bus transportation and a change of buses. It was really very difficult to get there, so I gravitated to the Lutheran Student Center on campus that held services on Sunday and mid-week prayer meetings. I attended services there, and learned two other girls from our house attended. We went together and attended regularly. I enjoyed all my classes and seemed to be keeping up quite well, despite the distractions with my roommates. Life was good at the university, and I began to feel right at home.

I received quite a few letters from home and friends, so I had all I could do to keep up my side of the correspondence. In no time it was the first of November and my friend with the airplane wrote and asked if he could fly down and pick me up for Thanksgiving vacation. Wow! Of course I said yes! We set up a time and date when I would meet him at the airport. I would take a taxi at the proper time. I was quite the talk of the house when the word got out. Teddy asked if she could catch a ride, too. I hated to turn her down, but I explained it was only a two seated-plane and there wouldn't be room

I had started to receive rush invitations from various sororities. I enjoyed going but wanted to see the process go through the whole cycle and see what I thought about it all before really deciding anything.

It had been a good beginning of my freshman year, and I couldn't believe it was nearly Thanksgiving time. I was looking forward to seeing my family and friends again and hearing all their stories of what had happened in my absence.

Thanksgiving vacation was a blur! There were so many things to do, people to see, and stories to tell that the whole week zoomed by. It was fun, but I was constantly torn. I felt I had to go out with my friend with the plane. After all he went to a great effort to bring me home, so we dated nearly every night. I had to have time for my friends from High School and spend time with my family. Mary and Ray and Nickie and George and family came, and they wanted to hear all about University of Illinois. It brought back many memories for them as they had been there many times. I also went out with my senior prom date, but we had to settle for a lunch and afternoon movie, as I pleaded family dinner obligations. I was one busy gal, juggling all those dates and visits. In no time, it seemed, I was back at school with a happy feeling about all the things that had happened during that visit. One of the girls from the house with whom I had been going to the Lutheran services was determined to set me up for a blind date. She was going steady with a fellow from the Camelot House, and there was a fellow from that house that she wanted me to meet. So I agreed to go. It was arranged that we meet at the Union Building and attend a dance there. It turned out that there were four couples at our table, so after introductions, we settled in for an evening of fun.

Well, let me tell you, in my opinion my date was a real dud! He was stiff and formal, not very talkative, but nice enough looking, pleasant, and a Lutheran, but other than that we didn't seem to hit it off. We exchanged dances with the others at the table, and I soon found I was very interested in the fellow across the table from me. I kept wondering if he was on a blind date, too. Oh, if only things had worked out differently, and he had been my blind date! I wondered if this was his steady girlfriend. Now was not the time to find out.

The evening ended, and sure enough my blind date called to ask if I would like to go the big Christmas Dance at Huff Gym, but I could honestly say that I had a prior date for that evening, and said no. So he never called me again. When I went to that dance, I saw the fellow I was attracted to on the blind date several times that evening and gave him a big smile of recognition. He nodded and waved, but that was that. Soon, it was time to go home for Christmas break.

This time I would have a longer visit, and it would not be so compressed. I had several dates. The "Fly Boy" was one, and I had several dates with him and the band leader I had dated the summer before was in town for Christmas, so I went out with him. I was not serious about either of them. I was shocked when I learned that both were serious about me and wanted me to make a commitment. I explained I was only seventeen and wanted to finish college first. I didn't date them any longer, because that was not the answer either wanted. I dated my senior prom date, as well. It was fun, but I felt I was just going through the motions until it was time to return to school. I felt I really belonged back at school. I had some papers to write and worked on that some of the time. Right after New Years, it was a relief to get back to school, go through finals, and finish my first semester at the University.

There were only a few days before the second semester would start, so I decided to stay there. There were more sorority rush parties, and I was invited to them, so I stayed and used the time to evaluate and consider my future living arrangements and whether I should change my course of study. I was running out of money, so I got a part-time job at a dress shop downtown. I would need to take a city bus, and I could work only Saturdays, so I thought I could swing it, as I had gotten very good grades my first semester, and now with football season over, I would have Saturdays free.

It was time well spent, as I received a bid to pledge Phi Mu, and I decided to accept. I couldn't move into the house until the next fall, as I had signed a one year contract at the Manor House, and there was not space at the sorority house for me until the next semester. It was arranged for me to live at the sorority house in the fall. I had high hopes that I would fit in better there. I liked the girls I had met and realized the house was much nicer than the Manor House. The atmosphere seemed much more serene and stable. The location was a little further from campus, but I thought I would be able to study there if I needed to without always going to the library every night.

During this time I arranged to meet with my counselor to discuss my course of study. I was uncertain in regard to my major. She assured me that if I followed the basic courses the first year or two, then I would be in position to select from a variety of majors at that time. I was leaning toward something in the medical field, such as Physical or Occupational

Therapy, so I decided to select the science courses recommended for these majors so I would be a step ahead, if I did choose one of these fields. After this brief break I was all set to begin my second semester with a few things resolved.

Now that I was a Pledge at Phi Mu, I was required to go there a couple of times a week for instruction and to get acquainted with the future sorority sisters. It was a joy to feel a sense of belonging. I found their requirements were easily accomplished and, in doing them, I became better acquainted with my future sorority sisters and the inner-workings of the house. I decided it had been a good decision to join.

My courses were going well, and I enjoyed going to work on Saturdays. My boss was a very nice lady, and she seemed glad that I was working out well for the store. It was fun. They carried a good line of ladies' clothes, so I found that I was soon selling as much as anyone else. With the addition of the extra money I made at the dress shop, I knew I could manage until the end of the semester.

In March, the Manor House made plans for a spring tea to be held on Sunday afternoon. I was interested to see that the Camelot House was on the invitation list. All the planning had been accomplished. The dining room was decorated with spring flowers, a punch bowl (fruit juices and ginger ale only), and lovely goodies carefully arranged on trays. Our guests began arriving when in walked the fellow I had met on the blind date, not my date, but the one across the table. We soon were chatting away. I'm really going to get acquainted with him this time, I thought. What fun! In a few days he called and asked me out and I was smitten. For me it was love at first sight. I had never felt like this before. Soon we were going out regularly.

Finally, I asked him if he remembered the time we first met. "Of course," he said, "but Camelot House has a house rule that if someone dates a girl, all the other fellows in the house are not to ask that girl out until they have not dated for at least three months."

That answered a lot of questions for me. It seemed that we both felt a strong attraction on that very first meeting. But the new romance was just beginning when I got an unexpected telephone call from home. It was the first and only time I ever remember Mother calling me when I was away at school. We wrote often, and in her last letter she had told me that Mary, my cousin, was going in for surgery and I was asked to pray for her. I had, but was so busy with all my activities that I did not give it much thought. Well, Mary had died! And Mother asked me to come home, as soon as possible.

I was in shock. I called the Dean's office and asked to be excused, explaining the circumstances and asked if I could stay home until after Easter Break, which would begin only a few days after the funeral. It was approved, so I called John to break our next date and explained why I was going home. I hoped that when I returned he would call me again.

I took a bus home as soon as I could. It was such a shock to all of us. She was so young, only thirty three. I learned that she wanted very much to have children but had been unable to conceive. She had scheduled that surgery in hopes that they could do something that would increase her chances of becoming pregnant. She chose a hospital in Wisconsin, as she was very well known in the Dixon Hospital. She wanted to keep her privacy and not let it be known that she was having this procedure. Something had gone wrong with the anesthetics and she died on the table. When I saw her, her face was so badly swollen that I hardly recognized her. What a shock!

Nickie and George came out from Chicago as well as Alice and Bob from Illinois and Jerry and Gerry from St. Louis. Lura and Cap could not come from California, as Lura was expecting and could not travel. It was a sad family gathering. Mary had been such a generous and helpful person to all of us. I remembered how much she had done for me when I stayed with them during the first part of my junior year at Dixon High School. She made me welcome in her home and helped me sew and had tailored some of her clothes for me. She was so good to us all. Mother was especially upset as she had imagined that Mary and Ray would always be nearby to help in any emergency. It was a terrible loss to all of us. Poor Ray, he was distraught with grief. Somehow we all got through it and the very sad and stark Easter that followed.

It was time to return to school for all of us; Mother to teaching, Anne to her junior year at Dixon High School, and me to return to the University of Illinois for the rest of my freshman year. It was a long, meditative, and prayer filled ride on the bus that returned me to Champaign-Urbana. Things can change in an instant and when we least expect it was the thought that kept recurring in my mind.

I was just getting settled from my trip back to campus when John called. It was so great to hear his voice. We talked about the last few weeks and set a date to meet on Friday night to take in a dance at the Union Center. There were so many things we shared and talked about. Our times together were filled with fun and exchanges of ideas and information. We began dating exclusively and spending every bit of time we could talking on the phone and planning the next time we would meet.

He was an only child and had graduated from Danville Illinois High School in midyear, so he was able to attend one semester at the University of Illinois before he reached his eighteenth birthday in April of 1945. He knew he would be drafted, so he signed up to join the Navy on that day. After he finished his semester, he left for training. He got as far as Hawaii when the war ended, so eventually he was discharged. He took some time off before enrolling again at University of Illinois on the GI Bill. He was majoring in Civil Engineering and was scheduled to graduate in January of 1950. The time flew by whenever we were together. I was really in love this time.

But there was one area that we carefully side-stepped religion. He was a Catholic, and I was a Brethren and/or Lutheran. Neither of us wanted to go there, but eventually we got around to discussing this one thing that divided us. I had a very hard time getting over this obstacle. My faith meant a lot to me, and I couldn't understand why it didn't seem to make much difference to him. I concluded that he wasn't a very strong Catholic and maybe he would change. Yet, I knew this was highly unlikely, because the Church taught that the Catholic Religion was the only true path to heaven.

The semester ended, and I had all summer to think things over. John was scheduled to spend the summer in Minnesota attending Surveying Camp, which was hands on training experience that is a requirement for a degree in Civil Engineering. We promised to write often, and we did.

I was eighteen now, so that summer I was determined to earn enough money so I would not have to work during the school year. I was able to get a job on line at the Borden's Cheese Factory through contacts from my dad. It was hard work. I had to punch the time clock before 8:00 a.m. and was out at 4:30 p.m. I worked on the assembly line changing jobs every hour. Eventually each of us worked every position on the line. At the beginning of the line we placed boxes on the belt; at the next position we placed a plastic liner open in each box. Then the boxes progressed to where the hot melted cheese poured into each box. There was a man there to make sure that all was working properly and that automatic shut-off filled each container with the right amount in each box. After they were filled, the boxes needed to be closed by hand, by quickly swiping the top of the hot cheese liners with our plastic gloved hands, but it still was very hot. Ouch! At the end of the line, tops were placed on the boxes and then all were stacked into packing containers for shipment. Most of the positions were filled by women who were seated across from each other, each doing the same task. We had to keep up, so at first I wasn't up to speed and the woman across from me had to work harder, but I soon was able to do my share. After each break time, we would progress to the next job, so it evened out, as some positions were more difficult than others, but I soon got used to each job.

I couldn't always remember where I was supposed to be, especially by the next day, but the other women always knew, and I was firmly told where I was supposed to go. There was always chattering as we did our jobs. I felt out of my element as most of the woman were forty or fifty years old and had been doing this type of job for years. It was boring after awhile, and I wondered how they could take this day after day. I knew that come fall I would be back at school. This was something to look forward to and allowed me to tolerate the work, besides the pay was great. The other women resented me, because I didn't have to join the union. I was a temporary worker and could work without paying union dues for a four month trial period. Of course, I didn't have union benefits, but I didn't care. I was making much more money than I had ever made before.

Once during one of our breaks, I talked a little with one of the other workers. I was talking about what I planned to do and about going back to school in the fall.

She said bitterly, "You think life is just a bowl of cherries. Just you wait! You will see what life is really like!"

I was taken aback by this remark. I could see that if I had to do this full time, with no other prospects in mind, it would be a very difficult life. After that I said very little about personal things and just stuck to the news of the day and the weather.

On weekends, I worked Friday and Saturday nights and sometimes Sunday afternoon and evening at the dairy-soda fountain where I had previously worked, so it was very busy. I didn't date much that summer, but I enjoyed the steady flow of letters back and forth from Johnnie, who was in upper Minnesota and was busy but a little bored on weekends. The good part was that my bank account was growing, and I had happy thoughts about the fall when I would return to the University.

On warm summer evenings, Mother, Daddy, Anne, and I would sometimes drive out to see the farm and walk down to the spring. It was great to see it and remember the old days. It was a summer to do a lot of thinking and reviewing in my mind about what I really wanted to do next. I wondered if things would progress with Johnnie and if he would be THE ONE! I hoped so, but I was concerned about our differences in religious beliefs. I would wait to see how that unfolded.

There were weekend visits from Nickie and George and family. In the past they usually had stayed at Mary and Ray's, but now we somehow managed to sleep everyone with us, but it was fun to see them. We all missed Mary! Soon the summer was gone, and I started planning what to take back to school and what new clothes I needed. Mother and Anne would be starting back to school about the same time. Anne would be a senior in high school, so she had to begin looking seriously at colleges.

In early September, I was on the bus to return to school, but this time to the sorority house. I knew I would really like it there. During my pledge semester I had become well acquainted with many of the girls and been assigned a roommate. We talked by phone about how we would like to decorate our room, so I had purchased my part. I was very excited about my return and especially to see Johnnie again!

What a joy to be back at school surrounded by the new friends I made the previous spring. Everyone was getting settled with new roommates decorating their rooms, unpacking and sharing their experiences of the past summer. There was much laughter and interaction between rooms. It all seemed just right. I felt secure and peaceful, yet stimulated by my new surroundings. It was then that I knew I made the right decision to join the sorority. And when Johnnie called, my day was complete. He asked about getting together and buying football tickets together. I told him about Block I and suggested that he sign up for it, too. Secretly, I thought it would be a good idea for us to share this experience, yet if our relationship would fall apart, we wouldn't be stuck with tickets next to each other. Naturally, I hoped that this would not happen, but I thought we should go a little slow, in case things didn't work out as I had hoped.

He agreed, so we arranged to meet at the Student Union later that day to catch up with each other's news. Yes, it was great to be back at school!

Peggy, my roommate, was a sophomore also, and loved to play tennis. We soon fell into the routine of playing a vigorous game of tennis before breakfast several times a week. The fall weather was warm and mild so we were able to play right up until nearly Thanksgiving time. We became very close friends and shared our thoughts and dreams. What a treasure to make such a good friend.

I was initiated into Phi Mu at a ceremony near the beginning of my sophomore year, as I had completed my pledge requirements last semester. It had its lighter moments, but ultimately, it was a very moving experience. Now I had a real sense of belonging and a better appreciation of the history and traditions of the sorority. Sadly there was one girl who had not made her grades for two semesters and was now enduring her third semester as a pledge. She turned up in my English History Class. One of the upper classman in our house asked me to tutor her in this class, so that hopefully this time she would make her grades. I enjoyed working with her, and in the end she did make her grades, but I benefited, too, as I got an A in that class. Drilling her about all the facts and dates helped me to learn it backwards and forwards. It was an enjoyable experience. She was initiated, but eventually she flunked out of school. She was a likeable, fun-loving gal, just not a good student.

I was seeing a lot of Johnnie. We talked often by phone but did not go out during the week, as he had a very challenging class load, being in engineering school. He was very serious about making good grades and completing his University degree. On Saturdays during football season, Johnnie and I spent lots of time together. After the football game, we usually went out for dinner and maybe a dance at the Union Building or took in a movie. One memorable Saturday his mother and father came over from Danville, only about thirty minutes away, to attend the game, and met us afterward. They took us both out to dinner. It was so interesting getting to know them. They were about the same age as my parents, as they had met and married later in life, also. His Dad had emigrated from Austria before the beginning of the first World War. He was a shoemaker by trade, which he had learned in Austria, and now owned and operated a shoe repair shop in Danville. Johnnie's Mother had been a school teacher and had taught for about twelve years before they married. I felt very comfortable with them, as they were friendly and kind, much like my own family.

I knew that I was really in love this time but wondered what would happen next. Was Johnnie as in love as I was? It certainly seemed like it. He proclaimed his love for me often, both very passionately when we were dancing or out on a date, and casually, ending our phone conversations with, "See you soon. I love you." I didn't want it to end, but I was still concerned about our differences in religion.

One weekend that fall, Johnnie was going home for the weekend and invited me to come along, so I went. I gained a real understanding about his parents and family life that weekend. They lived at the edge of town on a few acres of land, had a huge garden, orchard, chickens, and a barn which housed a couple of calves they were raising and planning to butcher later in the year. They had a country life style, which brought back memories of my years on the farm. I was very comfortable talking with his mom. We soon were chatting away like old friends.

In the course of conversation, she told me about her young life, how she met John, her husband, and their dating and getting married. She converted to the Catholic Church, when they decided to marry. That helped me understand why Johnnie didn't seem to be concerned about our differences in religion. I realized that he must just presume that in the end, I would just convert and that would be that. But, I had a real problem with doing it, since I held such different beliefs. Maybe she could do that, but I felt I couldn't go along with it, if I really didn't believe in what the church taught. This was something so important in my life that I could not lightly dismiss it. Should I stop seeing Johnnie? I was torn. I knew I loved him and wanted to spend my life with him, but this was a huge block for me.

On Sunday morning we all went to the Catholic Church together. It felt so strange and foreign to me with the Latin liturgy and the kneeling, standing, and sitting. I wondered if they really knew what was going on and understood it all, or if it was just a time for prayer and meditation. What really bothered me was praying to the Saints. I had been taught that when you die, you are just asleep, and that all the dead would wake up together, when the last trumpet is blown, as it said in Scripture. If they were asleep, how could they hear our prayer or do anything about it? I wondered if they had ever really studied and read Scripture. I had heard that members of the Catholic Church were instructed not to read the Bible.

I decided that I really had to find the time to discuss all this with Johnnie, before I became more deeply involved with him. Yet, how could I bring it up without presuming the he was thinking about marriage, or was he?

The next weekend was the big dance with Tommy Dorsey's Band. I was so excited to actually be going, as I loved the big band sound and especially Tommy Dorsey! It was all I had anticipated and more. What a wonderful evening. When we returned back to my sorority house, Johnnie asked if I would wear his pin. It was a popular thing to do to show we were a couple and going steady. I accepted, and we went to the jewelry store on campus the next day and had the two pins linked together, his Camelot and my Phi Mu pin. We both knew this was the first step toward engagement. He was finishing his junior year and next semester he would be a senior and hoped to graduate in January of 1950, which was a whole year away.

That Christmas I gave Johnnie a scarf and mittens that I had knitted for him, and he gave me a radio for my dorm room. He told me he knew that I loved music and was surprised that I didn't have one for my room. He suggested that who knows, maybe it would end up being our kitchen radio, after we were married. So now we began talking about how it would be and what our goals and dreams were. Finally we got around to talking about my concern about our differences in religious beliefs.

He explained that he had not really thought much about it until he was away from home during the war. It was then that he came to terms with facing the possibility that he might actually be killed during the war. His religious training gave him peace and a rather fatalistic belief, "that whatever will be, will be", and that God is in charge.

I shared my experiences with the Church of the Brethren and how deeply I had been affected by these experiences. I realized that it was true, that Catholics were discouraged from reading the Bible on the grounds that lay people did not have the education to properly understand all the conflicting statements that are included in Scripture. He had been instructed in catechism classes about the major points of the Catholic Church, and that was enough for him. It seemed to me that he was comfortable with his church and had no desire to probe further in regard to this issue.

Well, that was that. We didn't quarrel about it. We just had very different views about it. In the end we agreed to disagree about the finer points of religious beliefs. I realized that he would probably never change, and I didn't think it was likely that I would change. Could I live with the concept that we each would go our separate ways on Sunday morning, and could I really agree to sign a paper stating that I would agree to raise our children in the Catholic Church? Well, I had all summer to sort this out.

That summer Johnnie got a job working with the Department of Highway for the State of Illinois. I found a job in the State Hospital for the Mentally Disabled, which was located just outside the city of Dixon. I wanted to have some real hands on experience in an Occupational Therapy Department, as I was considering this as a career choice. I had taken some very interesting courses toward an Occupational Therapy degree, like Human Anatomy, Crafts and Sewing courses, and found the concept very interesting and challenging. I was determined to earn enough money to see me through the next year at the University of Illinois, so I also took a job on weekends at the hamburger & dairy bar where I had worked the previous summer. It turned out to be a very tedious and exhausting summer.

This hospital was dedicated to caring for the mentally impaired, which was mostly made up of patients who had a very low level of intelligence or had epilepsy. At that time there were no effective medications for epilepsy. If these people had no family members that were able to care for them, they became permanent residents of this state hospital. The patients that came to Occupational Therapy were selected on the basis that they were able to be in a classroom setting and benefit from learning to do simple to more complicated tasks. They ranged in age from five years old to adults. Some of the adults had lived normal lives until they had developed epilepsy. Over time a patient becomes disabled from repeated episodes of seizures, and their mental capacities become more and more diminished. When they have no place to go and could not care for themselves, they were sent to this state hospital.

I was amazed to see the great variety of activities that took place in this department. There was a great deal of needlepoint, basket making, and sewing. I remember one young girl who could not speak, only make a few guttural sounds, and was able to operate an elective sewing machine with dependable ability. She enjoyed mending sheets and did an excellent job of it. She could sew straight seams, so she was given this task, but was not able to sew more complicated seams that involved curves. Some of the patients with very low intelligence seemed to be very contented doing what we called shredding. They were given scraps of left over fabric cut in about three inch square sections. They patiently unraveled these little squares and the shredded material was used to fill the stuffed toys that were made here. They proudly showed us their little baskets of fluffy threads at the end of each session. It was a very good accomplishment for them.

All of these activities took place in a large building, and the patients were escorted to and from their resident building for morning and afternoon sessions. There were male and female patients who came. The young boys enjoyed basket making and wood working. They turned out some very nice baskets and lovely wooden toys for the nursery. I worked mostly with the stuffed toys and needlepoint. It was amazing to see how nicely they worked, as each concentrated on their own projects, and had the joy of accomplishment when seeing the finished product.

Sometimes a patient would have a seizure while at Occupational Therapy. The staff was trained to take care of them and help them through it. The concern was that they might swallow their tongues and choke or fall and hurt themselves. Sometimes they lost bladder control and someone was asked to accompany them back to their resident hall. They seemed to sense when a seizure was about to occur and would cry out or try to go to one of us for help. I soon learned to do what was necessary when this occurred.

One day I was helping some patients cut out the material for stuffed animals. Suddenly one of the epileptic women rose and came quickly toward me, with her hand grasping an open pair of scissors. As she approached me she fell and nearly pierced me with the open blade of the scissors, before losing consciousness. Fortunately, I was able to deflect the blade, but it was a very frightening experience.

The hospital encompassed about fifty acres, which was surrounded by a rather high stone wall. There was only one entrance to the grounds. The gate house, located at the entrance, was positioned to control all the traffic in and out of the grounds. There was not a concern that the patients would try to escape. Actually the patients were quite happy and content, as they were well cared for. It was more to control the entrance of unauthorized people from entering the grounds. The first building was the administration building, followed by the hospital for the bedridden patients, and the many dormitory buildings. The activities buildings included not only the entertainment hall and the Occupational Therapy buildings, but also the farm buildings, which were a very important aspect of the state hospital. Almost all the food used by the hospital was raised on the grounds. There was a dairy farm and huge gardens which happily occupied the time of many of the male patients. It was a very efficient and well run hospital.

A couple of times that summer when the garden produce was at its peak, the Occupational Therapy group was asked to help out by separating the green beans from the vines. The farming group brought in huge amounts of green beans that had been pulled up, vines and all. They delivered them to us and we sat in the shade and separated the beans from the vines. Later the farming group would come back and haul away the waste vines and take the full baskets of beans to the kitchen. Some would be used for dinner meals, and the extras were canned for future use.

One day I was sent on an errand, which required me to go to the nursery section of the hospital. I was shocked to see so many babies that had huge swollen heads. I was informed that these children were born with this condition, called hydrocephalic, and at that time nothing could be done about it. The life span of these babies was usually only a few months to a year. The baby would never develop normal intelligence and were seemingly unaware of their surroundings. They would never be able to walk or make intelligent sounds and were barely able to move their arms and legs.

I am happy to say that in today's world, there is no longer a need for such a hospital and indeed this hospital is no longer in existence. Now there are medications that effectively control epilepsy, so people with this condition can lead normal lives. Babies born with a hydrocephalic condition can undergo a surgical procedure that inserts a drain or shunt into the skull, which allows the water on the brain to drain away and to cause no harm. Children are still being born with less than normal intelligence, but now public schools have programs for special education and do quite a creditable job of preparing students to lead normal lives. Some are not able to support themselves but are placed in group homes, where together with help and direction, they can care for their basic needs. Indeed, that state facility has now been converted to a prison for non-violent criminals.

I was having a very busy summer working two jobs and writing letters to Johnnie often. He asked if he could come for a visit over the Fourth of July. I was delighted! It would be the first time that he would meet all of my family. I started making plans for that happy weekend. When he arrived he had a surprise for me. He was driving a brand new Chevrolet, which was purchased with a combination of his money, saved during the Navy years and his work during summers and an early graduation gift from his parents. It was useful during the summer, as he used it to drive to and from his job with the State Highway Department. Now that he was a senior at the University of Illinois, he qualified to have a car on campus.

We had a lovely weekend and my family really like Johnnie. I was so happy that we all had such a pleasant time together. Nickie and George and family came out for the day from Chicago, as did Alice and Bob and family, who came in for the day from Orion, Illinois. Mother fixed a cook-out picnic in the backyard. What a special occasion it was, and Johnnie fit right in with our family, but it must have seemed like an awfully big family to him, since he was an only child.

Later we took a picnic to the spring, long walks around town, and a drive through Lowell Park, talking endlessly about all the things that we had been doing while we had been apart. Now the fall semester didn't seem so far away. We both looked forward to returning to school, where Johnnie would have his own car on campus. It would be great fun going out on dates and to the big dances with a car to take us about. This would be his final semester, as he planned to graduate in January. I would be starting my junior year at University of Illinois. I couldn't wait until it was September.

Anne would be starting her senior year of high school in the fall, and she hoped to be going off to college in a year. Mother had recently purchased a better car, so she planned to drive me back to school when the time came. When Johnnie's parents realized that, they invited us both to come for a weekend visit. Daddy and Anne stayed at home. It would be too much for Daddy to make this trip, and Anne would be in school by this time, so she stayed home to cook and keep things going at home.

Mother and Johnnie's parents were nearly the same age, so they found they had a great deal in common and had a wonderful time getting acquainted. It helped that both mothers were school teachers, and John's dad was really a very comfortable person to be around. Initially I was kind of intimated by him, because he so closely resembled Johnnie. They made us very welcome and served lovely meals, mostly from food that John's dad had raised in his garden.

Soon, we were back on campus, going to all the football games, dances and having a wonderful time getting settled back into the routine of classes and all the things that go with dorm life. My sorority had lots of activities, and I was assigned a pledge as my little sister. I was responsible for teaching her the ropes, helping her get acquainted and getting settled in for the next semester.

I talked with my counselor about my class schedule. Having had the experiences at the Dixon State Hospital during the summer, I had a good feeling about Occupational Therapy as a professional choice but wondered if I would be able to finish the program. It called for my junior year at the University of Illinois and then two years training at the University of Illinois Medical Campus in Chicago. I was assured that my scholarship would fund most of the expenses there, except for room and board. I decided to continue with the program.

My courses included advanced sewing, woodworking, and a challenging anatomy course on muscles; we learned where they were located and their functions. I also took a medical terminology course, a medical records course and an art class, this one on architecture. It was a very heavy schedule, but I wanted to complete as much as I could.

I was happily in love, with Johnnie, and now I felt very comfortable about our future together. We discussed how wonderful things would be and where we would go after we were married, not if we would get married.

When I told him about my course of study, and that I would not graduate for more than another two years, he did not want to wait that long. He wanted a formal church wedding. I would like that, too, but secretly wondered how much it would cost and was a little apprehensive about how it could all be accomplished. I thought it would be a lot easier if we just eloped or quietly got married at some chapel on campus when I finished my education in Chicago. We agreed to think it over until the next date.

After much talking, Johnnie finally said no. He did not want to wait that long. He wanted to marry me as soon as he finished school and got a job. How about planning for next spring? I told him I would think about it. On our next date I said I had thought it over and I really wanted to finish school and get my degree. He countered with maybe I could do that after we were married. However, he would be capable of supporting us both, so it was really not necessary for me to plan to work after we were married. So it went back and forth. Now it was nearly Thanksgiving. Over that brief vacation, I talked about it with Mother. She thought it was a great idea for us to get married right away. She approved and the sooner the better. She did not have the time or the money to plan a big wedding and countered with the idea that when the time was right, just elope, and she would give us a wedding present of a refrigerator or something of that sort that we could use. I knew that would not be agreeable with Johnnie but decided to report what she had said.

When we got back together again, we talked about our future plans. Johnnie said that in time we would be able to buy all the things we wanted, but we could never have a real wedding if we didn't do it now. Well, I wanted the fun of a formal wedding, too. So I began to think about how it could be accomplished. In a flash, I thought, he wouldn't be at University of Illinois the next semester, so it would not be nearly as much fun. He would be working, and we didn't know exactly where yet. I could go home, work at the State Hospital, and earn enough money for a very nice wedding, for whenever we decided. And, we could still get together some of the weekends in-between. Ultimately, that was what we planned to do.

On one of our dates just before Christmas break, Johnnie gave me my Christmas present early, a gorgeous diamond engagement ring! I was overwhelmed! He told me that the Camelot club, his residence hall on campus, wanted to come over some night and serenade me on our engagement. I explained that Phi Mu had a custom that when someone became engaged, it was kept a secret for a day, until arrangements could be made for this announcement. I would ask my roommate to secretly go to the sorority closet and get "The Ring", which was a terribly gaudy thing, about twelve inches high, set with a huge glass stone. Probably, it had been used as a display item in a jewelry store, but, somehow, had found its way to our chapter house at University of Illinois. In the middle of the night, she would place it in the small high window that we all passed, as we trouped down to breakfast. Then everyone would know that someone in the house had a new engagement ring. The girls would have all day to guess who it could be. At dinner that night, the newly engaged girl would pass around a large box of Fanny Mae Chocolates that the prospective groom would have sent over, and in doing so would show her ring to everyone. We decided to do both things the same night. Sure enough the boys showed up right after dinner was over, so I passed the candy to them, also. What a night to remember!

Before we went our separate ways for Christmas, Johnnie suggested that he come up on the train before New Year's Eve, so we could have a short visit and we could return together on the train. In that way we began the New Year together. I thought that was so romantic. It was getting harder and harder to spend much time apart from each other.

Over Christmas with my family, our plans were discussed. Daddy really liked Johnnie. He recognized the fine qualities in him but was still concerned about our religious differences. He warned me that I should not let them talk me out of reading the Bible. I assured my dad that we had agreed to disagree about this one thing and that on Sunday morning we would each go our separate ways. Daddy knew that I really loved Johnnie and he could see that we were happy together, so he gave his approval of our marriage.

It was a good idea to take the train back instead of driving, as the weather could be uncertain at that time of year. The train ride back to Danville was lots of fun. It was much more comfortable than the bus ride I usually took back to school, but it took longer as we went into Chicago and then directly down to Danville. We planned to spend a day or so with his parents before driving back to school. Of course we had plenty to talk about whenever we were together. We arrived in Danville about nine o'clock at night, and his Mother and Dad were there to meet us. They took us to their house and, although they went to bed shortly, we stayed up to say goodbye to 1949 and welcome in the New Year of 1950, the year we planned to marry!

Back at school, we had only a few weeks left in that semester, which was filled with preparing for final exams, last minute papers, and very little time left to go out on dates. It all came to an end much too soon, and in no time I was on my way back to Dixon to resume my old job at the State Hospital and Johnnie, now a graduate of the University of Illinois, was beginning his real job with the Illinois State Highway Department in Paris, Illinois, about thirty-six miles south of Danville. The parties were over and now the work began.

As I resumed my work at the hospital, it hardly seemed that I had been gone at all. I was able to resume riding to work with the neighbor with whom I had ridden with last summer. I paid her a small sum to help her with the gas, and she seemed glad of the company on the trip. Now it was time to turn my attention to plans for our wedding.

I took my courage in both hands and placed a call to the priest at Saint Anne's Catholic Church, the nearest parish, to arrange for my required classes of instruction. It was scheduled for Tuesday nights, every week for eight weeks, with Father French, the pastor. So I began. The first night of my class, I arrived at the rectory, bringing with me a little notebook and my Bible. Father French answered the door himself and directed me into his office. He explained that he did not have a housekeeper at this time, as his brother, also a priest, was staying with him for a time while he recovered from a very serious illness. His brother rested a lot and he did not want to have an intrusion that would disturb his brother. It was his way of explaining that he was aware that the rectory was not very orderly, and the reason for it. So our talks began in a very friendly, easy going way.

I relaxed and told him about my situation and background, and it seemed that we were off to a very good start. He introduced the study booklet that he used and explained the topics we would be talking about in each session. I was instructed to read the chapter in advance and prepare any questions that I might have concerning the material. We chit-chatted a little and the hour was over. I felt a great sense of relief, as he had a way about him that was friendly and kindly, without any trace of superiority. It was a very good beginning. I soon found myself looking forward to our Tuesday night sessions.

Most of my friends from high school were off at college or had been married and moved out of town. I missed the friends I had left behind at the University of Illinois, the impromptu bridge games, chit chats, and most of all, my dates with Johnnie. But soon my life was as busy as I wanted. My work days were filled with projects and situations that needed all my attention and concentration. There was one friend from our neighborhood and in my high school class who was still there. She had become a hair dresser and now had her own beauty shop. We renewed our friendship and became very close friends. She had kept in touch with the girls that had not gone off to college, so now I was developing a new circle of friends.

I helped out at home, as Mother was teaching and Anne was in school. I helped with the housework and cooking. In the evenings, I wrote letters to Johnnie, and my time was filled. My Tuesday evening appointments were a nice diversion to my routine. I did my homework for the class and came very well prepared with Scripture passages that I quoted to explain my position and beliefs about topics that we were discussing.

Soon, it was the middle of March when I went to my final class. I thanked Father French and told him how much I had enjoyed the class but explained with a smile, "Well, you didn't convert me, but I still want to marry John."

He answered, "I didn't think I had, but I will be very happy to marry you, as I know that you really are a believer. I wish you both much happiness in your life together."

"Now," I began, "I realize that we can't be married from the main altar of the church, but I would like to see the place that the marriage will take place, so that I can visualize it, plan flowers, and seating etc. I think there will be about a hundred or more guests."

"Well," he paused, "that is a problem. As you can see, I could never get this rectory in shape for a wedding of any size, and there simply isn't any other space available in this parish. I have no choice, but to conduct the wedding at St, Anne's Church, as we do not have a chapel or side altar. Have you decided on a date, yet?"

"Yes," I replied. "We would like to be married at three o'clock in the afternoon on May 14th."

"I'll get my book." He turned and reach for his book and after consulting it, he said, "Oh no! That is a Sunday!"

"Well, what's the matter with that day? I can understand that you may not want to preside at a joyful occasion like a wedding, during Lent, or maybe on a Friday, but Sunday is a joyful day, and a perfect day for a wedding. In fact, in the farming community in which I grew up, it was a very acceptable day. The farmers didn't work in the fields, and the working people did not go to work, so they all were available to attend."

There was a little pause, and I sensed that he was turning this over in his mind. Suddenly a smile broke out on his face and he said. "I'll do it! But I won't tell the bishop. You don't want a Mass, do you?"

"No," I replied. "You see, there will be family members and friends that are not Catholic in attendance, so it would be best to just have the marriage ceremony. Now, who do I call to arrange for an organist and soloist and any other arrangements? Oh, I do hope you can come to the reception."

"I will certainly try to be there, if my schedule permits," he replied.

When I left the rectory, I felt like dancing with JOY. It was all set. Wow! And in that lovely church! Except, of course there were still lots of plans to be made: the flowers, bridesmaids, invitations, guests lists, and my dress! There will be lots to do from now on. I had already selected a lovely tea room near the river for a simple wedding reception. I visualized it to be like a high tea, with tea, coffee, punch and of course the wedding cake. Oh, wait until I tell Johnnie! I thought. I decided to break down and call him long distance when I got home. This was an important day, and I wanted to tell him all about it.

When Mother and Dad Hanzel found out about the date, they discussed it quite a bit. I later learned from Johnnie that Mother Hanzel said, "I can't believe they are going to be married on Sunday afternoon!"

But John's dad had replied, "Well, I think it's a great idea! I won't have to close the shop on Saturday. I may close up a little early, anyway. We'll go to early Mass and drive up there for the day, and I won't miss any work."

The letters flew back and forth. There was the Hanzels' guests list, and my guest list, with the help of Mother. Questions about the reception and the timing and food were resolved. Johnnie wanted to know how many bridesmaids I planned to have and reported that he was looking for an apartment for us in Paris, Illinois. I had already asked a couple of sorority sisters to be bridesmaids and of course Anne would be a bridesmaid, as well. I was shopping like mad for invitations, my dress, planning the bridesmaids' dresses, and flowers. It went on and on.

It was amazing to see how the whole plan was taking shape. My friend, the hairdresser, was a big help. She knew someone who could make the wedding cake, and she even arranged a bridal shower for me. I was so surprised. In addition she arranged to do my hair and anyone else's in the bridal party the day before the wedding. I asked her to take care of the bride's book, and she did a great job of it. How nice to have so many friends. The people I worked with at the hospital gave me a shower on the last day I worked. I was so pleased.

Finally it was May, and on our wedding day it was a beautiful day. The night before the wedding we had a rehearsal in the church and dinner after. Since Johnnie's parents didn't come up until Sunday, my parents came to the rehearsal but didn't go out to the dinner with us. They wanted to go home and be rested for the next day. It was just the bridal party and a few of my closest friends from Dixon, all about my age, so it was a lively party and lot of fun to start off the celebration weekend.

The wedding turned out to be better than I could have possibly hoped. I could not remember a happier day of my life! The reception was perfect and lots of fun. Father French did come and was a great guest. Nickie and George and family came, as well as Alice and Bob and family, and Jerry and Gerry and family, from St. Louis. My two Aunts, Daddy's sisters, were there and lots of other relatives and friends from the Dixon area. It was a wonderful day but disappeared like a flash. Soon we were on our way to begin our honeymoon. I was wearing my new going away suit with Johnnie in his new car, all covered with decorations, with shoes, and things tied on the back bumper.

We stayed in a nice hotel in Aurora about a two hour drive from Dixon for our first stop on our way to Niagara Falls, New York City, Washington D.C., and to do the loop around to get back to Illinois. What an adventure! Neither of us had ever been to these places, so we came armed with maps and plans. We met one of Johnnie's friends from Camelot, who lived in New York City. He had arranged for us to stay with his family in New York City, attend a Broadway Play and see the sights, as his wedding present for us. What a wonderful experience.

We were gone for two weeks. We stopped in Dixon to see Mother and Dad, bring them a little present from New York, and pick up the wedding presents. We also stopped in Danville for a brief visit with his parents, bringing them a small gift before driving on to the apartment I had never seen and to begin our life together.

Life In Paris

W e settled into our small, three room apartment in Paris, Illinois to begin our life together. I love to tell people that we started our married life in Paris—that is, in Paris, Illinois. Johnnie had been working in the office of the Illinois Department of Highway since graduation and had commuted back and forth from Danville, until recently when he rented the apartment and was somewhat settled. So, he became acquainted and knew quite a few people who lived there. It seemed that the social life in Paris (population about 12,000) centered around the Elks Club, so he had already joined. The Elks had both a city club and country club. The Country Club consisted of a nine whole golf course with dining facilities in the summer months. There were parties, dances, and bridge games, as well as the golf, so it was a wonderful way to meet people and great fun. During the winter months, the country club was closed and the club in town was then the hub of activities, which included a bowling alley, card room, dining facilities and a ball room. In no time we had become acquainted, and I began to feel right at home.

I unpacked the things I had brought from home, wedding presents, my clothes, and the radio. It was soon arranged to my satisfaction and really did not require much work to keep it neat and clean. There was a rather large living room furnished by the new furniture that Johnnie and I had picked out, which was the wedding gift from his parents. There was a very small bedroom, small kitchen, and bathroom, but it was certainly adequate. Our apartment was on the first floor of a large, white, two story house with a big wrap-around porch. There were two apartments upstairs, which were occupied by other renters, and the owners lived on the other side of the first floor.

Since there was a door from our kitchen that accessed the stairs to the basement from our apartment, the owners allowed me laundry privileges in the basement. One of the first things I did was to wash all of our traveling clothes. There was a Maytag wringer washing machine, which I certainly knew how to operate, and clothes lines in the basement and outdoors for use in nice weather. The washing I could do and my ironing, but I had never ironed a man's shirt before. Oh, my! Johnnie said he liked them done with light starch. This was in the days before wash and wear. I sprinkled them with water and rolled them up to do the next day. It took me about a half hour to do one shirt, and there were so many! First I would iron the collar, then I ironed the front for a while, and by the time I got to the back the front was messed up, and I still had to do the sleeves. They looked really bad when I finished. I hung them on hangers and hoped they would straighten out by themselves, but of course they didn't.

When Johnnie saw them he said. "Oh, I like them folded."

Oh, wow! I thought. *That will really mess things up.* But I said "Oh, okay."

The next day I tried again. There were about ten shirts that needed ironing. Ugh! That summer I had a lot to learn. I knew how to bake a few things, but regular cooking was something I hadn't done. But I thought, *Really? If you can read you can cook.* The first few months I poured over the cookbook, walked to town, which was a brief walk of four or five blocks, and purchased the items the recipes called for, and carefully planned what to have for dinner each day. Sometimes it turned out great, other times not so good. But I was learning. The time did not weigh heavily on me, as I was learning the tricks of cooking and ironing those awful white, and sometimes blue dress shirts, which he wore every day! Sometimes when he came home for lunch, he would change into a fresh shirt and pop the one he had only worn for a half day in the hamper. Maybe he was hoping that it would speed up my learning curve, but to me it was painful! If this goes on, I'll have ten or twelve shirts every week!

Finally in my distress I thought, *If only there was a book to show me how to iron these things!* When I put away the iron that day, I happened to look in the box and was amazed to find the very instruction booklet I needed!

Well, I poured over that booklet and looked at each step carefully. It even showed how to fold the shirt. How very fortunate for me! Hurray!

My learning curve improved dramatically. By the end of the summer I could iron a shirt in about fifteen minutes, and it looked very acceptable. Eventually, I could do it in about seven minutes. But, most importantly, they looked much better, so the six or seven shirts a week that I had now didn't take me nearly as long! Fortunately, Johnnie was very patient with me. Later, we laughed about it for years.

We played golf nearly every weekend together, and sometimes a nine holes, twilight game, during the week. Eventually, I became acquainted with some other gals and was invited to play during the week with them. Golf I knew how to play, but of course there is always room for improvement, so I had fun, and soon I was playing bridge with them, too. The summer flew by.

I had great conversations with my land lord. Her husband worked during the day. Occasionally we met outside and would visit a bit. She was very kind and wanted to make sure we were comfortable, and I assured her things were coming along very well. One day she asked me if we had registered to vote, and I explained that Johnnie had, but I hadn't.

Before I could explain further, she jumped in and said, "Oh, you must do it soon, as there will be an election this fall. It is very important that everyone vote."

"No, I won't be voting this year, but Johnnie and I will talk it over and he can do the voting for both of us," I replied.

Well, I really had her going. After that, she went on a regular campaign, to explain how it was our duty, etc., etc. This happened every time I saw her. I really couldn't register to vote, because I was only 20 and you had to be 21, but I didn't want to tell her that now, since she was having such a fine time trying to convince me.

Finally, to quiet her down, I said, "Well, maybe I will." I never did tell her the real reason. Johnnie and I laughed about that for years, as well.

Danville was only about thirty-five miles from Paris, so we went up several times in the summer to visit his family and sometimes they would come down, just for the day on Sunday. I was getting more confident about my cooking, so it was fun to have them visit. Mother Hanzel was such a wonderful cook that I wanted everything to turn out very well. When we went up there, I tried to help out in the kitchen, and watched like a hawk to help my learning curve in that department.

My mother was a wonderful letter writer, and we corresponded frequently. We always had a letter going back and forth in the mail. In those days we didn't call long distance very often, but I did enjoy the letters and was able to keep in touch that way. Anne had been accepted at the University of Illinois, but she did not get a scholarship. Now that Anne was the last one, they could manage, easily, to help her financially. Mother was still teaching and planned to teach for at least four more years. Now they had a better car, so she planned to drive down to campus and help get Anne settled. She wanted to visit us, too. I was delighted. I could arrange to put them up, as there was a Murphy bed that belonged to our apartment. It was stored in the closet, right out in the front hall, near our front door. There would be room to open it up in the living room; it would be a little crowded but fun to have them see our little apartment and Paris.

In late August, Mother and Dad arrived. They had dropped Anne off at the campus for orientation, so it was just two extra guests. Champaign Urbana is about sixty miles north and east of Paris. It was great fun to have them, and by that time I was a more confident cook, so it was a very pleasant weekend. We made plans to go up to Dixon in the late fall, before winter weather set in.

After they left and September began, I had a let-down feeling, like something was out of place. Here it was September, and I should be going back to school, too. I had been going to school every year in September since I was five years old. I had checked around and there were no openings for teachers in the area. With two and a half years at the university, at that time I qualified to teach in the lower grades, if needed. I could go on the substitute list, but somehow that didn't seem right. I knew it wasn't what I should be doing. I checked on the possibility of returning to the University by taking a bus to Champaign Urbana and then return, but the schedules were impossibly difficult, and I knew that Johnnie would not agree to have me gone for three or four days a week to attend classes. I still had my scholarship there; it was just a question of transportation. Soon the golf season would be over, and then what would I do all day? Housekeeping in a little three room apartment was no longer enough to keep me occupied. I had lots of time to think. I considered volunteer work, but where and what? I decided to pray about it, confident that God would know what was best.

I was aware of our expenses and our income, and I knew it was a tight budget. We were doing okay, but no matter how hard we tried there was not much room for saving. The prudent thing was for me to get a job, but I knew Johnnie's opinion on that subject.

One day when I was shopping around town, I noticed a sign in the window that announced the opening of a Singer Sewing Machine Center and a help wanted sign for a sewing teacher. "Oh. That's just the thing for me!" I thought. I went in and applied. Well, they hired me on the spot, as a sewing teacher, with a surprisingly comfortable salary. I would be required to go to Indianapolis, their corporate headquarters, for a five day training period, all expenses paid, plus my salary. They wanted me to start as soon as possible. I happily agreed.

As I walked home, I rehearsed in my mind how I would tell Johnnie. I fixed an especially nice dinner and then after dinner I broke the news to Johnnie. Well, of course he was not pleased, but after talking it through he finally agreed, but only if I would agree to deposit all my pay checks in a savings account. His point was that he didn't want us to become dependent upon two salaries. My big selling points were that I certainly had the time, and that the extra amount would help us save up for a down payment on a house.

I reported for work the very next day and helped with stocking the shelves. They set up the schedule for me to go to Indianapolis for the training class the following week. I took a bus over, only about ninety miles, and stayed in a hotel. All the schedules and reservations were made by them. It was great fun. I felt confident that I could do the work. This class instructed us about teaching others the use of all the attachments and the content of the various classes we would be teaching.

Eventually I taught classes in beginning dressmaking, which was included with the purchase of each sewing machine that was sold. There were classes in tailoring, home decorating, which included slipcovers, curtains and draperies, and teenage classes on using a pattern and sewing for beginners. In addition, they taught us how to demonstrate other items sold in the store, which included vacuum cleaners and their attachments. Part of my job would be to sell as much merchandise as I could and be qualified to demonstrate sewing machines when I wasn't teaching classes.

I loved it from the very beginning and soon found that I was quite successful in the sales department. I found that I had to schedule very carefully, so that I did not neglect things back in the apartment. I worked five days a week. I had a day off in the middle of the week, but was required to work every Saturday. Johnnie soon adjusted to this, as most Saturdays he had to work until noon.

We made it work and soon we both adjusted to it very well. I did the laundry and ironing, as well as cleaning on my day off. Most Saturday nights we went to the club for dinner or out to eat somewhere and to a movie, so it was our "date night". It was very rewarding to see our little savings account growing.

Mother wrote, diplomatically asking when she could expect to be a grandmother? I had secretly wondered about that myself. I responded, "Wait and see." I believed all things happen in due time. We were not in a hurry, and besides, I told myself, even birds build nests before they lay eggs, and we had such a small apartment. Mother and Dad Hanzel never asked, but I thought they wondered about that, too.

In early November we scheduled a trip up to visit my mother and dad. Armistice Day (now called Veterans Day) was on Saturday that year, so we had a day off on Monday. Mother had time off from school, as well. The weather was great and it was a wonderful visit. The fall flew by and soon the leaves were off. Johnnie was scheduled to a survey party for a projected new highway west of Paris. Sometimes, he would be gone for a couple of nights but was usually in the office on Mondays and Fridays. I was so glad I had something interesting to occupy my time. Currently, I had a couple of classes each week, so the store was a busy place.

Around the middle of December, I was walking home from work in the early evening, about 5:30 and it was already turning dark. I slipped on a spot of ice, fell, and broke my right wrist. Ouch! I was able to walk home, but by the next day it was really painful, so I had to go to the hospital for x-rays. Johnnie was notified and called in from the survey party, as I had to have surgery, to set it properly. This accident brought him home for a few weeks, since I needed help to dress. I didn't miss much work, as I could still teach sewing, but I really missed not being able to write or cook well, do the laundry or ironing, or even do my hair or nails.

But the good news that came from this accident was that Johnnie was in the office for the rest of the month. He heard all the latest news, including that Du Pont was planning to open a plant near Newport, Indiana, thirty-five miles east of Pairs. They were hiring workers of all sorts, like engineers, electricians, construction workers, and office workers. Johnnie took a day off from work and applied. He was hired and at a salary of nearly half again as much as his salary at the Highway Department. So, he gave proper notice and started work in Indiana after the new year.

It worked out very well. There were other people moving in, both at Danville and Paris, so soon Johnnie was in a five man car pool; then I could use the car four days a week. It was a real perk for both Danville and Paris, since many families transferred from other areas of the country, from various departments in Du Pont.

Soon, we were playing bridge and golf with people John met from his car pool and at the office. The plant was a heavy water plant, developed as part of the Hydrogen Bomb project. It was all very experimental, so they were all learning together. The extra money and benefits were wonderful. What a blessing. Every painful experience brings its own joyful side.

By spring our little savings account had really grown, and we started talking about buying a house. We were well acquainted by now and knew where we wanted to locate. Soon, we found a small, two bedroom house located on East Madison Street. It was in our budget range. It had a nice size living room, dining room, and kitchen, one bath, with two bedrooms, basement and separate garage. The lot was narrow, but deep, with space for a garden in the back yard. We went to see about a mortgage at the local Savings and Loan Company, but the manager was doubtful about us buying a two bedroom house. His reason was that a young couple like ourselves would soon have children and would out-grow this house quickly.

But this was all we could afford at this time, so it was finally approved. We pointed out that my earnings were going into the savings account, so we could live nicely on John's salary.

We moved into our very own house in early May, and we celebrated our one year anniversary there. It seemed huge to us after our little three room apartment. I was able to buy a sewing machine with my employee's discount and later a vacuum cleaner in the same way. I made new draperies for the living room and curtains for the kitchen. It was so much fun to have my own electric sewing machine at home. (I still have the same machine today, and it works very well, more than sixty years later.)

We tackled projects together, like removing all the many layers of wallpaper from the kitchen. I had helped Mother wallpaper, so I could hang the wallpaper when we were ready. The flower beds and garden were something we did as soon as possible and planted vegetables and flowers there. Oh, it was fun! Mother and Dad Hanzel were great resource people for this project, as Dad was a fabulous gardener. He generously brought down a few plants for our flower beds.

As soon as we could, we purchased a double bed to go into the extra bedroom, so now we could have over-night guests with greater comfort. The washer would have to wait. Now, I was going to the Laundromat on my day off, which was easily done, as I had use of the car more often, but an automatic washer was definitely on my wish list. We were very comfortable in our home, but suddenly our needs were expanding, as we would like furniture for the dining room, and we were always coming up with things we would like to have or do.

It was difficult to save, even though our Building and Loan payments were less than our rent had been. Owning a home had additional bills such as real estate taxes which were due soon. We wanted to paint the outside of the house but would wait another year, hoping that Johnnie could do it himself, as it was only one story. But we would need to buy ladders. Oh, the joys and the downside of home ownership.

The golf season was in full swing, so we did find time to play golf after we were settled. Our new neighbors were very friendly, so our friends took a big leap in numbers, with the addition of all of the new Du Pont friends. After we purchased a drop leaf dining room table and chairs, we were ready to do more entertaining.

The Hanzels gave us an old card table, which had been well used. I won a new card table as a prize from Singer, as I was the highest salesperson for the Vacuum Cleaners Sales Contest for our district. Now, we could have two tables of bridge at our house. My cooking level of expertise was improving, so we had an occasional dinner party. Life was good!

I found a Christian Church home nearby, which I found comfortable. Soon I was singing in the choir. I felt quite at home and felt better about going to church, especially now that I didn't have to sit alone. I had my place in the choir loft. Sunday mornings, Johnnie usually went to the early Mass, so I could have the car to go to my church, but it was within walking distance, if necessary. Our Sunday schedule was settled, and we didn't have any problems in that department.

Early in the summer, Mother and Dad came down to visit us in our new home and heartily approved of our choice. It seemed so right for us then, and we had a very happy summer getting settled in and making decisions on what to do first and what would have to wait awhile.

Anne had a summer job, so she could not come, but she promised to visit us sometime soon. It was nice to catch-up on all the family news. We planned to come up for a visit, sometime before school started again. I wanted to see the farm and the spring again, so we set a date for that. Our calendar was filling up fast.

In the fall I started to do more sewing and decided to make an outfit for Anne for school. When she came to visit, it was nearly finished, and I checked it for fit and length. She was very pleased with the results. I was really enjoying my sewing machine and started to tackle other projects for the house.

Soon, it would be time to plan for Christmas. It would be such fun decorating for the first Christmas in our first home. But there was a huge surprise in store for all of us. I began to suspect that I was pregnant, so in late December I consulted a doctor. He confirmed my suspicions. The baby would be due in the middle of August. We were thrilled but decided to wait and tell our families until after Christmas. Later, we would announce it to everyone else.

Right from the start I thought the baby was a girl, and soon we were calling her Henrietta Hanzel. It was fun talking about her by name. Later when I was talking to Mother she said, "Are you really going to call her that?"

I laughed and said, "No. It's just a joke. It is nicer to call her by name, rather than calling her 'the baby' or 'it'. When she gets here we will decide. We have to see what she looks like first."

I was busy making maternity clothes for myself. I planned to work at least until hot weather but only if I continued to feel well. I didn't show yet, but I wanted to be prepared for when I would need the clothes. We were saving our money, so that we could do some of the things around the house that we planned. I hoped that we could soon buy an automatic washer. We would need it when the baby came. Credit cards were something that Johnnie disapproved of and were not common at that time. We would need a basket for the baby right away and later a crib. At first we planned to have the baby in the little basket in our room, but when she was older, we would put her in a crib in the spare room.

In March Johnnie was sent to Wilmington, Delaware for a two week training program. While he was gone I got busy and painted the spare room pink for Henrietta. It turned out a brighter pink than I had envisioned, but it was clean and bright, and cheery. Johnnie was so surprised when he returned.

"Are you really sure she'll be a girl?" He asked.

"I'm sure. I don't know why, but it just seems like it will be."

The ladies in my current sewing class thought it would be great if it would be a girl, as they envisioned me making cute, little dresses for her.

At first I wore my shirt tails out, and I didn't show, but by April, I wore maternity clothes all the time. It was much more comfortable. I told the manager at this time. He was very sorry that I would be leaving, as he was happy with the job I was doing. I was sorry to leave and decided that I would work as long as I felt well. Johnnie did most of the garden planting that spring, as it was a little much for me to do it, but otherwise I kept up with my regular routine.

In April I was definitely feeling signs of life. The doctor said I was doing fine, but I began to feel tired, and the heat really bothered me. In late May I received a letter from Alice saying that Bob was working out of the country, and she thought it might be a good time to visit. She would bring the two girls and wondered if that be too much for me. Diane would be out of school by then, and maybe I would like a little company to pass the waiting time.

I thought it over and decided that by then it would only be two months before Henrietta would arrive. By then I would be ready to take it easy. I scheduled my sewing classes to be completed by the middle of June, and then I would retire. Johnnie was very glad. He thought it was high time I stopped working. I would have two months left to shop for baby clothes and get things finished around the house, in order to be ready for the big event.

We decided to buy the washing machine now as it was harder and harder for me to load up the laundry and lug it down to the laundromat each week. It was a joy to finally have it delivered and hooked up. I would hang out the laundry in good weather or in the basement, if necessary. Things were coming to a close for me at work. I had worked for Singer for nearly two years, and Johnnie had worked for Du Pont for about a year and a half. We had excellent medical and hospitalization coverage with Du Pont, so that was not a concern for us. Things were coming together very well, and I was looking forward to Alice's visit.

She and the girls arrived in early July. It was a relaxing and enjoyable visit. However, it was extremely hot, as it can be in the summer in Southern Illinois. Actually it was a relief when they left.

When Alice returned home from Paris, she called Mother and alerted her that I didn't look well, and she should plan to help me, at least a week before the baby was due. I learned about this much later. I wasn't around pregnant women and didn't know what to expect. I thought I was doing just fine.

Mother wrote and said that Anne was home from the University, and she could be with Daddy and take care of the housework, so she wanted to come down early, maybe as early as the first part of August. Then we could have a nice visit before things got hectic with the new baby. Maybe the baby would come early, she wrote, and she wanted to be there for the big event.

I wrote back and invited her to come whenever it was best for her. Mother arrived the first day of August. She took the bus, so Anne would have use of the car in her absence.

It was wonderful to have her with me. She didn't let me do a thing, and we had plenty of time to talk and talk. I was encouraged to take a nap every day and was surprised that I found it very nice to have someone with me in the last few days. She insisted on doing all the cooking and kitchen work, and I found it very comforting. I guess I was more tired than I realized.

Now, I was on a weekly schedule to visit my doctor, so Mother went with me for a visit or two. He assured us that everything was fine and the baby should come at any moment. One night Johnnie and Mother and I decided to go to the movie in town. It was an Oscar Hammerstein movie with lots of music and dancing. It was great fun and we came home about 9:30. When I got home I decided to go right to bed. I was just settled in when my water broke. What a mess! Johnnie called the doctor, and he told us to go straight to the hospital where he would meet us.

I had started to feel cramps or labor pains, but it wasn't too severe. They brought me right to a room and gave me something to induce labor, as I had lost the water. They wanted the delivery to occur as soon as possible. I went into normal labor, and Johnnie and Mother were there with me for most of it. It wasn't too bad, and I tried to relax. When I opened my eyes, I was startled to see how worried Johnnie looked, and I became a little frightened. I ask him to put cold cloths on my forehead, and I kept my eyes closed. Then I could relax. By early morning, a six and a half pound baby girl was delivered safe and sound. I was so joyful to hold my first born and to know that all was well.

But Johnnie and Mother had been terribly worried about it all. The doctor told them that there was a great danger that the placenta would come first, and in that case, when it detached first, the baby might not survive. This is called Placenta-Previa. I was happily unaware of this. Now, I understood why every time I tried to talk and opened my eyes, I saw Johnnie looking so worried. I chalked it up to his sympathy for me, because I was in pain. I think they had a worse night than I did. They say "ignorance is bliss", and in this case, it was true.

I was kept in the hospital a little longer than usual, because the next day I started running a fever. I was given an antibiotic, but it took several days for that to clear things up, and then my temperature began to return to normal. As a result I was unable to nurse the baby. It was a restful week for me. All I did was rest, have visits from Mother and Johnnie, and hold the baby from time to time. It was a very peaceful, joyful interlude.

Six days later, Janet Elizabeth and I returned home to our little house on East Madison Street, and it was so wonderful! Mother was there and wouldn't let me do anything but take care of the baby. I had her to help me every step of the way. Mother was determined that I would be able to nurse the baby, but the fever had dried up my milk. Johnnie scurried about to purchase the required formula, sterilization kettle, and the bottles, so everything was on hand. Janet was a nice size baby and she took to the bottle right away. I had been giving her bottles in the hospital some of the time, so it was an easy adjustment for me, except that it was every four hours, night and day at first. Oh, well, it was still enjoyable. With all the help, I was really well rested, so our home coming was peaceful and joyful.

Once I got the hang of it, it was lots of fun giving her a bath. But dressing her was something I struggled with at first, as her little arms and legs were so tiny. I was learning to fold the diapers to just the right size to fit her and pin them on, not sticking her with the pins! I had to be very careful to support her head at all times in the bath and while I held her. There was a lot to learn. It was wonderful to have Mother there to show me the ropes.

Mother arrived the first of August, and Janet was born on the eleventh, so a week after we came home, it was time for Mother to leave. Her school started right after Labor Day. She had much to prepare to get ready for the start of another school year. By then I was strong and ready to be on my own. We had a baby scale and we could tell the baby was gaining and thriving. Wonderful! The whole experience was a very blessed time from the very beginning.

Mother and Dad Hanzel visited as soon as they possibly could. They were very excited and pleased to be grandparents. Janet had a lot of very loving visitors in the first few weeks we were home, and it was pure bliss.

Soon, it was time for my six week check-up and another visit to the doctor, for Janet as well. I was driving by then, and thanks to the Hanzels and other friends and family, we were now fully equipped for the baby, including a car bed for the car that could later be changed into a car seat, as well as darling little dresses and sleeper sets. It was a joy to get us ready for our little outing.

Everything was fine with Janet, but I was surprised to learn that things were not fine with me. The doctor informed me that there seemed to be a "growth" in my abdomen. It was not in my uterus but outside of it. The uterus had returned to its normal size, but this other "thing" was definitely there. He said he wondered about this all along, since he thought I was farther along in my pregnancy than I was when I first visited him. The other signs were right on schedule, such as first signs of life and the actual birth.

He assured me that sometimes this happened and that he wanted me to come in every month for an examination, to see if it would change in size. He said that sometimes they just disappear by themselves. I was feeling very well and could hardly believe that anything could really be seriously wrong with me.

Johnnie and I talked it over. I said, "Let's not worry about it. You will see. When I go in next month, everything will be absolutely normal."

Every month I went in for a check-up, and sometimes it was a little smaller, then next time it was a little larger, but it always was there. When

Mother Hanzel heard about it, she insisted that I make an appointment for another opinion with her doctor. Danville was a much larger city than our little town of Paris. By this time several months had passed, so an appointment was made for a Friday. I planned to make the first trip with Janet to Danville and stay the weekend with Johnnie's parents. Johnnie was able to catch a ride with one of the car pools from the plant that went to Danville.

It was quite an adventure for me. We planned that the baby and I would drive up Friday morning, only about an hour's drive, and then Grandmother Hanzel would take care of Janet while I went to the doctor. I had to stop a couple of times on the way up, because Janet would be crying. This was something she rarely did, unless she was hungry or wet or over-tired. She actually vomited a couple of times. She had never done that before! I couldn't understand what could be wrong. When we finally arrived, I was a little pressed for time to make my appointment, so I left shortly after arriving. But as soon as Janet was there, she settled right down and was her normal happy self. I was puzzled, but I had to leave for my appointment.

The doctor was as puzzled as my doctor had been about my "growth." He suggested that I return in a month and see if there was any change.

Well, well. I thought, *That's just what my doctor said.* But, I dutifully made an appointment for the next month, since there was pressure from the senior Hanzels to give him a fair chance for a diagnosis. It seemed I was right back where I started. His findings were the same as my doctor's.

Janet was fine when I returned. We all enjoyed the weekend. But when we drove back to Paris on Sunday afternoon, Janet got sick again. It must be that she gets motion sickness in the car, we decided. It proved to be true. We hoped she would outgrow it, but she didn't. We found that it helped to have her sit in the front seat and later the doctor prescribed a medication that would lessen her symptoms. Poor little girl! We felt so bad for her.

We had wonderful fall weather that year, and I enjoyed taking Janet out for rides in the lovely baby carriage that Mother and Dad Hanzel gifted us. I had a friend, Georgia, who had a baby a few months before Janet was born. We would meet at the corner nearly every nice day and take our babies for a little outing. Sometimes she would stop over at our house, or I would stop at hers for a visit. It was great fun comparing notes on how they both were doing.

One day as we were out for our stroll, I said, "I had a dream last night. Now I know that I'm going to have another baby. It will be when Janet is about two or three years old."

This was something that we had talked a lot about before, as we both wanted to have another baby, but not too soon, and we wondered if or when it would happen. So I proceeded to describe my dream. In my dream, I was standing at the changing table by the window in the kitchen, as it was then. I had a "new" baby on the dressing table, changing its diaper. Janet was playing outside, near the kitchen window, when suddenly the window broke and my hand was caught in the window. I was puzzled at first, as the window was broken, yet my hand wasn't bleeding, but it hurt terribly. And I couldn't get it loose. I couldn't reach the phone. I wondered what to do. I decided that, although I had been talking with Janet through the open window, she was too little to send to the neighbors. What should I do? Then I woke up.

We were puzzling over the meaning of this dream, when Georgia asked, "Was the baby a girl or a boy?"

"I don't know." I replied. "It was just a baby, all wrapped up in a little blanket."

"Well," she replied, "you should have looked before you woke up." We both laughed about that.

Time went on. Christmas came and went, and it was a joyful occasion with a new baby in the house. I tried not to worry about what could be going on with my body, and the Danville doctor had no solution, other than wait and see.

It was the middle of February when one morning I got up as usual, to fix Johnnie breakfast and see him off to work. It was still dark and the baby was sleeping well, so I decided not to wake her and went back to bed for a little snooze myself. About an hour later a terrible pain woke me up! It was in my stomach and it felt really awful. I heard the baby, so I got up to take care of her, but the pain was so severe that I could barely cope. I staggered out to the kitchen to heat a bottle, and it seemed a little better when I sat down and fed Janet. Yet it came back soon and much stronger this time. Johnnie was an hour and a half away at work by now, so I decided to call my next door neighbor, Helen, who came right over.

She took one look at me and said that we must call Johnnie immediately and decide what to do.

Johnnie rushed home (he got a friend to drive him home), and he called the doctor in Danville. He instructed us to go right to the hospital in Danville, as soon as possible, and he would meet us there. Johnnie had to pack a bag for us and also pack up things for Janet.

It was then that I said, "There is no way I can ride that far in a car! I am in agony! You'll have to call for an ambulance. I'll have to lie flat or I won't be able to stand it."

"Really?" Johnnie said in surprise. "Are you sure? I have no idea what that will cost and who to call."

"I'm sorry, but it is absolutely necessary this time."

I was usually so frugal that this admission frightened both Johnnie and Helen. Between the two of them and several phone calls later, it was all arranged. Helen was a big help during this time. It was decided that Janet would stay with Georgia and Tom, our good friends. The ambulance arrived promptly and I was loaded aboard. Johnnie would follow in our car.

When we arrived at the hospital the doctor was there shortly after. He talked with me and did a short examination. Then he turned to Johnnie and said, "Is she usually this sensitive to pain?"

"Oh! No!" Johnnie replied. "I was with her during most of the time she was in labor and delivery, and she was a brick. I think she must really have a lot of pain."

"Hmm." He consulted his records and then said, "I am going to order a dye test now and hope that the x-rays will show me what's really happening. Is she allergic to anything that you know of? Has she had anything to eat in the last few hours?"

When the reply was negative to both inquiries, the doctor said, "I will make the arrangements as soon as possible. In the meantime I will order something for pain."

When he left the room, I asked about Janet. He said Georgia and Tom would take care of her until he and his mother could bring her to Danville. In that way his mother could care for her. I was greatly relieved that she was being so well cared for, and after the nurse came in with an injection, I was a little bit more comfortable.

The test was conducted on a tilt table and was most uncomfortable! Dye was injected in my veins and as the dye traveled, it helped illuminate the problem. When I was back in my room, the doctor explained what they had found. He said a large cyst was attached to and wrapped around the ovarian tube shutting off the blood supply to one ovary. No wonder I had experienced such extreme pain.

Astoundingly, these cells contained teeth and hair and were probably cells that had remained dormant all these years but should have been my twin, not Janet's twin! This cluster of cells was probably very small until I became pregnant. The increased level of hormones in my body had stimulated them to start developing and continued to grow for the last several months. Surgery was indicated to remove this.

He went on to say that he would do an exploratory examination and make sure that everything else was normal. He also recommended removing the appendix as a precaution against any further surgery in that area. Most likely the affected ovary would be removed, but, hopefully, I would still be able to have additional children. Although, he cautioned, it was a risk he felt we should take. The surgery was scheduled as soon as possible for the next day.

I was stunned at this news. Johnnie was with me and was wonderfully supportive. I shed a few tears, wondering if I would have more children. Then through the tears I said, "I really want to see Janet and hold her, before I go under this comprehensive surgery. I'm sure they will do the best that they can, but what if...?" I became desperate and threatened, "I won't sign the papers unless I can see Janet and hold her before I go to surgery!"

Johnnie replied, "I will talk it over and maybe Mother and I can go down to Paris this afternoon and bring Janet back up here. Would you like that?"

"Oh, yes!" I said. And that is what they did.

But getting permission to bring Janet into the hospital was another hurdle. I was in St. Joseph's Hospital. The next thing I knew, the head Sister came floating into my room in full habit, to explain the rules of the hospital. It was never allowed that a five month old child could visit in the hospital! It just was not done in those days! She was very firm.

But I was just as firm, and in the end she finally agreed. But it would have to be after visiting hours and only for a few minutes. I was so relieved! But I was still dealing with the shocking news and my concern about the surgery.

I was given another injection and I finally felt peace. I prayed as I fell asleep that He would take care of everything, and I put it all in His very capable hands.

That evening both Mother and Dad Hanzel came to visit during visiting hours but left shortly, explaining that Johnnie would come after visiting hours and bring Janet. Later, Johnnie and baby Janet arrived. It was such a joy to hold her and see her again! It gave me great peace to know that she would be in good hands. Now, all I had to do was just get through the surgery and get well.

After they both left, the Mother Superior came in to see how it had gone. I thanked her for allowing me to see my baby, but I was crying and explained that I was afraid I would not make it through the surgery, and if I lived through it, would I ever be able to have any more children?

"It is all in God's hands," she said firmly, "and I am sure that the staff will give you the best of care possible. As to having more children, you should be thankful that you have one healthy baby." Then, she floated out again.

I thought over her words. At first I thought it was a little harsh, and then I realized, I was feeling sorry for myself! Yes, I was thankful for the many blessings that we had. So, I prayed, "Help me be strong and get through this surgery. It would be so hard to leave Johnnie and Janet to struggle along alone. Take care of all of us."

The next morning I was taken to surgery before I had a chance to dwell over the situation, and I was soon feeling peacefully fuzzy. I knew that Johnnie was there holding my hand as they wheeled me into surgery. The next thing I knew, I was back in my room, and it was all over. I was pretty groggy, but wanted an update. Johnnie reported that everything was fine, and he thought there was a very good chance, that I would have future pregnancies.

That evening the doctor made rounds and we talked. He had not realized how terribly painful it must have been for me. He reported that the left ovary was fine, but he had no choice but to remove the right ovary, as it showed a great deal of damage. The cyst had its own long tube, which was attached to the right ovary. As it wrapped itself around the ovarian tube, it had scarred that ovary, as well as cut off the oxygen supply.

However, the surgery was very successful. Because he wanted to check out everything and remove my appendix, the incision had to be quite long. He assured me that he thought my recovery would be excellent. He also warned me not to become pregnant, until at least a year following surgery. I would be discharged from the hospital in about a week, but I could not return to my usual activities, for at least a month. No heavy lifting, going up and down stairs, etc. He wanted to see me in his office in a month.

I was extremely relieved to talk to him myself and get a clearer picture of the surgical outcome. Johnnie called my mother, but talked her out of coming. Indeed it would have been very difficult, as she was teaching and taking care of Dad. He also called her again, after the surgery, to tell her that everything was fine. I had much for which to be thankful. I felt my strength coming back. I was cozy in bed, as long as I did not move very much. It was very uncomfortable when I moved. All I had to do was get well. Even the reports about Janet were comforting, and she and Mother Hanzel seemed to be getting along just fine.

The first day I was allowed to sit up in a chair for a few minutes while they made up my bed with fresh sheets, I realized how really weak I was. Dad Hanzel stopped by to see me during his lunch hour, and I just sat there like a stone. He chatted along about the baby, but it was all I could do to smile and make a few comments, barely holding on until I could get back to the comfort of lying down again. It was then that I realized that recovery would take longer than I thought. Soon I was allowed to walk a bit, so things began to look better.

It was decided that we would all stay in Danville with Mother and Dad Hanzel for a month. I would be available to go to my one month check-up. Johnnie arranged to drive to the plant with some of the others from that area. It all worked out very well. The DuPont people had been very supportive of John and me. They sent flowers and cards and had assured John that the medical insurance would cover most or all of the medical expenses.

Everyone was wonderful! I received lots of cards and letters from my friends in Paris, the bridge club girls, and golfing friends, and letters and cards from Mother and the family. *I would have a lot of thank you cards to send when I felt better*, I thought.

When I was released from the hospital, I could see how much Mother Hanzel enjoyed baby Janet. She was at a wonderful age, when every day she could do something new, making cooing sounds, reaching, smiling, laughing, and trying to turn over and crawl. It was wonderful to be there and receive such love and care. I was not allowed to do anything but take care of Janet a little. I hoped that soon I would be well and we could return to Paris.

It was wonderful to begin to feel really well and strong again. I had not felt this well since the beginning of about the third month of pregnancy. Janet was now sitting in a high chair and being fed beginning baby foods and cereal. Life was good, and my incision was healing nicely. As winter turned into spring, I felt my spirits soar with the first green blades of grass and the early spring bulbs starting to bloom.

Soon we were back in Paris, and Georgia and I were walking every nice day with our girls in strollers now. I started to think about our garden and what we would plant. Yes, life was very, very good. "Thank you, Lord for helping me back to really great health and strength," I prayed.

I began to wonder if and when Johnnie would ever bring up the subject of Janet's baptism. I felt it was his responsibility to arrange for this, and I suppose he hesitated to bring it up for fear it would be divisive. I was not worried about it though, as I had baptized her in one of her early baths. I had been taught in my instruction classes that in cases of emergencies, anyone could baptize. I didn't want to take any chances, so I had done it secretly myself.

At last, when Janet was nearly eight months old, Johnnie brought the topic up. I asked what he wanted and who would be the Godparents. The wheels were put in motion. Soon the date was set. It was accomplished quite easily, but we were a little embarrassed that Janet was so much older than the other babies being baptized that day. Indeed, the priest commented on it that Janet looked around and seemed to take it all in. But she didn't cry or make a fuss, like the other babies.

We had a little party at our house later. The Godparents were Eleanor, a neighbor that I had known since our apartment days, and Bob, Johnnie's best man, whom he had known from his kindergarten days. He and Phyllis were living in another town in Illinois about fifty miles away, so it was a grand excuse for a party. I think we were both relieved that this was accomplished simply and without controversy.

One day I received a long letter from Mother. Now that school was out, she was spending more time with Dad. She became alarmed by his health and took him in for a complete check-up. The conclusion was that Dad definitely had Parkinson's disease. There wasn't much they could do for him. At that time, there were no medications available for this. It was very frightening for us all. It was usually a long, lingering, and debilitating condition with progressive loss of function.

At that time, Anne had completed two years at the University of Illinois in Physical Therapy, but it was a five year course. Mother wanted very much to continue to teach, in order to help pay her bills, but now, with this diagnosis, she wondered how it would all work out.

Our letters flew back and forth. Mother wrote that they were thinking of selling both of the houses they owned and buying a larger two story home that had an apartment, one up and one down. They would rent the upstairs apartment, but at least there would be other people around if Daddy needed something while she was teaching. Indeed that is just what they did. It was a very well built house, with a huge wrap around porch. It had more built in modern conveniences, and it would not require Daddy to go up and down stairs. In the future, that might be too difficult for him. Their plan was to move in early August. I wanted to help in some way, as it would be quite a job moving.

Alice wrote and suggested that she and I meet in Dixon after they were somewhat settled and help make curtains, draperies, slipcovers, or whatever was needed. Great! I wrote back and we started planning in that direction. The result was that Johnnie drove us up (Janet and me), and we stayed for a week. Johnnie came back and brought us home the next weekend. What fun we had. It turned out that Janet celebrated her first birthday in Grandma's new house. It was amazing how much talking and the amount of sewing that got done in that week. I was able to rent a portable sewing machine from Singer, and Alice brought hers from home, as well as her two girls. So Diane and Cathy played with Janet while we all sewed and talked. And talk we did non-stop!

I liked the house very much. It was in a lovely neighborhood but only a few blocks from downtown. I could see that it was going to be very nice in many ways. By the time we left, the books were all in their bookshelves and everything was in order, with new curtains and draperies in the living room, dining room, and kitchen, and the living room sofa and chairs were sporting new slipcovers. While Alice and I sewed, Anne and Mother did the house work, and we all had a fine time. Dad tried to stay out of the way but spent a lot of time playing with the little girls on the large front porch.

There were many changes in our world at that time in the summer of 1953. Now we all had TV's. Many were built in huge pieces of furniture. They took up a lot of space and dominated our living rooms. Of course they were black and white back. Color was not available; and it was thought to be way off in the future and not at all likely in our life time. In Dixon and in Paris, rabbit ears were not enough to pick up the signal, so we needed tall TV antennas. They were located high above the roof lines. Indeed, all about our towns, these things sprung up everywhere like mushrooms.

Eisenhower was now our president and enormously popular. The only cloud on the horizon had been the Korean War, but it ended July of 1953. Johnnie had wondered if he would be called up to serve. He might have been given an exemption, as he worked for DuPont in the explosives department, but he was never called. It was scary, never the less, as now in the Atomic age we surely hoped these terrible weapons would never be used again.

We tried to go about our own business and trust that things would work out. But it was impossible to ignore these events with nightly news blaring in our living rooms. There were only three major networks, ABC, CBS, and NBC. Local TV stations were starting to broadcast from local towns, but their programs were very limited. At that time, programs were only broadcast from about 7:00 am to about midnight, when the stations would be off the air but leave a test pattern to signal the end of the day and time to go to bed. Most of the time we were all in bed, well before that came on.

Christmas came and went. It was such fun buying things for Janet, as she was excited with every toy and package that she unwrapped. I was busy sewing, making dresses, and even coats and bonnets to match for her, as well as most of my own clothes. I was playing in a bridge club once a week with the girls in the neighborhood. My time was happily filled with housework, taking care of Janet, and teaching her little songs to sing. I made a lovely, long dress for myself to wear to the New Year's Eve Party at the Elks City Club. Johnnie had played a lot of golf during the summer, but I had not gotten back to golf yet. I didn't miss it, though, as my time was happily filled.

My surgery had been in February, so it was now almost a year ago. We both wondered if I would be able to conceive when all the restrictions were off. It was a relief to stop counting the fertile and non-fertile days and just let things happen when they would. Yep! By April I was sure I was pregnant, and it was confirmed by the doctor, but it was not to be. By my third month, I suddenly had a miscarriage. I was devastated. My doctor was very supportive and said not to worry. By this happening, it was likely that any adhesions that were still there had been eliminated. However, if I did become pregnant again, I would have to be very careful to take it easy around the third month, so that it would not spontaneously happen again.

Well, all our concerns about fertility were unjustified. By late fall I was pregnant again, and, though I had a difficult pregnancy and had to have complete bed rest during the third month, John Robert, whom we immediately called little Jackie, was delivered safe and sound in June of 1955. He thrived and was a strong, healthy baby. Mother came down briefly, but because Dad was not as well, she could stay only a short time. I was used to babies by now, so it was not as difficult this time. Johnnie quickly arranged to have him baptized at about ten days old, and I thought it was a good thing.

I did not mind going to church alone. I had stopped singing in the choir some time ago, as I had been incapacitated with all the pregnancies and the children. Johnnie still usually went to early Mass, while I was busy taking care of the children, bathing the baby, and feeding him and playing with Janet. When Johnnie came back, he had his breakfast and I had time to get ready for church. I was back in time to fix lunch for all of us. Sometimes the Hanzels would come down Sunday afternoon, and that was grand. So going our separate ways on Sunday was a very convenient, comfortable schedule for both of us. It had all worked out very well.

Johnnie had built a sand box for Janet, and it was located just outside our kitchen window. She loved playing in it. One Saturday morning Johnnie had gone to play golf and Jackie was about a month old. It all happened, just like in my dream. I was getting Jackie up from his nap and changing him in the kitchen when Janet wanted to play in the sandbox. I said it was okay. I would open the window, so we could talk while I cared for the baby. I knew that the lower window would not open, as it had been painted shut, but we always opened the upper pane from the top down.

When I tried to open it, the sash cord broke, and it came crashing down. Somehow it trapped my right hand between the upper and lower sash. It really hurt, and I could not get my hand out, nor was it bleeding. I could reach the baby and I could talk with Janet, but I could not reach the phone. Janet was not yet three years old. What to do! I was trapped.

I began screaming, "Help! Help!"

Finally, one of the side neighbor called out to me, "Are you alright? Or are you playing a game with your children?"

"No!" I said. "Please help me! I am trapped here!"

They came right over and were able to free me from the window. When they released me and the blood started to flow again, I nearly passed out. Johnnie was called off the golf course and took me to emergency room. Nothing was broken. I only had a very sore hand for a few days. The whole thing was a very strange co-incidence, because I had experienced the same thing in my dream.

I puzzled about it when Mother and I were together. She said she experienced similar dreams, which had forecast future events. She shared some stories about her experiences. Not all dreams are like that, but I knew this too happened during biblical times and was recorded in the Bible. I had a new awareness that we all need to look at some dreams as a sign from God as a warning about things to come. Indeed, when it happened, I immediately recalled my previous dream and it made me feel calmer, because I felt sure that everything would work out fine.

For Christmas, we decided to spend it in Dixon. We had spent many Christmas holidays with the Hanzels in Danville, so it was clearly the right time. Dad was continuing to decline and becoming a handful for Mother. It would cheer them both up to be there with our two children. Indeed it was a lovely holiday time and much fun for us all. Dad was particularly pleased to have a grandson. They had wanted a boy in the family for such a long time.

The New Year of 1956 was a year to he remembered, as it ushered in many changes in all of our lives. Because Daddy was not well, we decided to go to Dixon for Easter weekend. Johnnie had vacation time coming. We took a long weekend and drove up on Holy Thursday. I began to suspect that I was pregnant again, and we thought this was a good time for a visit, in case travel was prohibited later in the year.

Mother and I wanted to attend Good Friday services, which were between noon and 3:00. It was the custom in Dixon for all the Protestant churches to take turns hosting this event. Each pastor would prepare a sermon on the last words of Christ on the cross. There would be music from the various choirs in between sermons and hymns. Most people stopped in for a segment or two and then went about their Easter preparations. Johnnie offered to stay home and take care of the children and visit with Dad, while Mother and I made a visit for Good Friday and stopped by the grocery to pick up the last minute things for Easter Dinner.

The sermon that we attended happened to be on the words Jesus spoke to one of the thieves that hung on the cross next to Him. He said, "This day thou shalt be with me in Paradise."

Of course I had heard those words many, many times before, but, suddenly, it took on a whole new meaning for me. Wow! Maybe when people died, they weren't just asleep. Maybe they were aware of things and were thinking people, only in a different way in Heaven. It started me thinking. Maybe the Catholic Church had been right about this, all along.

On the way home I asked Mother what she thought. She indicated she didn't know and that no one would really know until they died. But, it didn't affect our behavior here on earth. Our goal was to be sure to get to heaven and that someday, it would all be made known to us. It deeply touched me and started me on a new path of thinking. However, I didn't have time right then and knew I would think about it later. We enjoyed the rest of the Easter weekend together.

Mother shared news about Anne. She would graduate from Washington University in St. Louis with a degree in Physical Therapy in June of 1956. She hoped to get a job as a Physical Therapist in the St. Louis area. She was recently engaged to a medical student, who would be a doctor in a few years. They were thinking about getting married sometime this summer, maybe as early as June. I didn't tell Mother then, but I thought I might be pregnant and traveling might not be possible for me, but I decided to wait until I was sure, before I told her.

When we got home I scheduled an appointment with my doctor and he confirmed that I was pregnant and the baby would be due sometime in October. I was delighted but wondered how it would all work out, in our tiny, two bedroom house with two children now and a third baby coming. Well, we could have the baby in our room at first, in a baby basket. But it was going to be a little crowded. Wow! I laughed. Apparently, I didn't need to worry about having more children. That one ovary was doing just fine! Maybe the banker that gave us our first mortgage had been right, too. Three bedrooms would be wonderful right now.

Spring was lovely in Paris, and we talked about our garden and how things would be with another baby on the way. How blessed we were. Anne wrote and invited me to be her maid of honor, but I had to decline, as now I was sure I was pregnant, and I could not make any other commitments. Indeed, by early June, I had some difficulty and was put on full bed rest for a month. Mother had arranged to go to Anne's wedding. She would only be gone for a few days and Aunt Emma, Dad's sister who lived in Dixon, had offered to come and stay with him while Mother would be away. That worked well, but I realized my going was out of the question.

We found a woman to come in everyday to help with the children, house work, and the cooking. I could read stories to the children and help as much as I could, but I was not allowed to be up at all. Sadly, in late June, I went into labor and it could not be stopped. I delivered a 2 lb. 5 oz. baby boy. We had decided that if this baby was a boy, we would name him Jeffery Alan. We had decided that we would name all our children with names starting with the letter "J". I had many names picked out, in case it would be a girl, but we had planned that if this one was another boy we would name him Jeffrey.

The doctor told me he was born alive, but, in his opinion, he did not expect the baby to live very long, as he was only a six month baby and under developed. I felt devastated, as did Johnnie. I wanted to see him before they placed him in the incubator, so I saw him briefly but was not allowed to hold him. I cried and cried. And so did Johnnie. We didn't want to wait but have him baptized immediately. Johnnie asked if I still wanted to use that name, and I said absolutely. That was the least we could do, to give him a good name. The nurses and doctors took care of his baptism.

When he lived until morning, the doctor came in to talk with me. If Jeffery had any chance to live at all, it would be best to transport him to The Premature Baby Center, in Springfield, Illinois. He could make no promises, but we decided to give him every chance that we could. By then I was feeling able to go in and see him in the incubator and say a sad good bye. It was the saddest thing I had ever done.

I was released from the hospital in three days, and it was very nice to be home again but my heart was heavy. I prayed and prayed for him to live. I felt very guilty, because maybe I could have done something different and carried him a little longer. We called the hospital every day, and every day he was still alive. But, on the sixth day, he died. Then there were decisions to be made. We would have a funeral for him but what about burial? Mother and Dad Hanzel said they had a burial plot in the Gundy Cemetery, near the family farm they owned near Bismarck, Illinois. Mother Hanzel's parents were buried there, and there was space available. It was what we decided, but it was such a sad time in our lives.

For the rest of the summer everything seemed flat and uninteresting. I took care of the children and went about as usual, doing what had to be done, but I was still grieving inside. Everyone was very kind to me and I received many flowers, letters, and cards. One day Johnnie came home from work and said, "I am going to throw out all those flowers now! I can't stand the looks of them for one more day."

I agreed, and at that point, it appeared like we would be getting back to normal, as much as we could after losing a child. Mother wrote to tell me all about the wedding. In addition, she decided to work one more year, as she wanted to save money for their retirement. After all, Mother was only fifty-nine years old and enjoyed teaching very much. She arranged for someone to come in every day at noon to prepare Daddy lunch and make sure he was alright. He usually slept a great deal in the afternoon. The school year would start right after Labor Day.

Exciting news in the medical world was announced right about that time. It appeared that Dr. Salk had been working on a medication for the prevention for Polio, and it was now available for everyone. We all made arrangements to get our sugar cube, which contained the preventative medicine. Sadly, it was too late for those that had already been crippled or died from polio, but it was wonderful to know that, now, this marked the end of polio!

In the middle of September I received a call from Dixon with news that Mother had fallen at school and severely broken her right arm. It was a very bad break. After much discussion it was decided that it would be best to take Jack and Janet and stay with her so I could help. As soon as possible, Johnnie drove us to Dixon to stay for several weeks until things were better. Johnnie drove right back the next day. I didn't need a car, since I could use Mother's.

Things were very difficult for Mother. The break was painful, and she was suffering. It was difficult to get dressed or to do most anything. I was so glad I could help. There was much to do, in addition to watching Jack, just over a year old and walking but still in diapers; and Janet now three, who tried to help. There was laundry, the house to keep up and meals to tend to as well. It turned out to be just the thing I needed to fight the depression I felt. Being so busy and involved, helping others, and caring for my children all added to the positive impact and snapped me out of despair.

Mother and I had plenty of time to talk, and she finally agreed that this was the time to turn in her resignation. She had taught for over twenty-five years. Now she was eligible to receive a very good teacher's pension. With the farm income and the income from the rent of the upstairs apartment, they would be fine. Anne was married now and working. Mother was so glad that she had been able to see Anne through the five years at the University. She really earned her retirement! We enjoyed many long talks in the evening after the children and Dad were asleep in bed. It was a healing time for both of us.

Mother said that she felt that when you break a bone, it is a sign that things are about to change. She pointed out that when I broke my arm, Johnnie was moved to the home office and heard about the opportunities at DuPont. Now that she had a broken arm, she felt that it was a sign to stop teaching and stay home and take care of Dad. I agreed, but I wanted to stay until she would be able to function better and drive the car. All these things would make life a lot easier. I ended up staying longer than I expected; however, it was time well spent, and we were healing together.

Finally it was time to return to Johnnie and my life in Paris. I was renewed. I called Johnnie and we arranged to have him come the following weekend and take us back home.

Many things happened during my absence, and it was time to catch up, not only around the house but with my friends. Johnnie and I talked, sometimes long into the night. He had news about the plant, and it affected our future. He had been waiting until I came home so we could discuss the details.

He learned the plant at Dana would soon be closing, but it was not to be announced for another month. Some people were already transferred to the new plant in South Carolina. John had been told that they would guarantee his job at DuPont, but they wanted him to stay on until it was closer to the time of closing the operation, in order to help put the plant into "moth balls".

Where he would be and with what department was still not determined. He agreed to stick it out, and I was happy with his decision. He had been given a great opportunity with DuPont, and we were confident that the relationship would continue to be satisfactory for all of us. There were still many unanswered questions.

The next day as I worked around the house and cared for the children, I was praying for the transition. I knew my dad was getting more and more frail. I hoped that we would not be transferred somewhere far away. I wanted to be within easy driving distance, in case I was called home again. Also, what about our little house in Paris? I prayed, *When the time comes, please, Lord, help us to sell it quickly. Whatever is going to happen, help us be prepared for whatever it will be. I place my trust in you, Lord.*

It was soon time for the DuPont Christmas party, usually a very happy and pleasant event, but not this year. The announcement had already come down. Some had been assured of a job, and some had refused. Some had not been given that option. Whatever was going to happen, it seemed likely that this was going to be the last Christmas party for the Dana Plant. It was a sad ending for 1956. It was truly the year of change and uncertainty. But one thing was certain—this was the end of our years of living in Paris!

The Transfer

The year of 1957 began with the news that John was transferred to an Elastomers Plant in Montague, Michigan. We quickly got out the maps and discovered that Montague and Whitehall were twin cities or rather, twin small towns near Lake Michigan, and just a few miles North of Muskegon, Michigan. Johnnie was scheduled to travel there as soon as possible and check things out. If it all went according to plan, he would start work there shortly.

We talked and talked about how it would work, what we needed to do to accomplish the move, and what help the company would provide for us. After further investigation, we decided that this would be an ideal situation. We would be within a day's drive to Dixon or Danville. It was amazing to study the map and realize that the distance was almost the same to both places. What a blessing, not to be transferred to some far-away place like California or way down South where it would be difficult to drive over in case there was an emergency. We both realized that my father was not well, and Mother may need help again. Also, Johnnie was an only child, so if his parents had an emergency, it would be up to him to go.

The company offered to pay all our moving expenses, which included packing everything and transporting all our furniture and things to our new destination. We needed to sell our Paris home and, hopefully, buy a home in that area in Michigan. When John was in Michigan, he planned to stay in a motel and spend some time to see the area, house hunt, and get acquainted with the plant staff, and the new job responsibilities. We had many questions, but in time we felt confident that this would be workable. Johnnie was looking forward to getting away from the closing of the Dana plant, as he said it was like watching a slow death. It was time to move on.

I helped him pack, since he would leave shortly for Michigan with an opened ended plan as to when he would return. He had been told that he could come home every two weeks or so for a few days, so that was something to look forward to. I would be contacting a real estate agent and preparing to put the house on the market. Johnnie planned to call me as often as he could, especially when he had news to report. I would have liked to go up with him and scout around for our next home, but with two small children, it was not possible. We each had our separate responsibilities.

After Johnnie left, I took some time out to pray about all that had transpired and what I should do next. I realized that my prayers had been answered. We would not be much farther away from Dixon than we were now. And both sets of parents, John's and mine, would be pleased with the news. But clearly it would be a big change for all.

John's dad had been trying to sell his business, as he hoped to retire and take things a little easier. It seemed that there was no market for his business, so he was in the process of selling his equipment and closing the shop in the next few weeks. He had turned 65 on Dec. 23rd, and my mother had her 60th birthday one day later on Dec. 24th, and now, both would be retired. Mother would have her teacher's pension and Dad Hanzel would have Social Security. Also, they both owned farms, so their situations were somewhat similar.

After my prayer time I felt refreshed and secure and now had some direction. I felt that all things would work out. I just needed to do my part. I called a real estate agent and put the wheels in motion for selling our home. I tackled some of the things that needed doing around the house before the children would wake up from their naps, and want my attention.

I heard from John quite often. He seemed to like the area very much, and he was interested in the plant and the workings of the staff there. He was just beginning to look around at housing. White Lake was larger than he thought it would be, and it was really a very pretty area. Montague and Whitehall were very small towns, built around White Lake, with Whitehall on the south side and Montague on the north side of the lake. White Lake did not connect to Lake Michigan, but it was nice for boating, fishing, and swimming. That sounded lovely to me.

After he had been gone a week or more, I got a phone call from him in middle of the day. He said, "Have you heard the news yet?"

"What news? " I asked. "I haven't had the radio on."

"Good!" He said, "I was afraid you might have heard. There was an explosion at the plant today. Now don't worry. No one was hurt, but it did quite a bit of damage to the plant. We will all have to pitch in and help clean up the mess. There will be lots of things that need rebuilding, but it was so fortunate that it was not any worse than it was."

He went on to explain exactly what had happened and updated me on what he had done since our last visit. There were several houses he was interested in, and he was all set to tell me about them, since he was coming home by the weekend for a few days. Things were on hold for a while, until the plant was up and running again. I was delighted to know that he would be coming back for a long weekend, as I really missed him,

While he was home we had a meeting with the real estate agent and signed the necessary papers and decided on a fair starting price and other details. His timing was great, as all of these things were easier with him at home. We had done quite a lot to the house since we purchased it four years ago. We had put in new kitchen cabinets and a sink and had repainted or wallpapered nearly every room in the house. We had converted the furnace to gas from coal burning, removed the old coal bin, which gave more space to the basement, and updated the old water heater to a new automatic gas one. The real estate agent planned to start showing the house soon. We were optimistic.

Johnnie had located a house that was under construction and the builder hoped to complete it in a few months. Johnnie was quite excited about it. It was a three bedroom ranch with a large living room with a fireplace and large kitchen with lots of cupboards and counter space. The kitchen included an eating area. There was an attached garage and full basement with connections for a washer and dryer. After coping with repairing and redoing lots of things in our current home, the newness of this house was very appealing. It was in our price bracket, so that seemed like a good choice.

The short visit was over too quickly, and soon it was time for the children and me to say good bye to the one we all loved so much. Janet was four and a half and Jackie was twenty months old. When he had left before, it seemed like Daddy was just going to work, and he would be back that night, but this time they were very concerned about his leaving. It was hard get them to understand what was happening and just where he was going, but we tried to assure them that soon we all would be together in our new home.

I tried to spend extra time with them, playing little games and reading stories, but it was difficult to fill in for John. I missed him, too. The frequent phone calls helped me a lot, but it was hard for the children to understand. It showed up in many little ways, in short tempers and misbehaviors. Once I was talking on the phone with a good friend of mine while the children played with their toys in the living room. Jackie came out in the kitchen and tried to get my attention, and I told him to wait a minute, please. He stamped his feet and said, "NO! Come now!"

I replied, "Jackie, wait just a minute and I'll come. I'm talking on the phone."

"No!" He screamed, and with that he gasped and started holding his breath. When he started to turn blue, I quickly put down the phone. Immediately he passed out and fell to the floor. Of course when he became unconscious, his breathing returned to normal and he was okay. But, it was a frightening and learning experience for both of us. Later, I talked to my doctor about this incident, and he told me that some children do things like that and not to become overly concerned. He assured me that my reaction had been correct. I was beginning to realize that each child is born with their own personality, and children, even from the same family, can be very different from the beginning. Janet had always been even tempered and co-operative, but Jack had a mind of his own!

God was very kind to us, because soon things began to gel. We received a very good offer for our Paris house, and John negotiated with the builder. He thought it would be available for occupancy by Easter time. There was a winterized cottage for rent on the lake that was fully furnished and available, so Johnnie rented it until our house would be ready. Our furniture would be put in storage until move-in day. Everything came together quickly. The packers came and the moving van was scheduled. John was home in time to sign the papers for selling our house and help with the move. Near the end of February, we loaded the children with our clothes and their toys etc., and we were off to drive to our new location in Michigan. The movers would drop off the few items, like my sewing machine, a crib for Jack and a few other things that we would need in our rented house. I was excited to see the new house Johnnie had picked out for us. I thought that having the sewing machine was a good idea, as it would enable me to get a head start on making draperies and curtains for the new house while we waited for its completion.

It was a long trip with several necessary stops along the way, but we arrived at Whitehall just at dusk. We had a simple supper, thanks to carry out, and it was early to bed for all of us, as we were exhausted. The next morning, John and I were up early to really check things out. I was amazed at this "cottage" on the lake. It was a large two story house, fully furnished, with a mishmash of furniture that seemed like a collection from someone's attic. The kitchen was huge and had plenty of furniture in the eating area with a connecting pantry full of dishes of all kinds. There certainly were plenty of pots, pans, and dishes to serve a great number of guests. In the living room, among all the mismatched chairs and sofas, I was amazed to spot a large painting of a very attractive, totally nude woman that was hung above the fireplace in the living room. I told Johnnie that "it" would have to go, but he explained that we were told not to remove or change anything.

Off the living room, there was a large porch overlooking the lake. There were plenty of places for the children to play. The four bedrooms upstairs were more than adequate for our needs, so all in all, we decided that it would be fun to camp here until our house would be finished. I didn't think we would be doing much entertaining, but if we did, it was going to be interesting to see people's reaction to "The Painting".

The view of the lake was really beautiful. The snow was about four or five feet deep. The lake was frozen over for about thirty yards where we could see ice beginning to thaw. Yes, it was going to be a lot of fun here, and, after all, it was only for about six weeks or so, we thought.

It was Saturday, so John called the builder. He arranged for us to meet at the new house. First we had to get the children up, fed and dressed, but I could hardly wait to see our new home.

The house was located several blocks from the lake and not too far from the "down town" business district. This area included a collection of a few stores and offices and was very small, even compared to Paris, Illinois. Our house was on a pleasant street, surrounded by well-maintained homes of a similar size as ours. Our house was a small, compact brown ranch that still looked a little raw, as there was no landscaping in place.

The living room had a lovely stone fireplace and floor to ceiling corner windows at the front of the house. The kitchen was also on the front of the house with the three bedrooms across the back of the house and the bathroom at the end of the hall. I was pleased to see that there was a clothes chute in the bathroom to send the laundry down to the basement area where the washer and dryer would be located. The only feature that I found strange was that the entrance to the basement was located in the garage. You entered by going out into the garage from the kitchen. The staircase was there, leading to the basement. There was a door at the bottom of the stairs, so the basement would stay warm in the winter, but it would be a chilly walk, going from the kitchen to the basement. Oh, well, I thought, it will probably be okay.

My main concern was whether or not the house would be completed in the promised four to five weeks. The bathroom and kitchen were incomplete, and the walls needed to be painted and the carpeting installed. The builder assured us that it would be done soon. He had waited so that I could select tile for the bathroom and the counter top color for the Formica in the kitchen. The landscaping would have to wait until spring. There was a great deal of snow on the ground at that time. We were assured that the house would be ready for us in time.

I was very happy to finally be there and visualize the finished product. That night John had arranged for someone to take care of the children while we went out to dinner with some of the DuPont people from the plant. It was a lovely introduction to Whitehall & Montague.

The plant was nearly rebuilt and production would begin once again. When that happened, John would be placed on swing shift, as would many other employees of the plant. John explained that he would be on days, 7:00 am until three pm, for a week then moved to afternoons, 3:00 to 11, and finally nights, from 11:00 to 7:00am. It was important that the plant be kept in production, around the clock, seven days a week, with no interruptions in the process. There would be a long weekend at the conclusion of each cycle before the cycle would be repeated. That was stunning news to me. He had never been on the swing shift before, so it would be an adjustment for everyone. I wondered how this would work!

Well, as with everything in life, there are advantages and disadvantages in every situation. Johnnie would be able to sleep, undisturbed, during the day, as the bedrooms were all upstairs here, and he would not hear the children's noise or mine. I hoped that it would be the same when we moved to the new house. At first I thought I was adjusting very well to this move. Johnnie took our car to work every day, but I could use it after 3:00 when he got home, to grocery shop or for appointments, and with the next shift, there would be time in the morning before John went to work at 3:00, but on the night shift, he would need to sleep a great deal of the day, so if I went anywhere at that time, I would have to take the children with me.

As it worked out, I found that our social life was the area that was out of whack. It was impossible to plan on a Saturday night bridge party or dinner party. If I tried to set up something in advance, I worried that the ones I wanted to invite were on a different schedule. Besides, who was there to invite? Our "cottage" on the lake was not conducive to entertaining, especially people that you were just beginning to know. In the end, all social activities were put on the back burner until we would move into our new house.

I missed my friends from Paris. I had no new friends and very few opportunities to meet anyone. The neighboring cottages were not occupied at this time of year. I spent a lot of time with the children, and during nap time, I sewed, making the draperies for the living room and curtains for the kitchen. It became very lonely for me. I missed fixing dinner at the regular time and our evenings together. Of course, it was a physical adjustment for John, as his sleep pattern was constantly changing. I did keep up a constant flow of letters back and forth to Mother and to the Hanzels in Danville so that helped.

Before I realized what was happening, I slipped into a serious depression. I looked back at the loss of our baby, Jeffery, as if somehow I might be to blame for his early arrival. I was still in grief from this loss. Spending long hours alone only increased my sorrow. For the first time in my life, I found it difficult to choke down food. I lost my appetite, and, as a result, I lost a lot of weight in a very short period of time.

One day when I had the car and Johnnie was there to take care of the children, I went for a long drive to think things through and to acquaint myself with the area. Then I decided to drive by the house and see how it was coming. To my dismay, there was no activity there. I peaked in the windows and it didn't seem like there had been much, if any, progress. We had been in town over a month now. So I went right home and asked Johnnie when he had last spoken to the builder. He really could not remember, as he had been busy at work and adjusting to his new work schedule. It was a red flag for both of us. He called the builder, and there were several excuses, like they were waiting for materials to arrive. At the present, the work crew had started another job in the meantime. It was very difficult to pin him down on just when the house would be ready for occupancy.

The idea that I was trapped here, for an indefinite period of time, only increased my discouragement. I didn't want to burden John with my little troubles, and indeed, it seemed there were very few interludes when we could have a really deep conversation about anything. I was frustrated and didn't know where to turn. I then realized that in the move, my schedule had been so seriously interrupted that I had neglected my prayer life. So, at the first opportunity, I reestablished a prayer time. I took the time to pour out my heart and plead with Him to reach out and help me in some way, so that I could shake this feeling of deep sorrow and loneliness. I asked for guidance and wisdom to help me through this difficult time of my life.

It was the first of April, and for my birthday Johnnie surprised me with a night out with some of the friends he had made through DuPont. It was a wonderful evening. That seemed to be the turning point. Signs of spring began popping up around the lake. One day when Johnnie was home during the day, we spotted a deer that was trapped on a piece of ice floating on the lake. We tried to think of some way to help him. We ended up calling the fire department and in a short time the doe was rescued. The children were fascinated with having a front row seat to all that had happened. Wow. That was a first for all of us.

The thought suddenly occurred to me that I had been trapped on my own little island and needed to be rescued. I wanted to be picked up, rescued, and turned around to head in the right direction. I took a great deal of comfort in that thought. Hope took root and began to blossom. I soon realized that I might be pregnant. Oh, new life within me, could it be? I asked Johnnie to locate a good doctor for us. I made an appointment and found that it was true! I found a surge of excitement and happiness. The baby would be due the last part of November, maybe just in time for Thanksgiving. How wonderful! This time I would take every precaution and surely everything would be fine.

We received a letter from Mother Hanzel telling us that they would be returning home from Florida soon, where they stayed for the winter. They would be busy getting settled, and Dad wanted to put in his garden as soon as the ground would be ready. Then they wanted to visit us. I hoped our new home was ready by then. I wrote back promptly and said that we would love to have them come and visit us anytime. We had plenty of room for them, in either the "lake cottage" or our new house. It was something to look forward to and plan for their visit. We decided that we would not tell them about the new baby just yet. It would be better to tell them in person. I would tell my parents about the same time. Looking forward to their visit perked me up.

There is something special about the spring, the budding trees, new leaves, and new blossoms coming forth that really lifts your spirits. The snow was melting quickly, and patches of green grass began to appear. At the first opportunity, we stopped by the house to view the progress. We could see that some work had been done, but it was weeks, maybe months from being completed. We were so disappointed, as we wanted so much to be moved in soon and be surrounded by our own furniture and really begin to live in a more settled way.

Easter came and we celebrated that lovely time of year. Since coming to Whitehall, we had been attending the Catholic Church together, as it seemed easier that way with the swing shifts and our constantly changing schedules. It had been a very snowy winter, so the driving was a little uncertain. Janet, now four and a half and Jack, nearly two, loved to go anywhere and quickly learned to be still in church. I had not had the time or the motivation to search out a church home for me. For now, this is what we did on Sundays.

It turned out that it would be May before the Hanzels would be able to come up for their visit, so we suggested that they come up for Mother's Day, which was May 12th that year. I tried to spruce up our rented cottage and make it as presentable and comfortable for their visit as possible. It would be Johnnie's long weekend off, between shift changes, so we were looking forward to their visit and a little change of pace.

They arrived on Thursday evening looking very fit and tan after spending three months in Florida. We had a fine time showing them about our new surroundings, our unfinished house, the DuPont plant where Johnnie worked and the lovely lake views of White Lake and also Lake Michigan, as we were only a short distance from the shore line.

We were all sitting at the breakfast table after returning from Sunday morning Mass when my mother called to tell us that Daddy had been admitted to the hospital with a severe case of pneumonia and was listed in critical condition. Of course I needed to be there. This brought a pleasant, care free weekend to an abrupt halt. I was concerned, being three months pregnant, and wondered about the risk of a car ride of at least eight hours of driving time. We placed a call to my doctor and he called us back promptly. He assured me that I would be fine. He was aware of my past history but cautioned me to take it as easy as possible under the circumstances.

The Hanzels were happy about our news of a new baby but concerned about the stress of the situation and about the drive to Dixon. They helped clear the table and packed up their things and left for their home in Danville as promptly as they could. It was nearly noon when they left, so John and I sat down to think through what had to be done in order to leave. He had to call the plant and arrange for some time off. I had to pack our clothes to take and all the things for the children, not knowing how long we would be gone and what we would need for the trip.

We decided that the best thing to do was to call Mother back and tell her that we would be leaving in a few hours, but we would probably not arrive until late that night. It would be easier if we could drive at night traffic wise, and also, the children would sleep most of the time. The children went down for a brief nap and we packed. We managed to leave at about four o'clock, which put us in a little after midnight, Dixon time. We decided not to tell Mother about the new baby until a later date, as it would just add complications to an already stressful situation.

Mother had been resting in a chair until we got there. She was glad to see us but looked tired and worried. She spent much of the day with Daddy at the hospital, but there had been very little change. He was still running a high fever but was resting comfortably. He was on antibiotics and oxygen, so they were doing all that they could. We visited a little, but we were all tired, so soon everyone was bedded down for the night.

When we woke up the next day, Mother had left a note saying she had gone over for a brief visit at the hospital and would be back soon. She reported that Daddy had a good night and was still fairly alert, but his fever was still high. The next few days brought very little change. We took turns staying with him at the hospital and taking care of the children.

On Wednesday morning, Johnnie decided to return to Michigan and go back to work. The nurses had said it could go on like this for days, and it could go either way. I hated to see him go, but I knew that it was best that the children and I stay there to watch and wait and help in any way that we could.

The days slipped by with Daddy going in and out of consciousness. Mother and I took turns spending time with him at the hospital. Usually Mother would get up early and be at the hospital before I could manage to get the children up, fed, and dressed. It was only about a four block walk to the hospital. Mother would come home for lunch and then I would go over for the afternoon shift. The nurses and doctors didn't have much to tell us. His temperature climbed to 106, which was very upsetting for us, but all we could do was watch and wait.

On Friday afternoon, Daddy did not speak at all or did not seem to be aware that I was there. I hoped that he was getting a good rest and would awaken a little better, but it was not to be. Before five o'clock, Mother arrived and said she wanted to stay for a while. The next door neighbor had agreed to stay with the children until I got back. Mother had eaten a bite and suggested that I go back and take care of the children. She wanted to see if he would come around. I returned home after a brief visit with Mother to take care of the children. When they were in bed, I tried to watch a little TV or read, but I really couldn't settle myself. It just didn't seem right, so I spent the time praying, asking for His will to be done and for the strength to do all that I could in this situation.

At 9:30 the hospital called and said he had taken a turn for the worse and that I should come. I asked the next door neighbor to come over and I went to the hospital to be there with Mother. We tried to talk to him, but he seemed to be in a deep coma. All we could do was to watch, pray, and wait. It was after midnight when he drew his last breathe. The nurse came in and confirmed that he was gone. We stayed until the funeral home people arrived to take him. We made funeral arrangements.

When Mother and I were back at the house, she told me that while she was sitting by his bedside, Daddy had suddenly sat right up in bed and said, "Why, Otto!" Then, he lay back down and apparently fell back to sleep. That is when she had called the nurse and asked that I come over as soon as possible.

Mother said that she had heard that when someone dies, a person comes to them and accompanies them to the next world, but she had never really believed that it happened. But now she did! Otto was Dad's brother and he had always wondered what had happened to him, because after he left Dixon, none of the family had ever heard from him again. Apparently Otto had been designated to be the one to come for Daddy. It was comforting to know that he had passed so peacefully, but this was a stunning incident! I was comforted by this. I knew the depths of my dad's faith and belief in scripture. I knew he really did believe!

The next morning I awoke early and called Johnnie before he left for work. He said he would make the arrangements and probably would drive over on Sunday. He would call me back as soon as he knew for sure just when he would be coming. This was just one of the many calls that Mother and I made that morning to family and close friends. Mother made out the list and I did most of the calling. Mother had been in touch with the pastor of the Lutheran Church and the funeral was tentatively set for Tuesday morning, with a luncheon and the reception after in the parish hall, which the ladies' guild would be arranging. The children slept a little late, so that gave us time to accomplish most of the calls. Later, we arranged for someone to stay with Janet and Jack while we went to the funeral home and the Franklin Grove Cemetery to make all the final arrangements.

It was a relief when all the details were accomplished. By early afternoon, things were pretty well in hand. Mother had drafted a tentative press release, so we prepared and delivered it to the local newspaper. By evening we had done most of the things that we needed to do. Visitation at the funeral home would be Monday afternoon and evening, and the funeral would be at 11:00 Tuesday morning in the church.

Sunday, the family gathered. Alice and Bob came over from Iowa, Nickie and George from Chicago, Anne flew in from California, but Arthur, her husband, could not get away. He was a doctor now, and in practice with his brother in the San Francisco area. John came in Sunday afternoon. It was wonderful to have most of the family there, even though it was a sad event that drew us together. It was a great relief for me to have Johnnie there. He was great with the children, and it took some of the pressure from me. I was grateful to feel that I was getting along so well. I had a sense that God was in charge and that things would be okay, and the baby would be fine through all of this. Mother never guessed that I was pregnant, but after Alice arrived, she took me aside. She had guessed it right away, but I asked her please to not tell anyone else until everything was over.

Looking back, it was kind of a blur, and only a few things stood out. I remember thinking how well Mother was handling things and how helpful everyone was, from the ladies of the parish and the luncheon they served to all the family and friends. Of course, Dad's sisters, Aunt Emma and Aunt Annie and Uncle Floyd, were there. There was a huge attendance at the funeral, as they had lived most of their lives in the Dixon area. The neighbors sent in lovely flowers, food, and desserts, so after the grave side services, which took place after the luncheon, Mother invited everyone back to her home, where we served a light supper.

That evening Nickie and George drove back to Chicago and took Anne with them. She planned to fly back to California from Chicago. Alice and Bob went back Tuesday night, also, but we planned to drive back the next day as we had the longest drive. It was hard to say goodbye to Mother. I knew she had lots of things to do, but we really couldn't stay any longer. It was difficult for Mother, as she had never lived alone. She had never left home. When her sister and the children came to live, she took charge of things. Later she married and had children of her own. One by one, we all left, but she still had Daddy. There was always someone that needed to be cared for. Now, this would be the first time in her whole life that she would be living alone. She had been married 28 years, raised eight children, and was now only sixty years old.

When we got home and I settled in again, it seemed I had been away about a month, because so much had happened. It seemed strange somehow that we still lived out on the lake. I had not made many friends, so it was like coming back to a location I hardly knew. My limited social life was brought home to me when I got our first mail after returning from Dixon. It contained only one letter of condolences, and it was from the man that delivered John shirts from the laundry. How sad that this was the only person outside the family that I had regular contact with. I missed my nice automatic washer and dryer, which was still in storage. Laundry was a bit of a problem, because I did our laundry at the laundry mat. Early on we had decided to treat ourselves by having the laundry service pick up John's shirts and deliver the fresh ones to our home each week.

It was a nice treat for me as John wore a dress shirt and tie to work, and sometimes, with the inconveniences of the lake house, I would run behind with the ironing. It was a wake up call for me. I must get out more and develop a circle of friends. I had not written to my friends from Paris for a while, so I had some catching up to do there.

At the first opportunity, I loaded the children in the car and we went over to visit our, as yet, unfinished house. It was a lovely day in late May, so we walked around the yard a little to see what might be coming up. I hoped to see someone from the neighborhood out and about. The house was coming along. At last they were working on finishing up the kitchen counter-top and the bathroom cupboards. The builder himself was there. He told me that he thought it would be ready in a month or so. I told him that we had decided that it was about time that we contacted an attorney, as we clearly had been misled on the amount of time it would take to finish this house. That seemed be the right thing to say to him, as he immediately apologized for the long wait, and said he would personally see that we would be in at least by the first of July. I said I would like something in writing to that affect and stayed there until he provided it.

As I drove home, I thought, Good heavens, by July I would need my maternity clothes and we would all need our summer clothes. How had we let this thing slide and go on and on without taking any action! I called the storage company and said that I would need to get into the storage area to retrieve our summer clothes and made an appointment to do that.

I was ready to take action. No more living life like a hermit without any social life. Sure, it has been difficult, with the swing shifts and all, but others had to cope with this. I would have to reach out to the others from the plant and try to become better acquainted in this area. I had no neighbors here on the lake, but I must get to know the people in our new neighborhood.

I sat down and wrote a long letter to Mother. I knew that she was very lonely, as I had just received a letter from her. I suggested that she come over and visit us and help us with the move into our new house the first of July. Also, I told her that I was expecting a new baby in November and had not wanted to tell her under the circumstances, but I had just seen the doctor and he said everything was progressing normally.

In a short time, I got a glowing letter back from her and she said she was looking forward to coming and would come a little before then to help out. She didn't want me to get too tired.

The draperies for the new house had long ago been finished. I got my maternity clothes out of storage and washed and ironed everything, so they would be fresh and ready to wear. It was none too soon. I was already four months along and had to wear my blouses out and loosen the waist bands. Oh, how happy I was to be expecting again, and this time, I had every confidence that things would go along well. The more I saw of the new house, the more anxious I was to finally move in.

At last it began to seem possible that we would soon be settled in our new home. It would be great to see our own furniture again. The house had some very nice features we had never had before. There was a lovely stone fireplace in the living room, and the large, corner, picture windows were going to be very pretty. I had carefully selected the fabric for them, so that the carpeting would go with them very well. Also, there was a laundry chute in the bathroom that would take the dirty clothes right down to the laundry area in the basement. Oh joy, to have my laundry equipment back again. I was looking forward to the large kitchen cupboards and the much larger counter space.

Sure enough the house was finally ready and we moved in a few days before the first of July. Mother had arrived early as planned, and she was a great help. All I had to do was direct the movers to place the furniture where I wanted them. The unpacking went smoothly. It was like Christmas morning, opening all the boxes to see what was in them and putting things away in the new cupboards and closets. The children were delighted to see their toys and their bikes and tricycles again.

The best part of moving was meeting all our new neighbors. They had been wondering when we would move in, and everyone was very friendly and welcoming. At last the children had friends in the neighborhood to play with. The houses on our block were mostly ranch style and about the same size as ours, built in the last few years. This attracted families with young children. Some were old enough to baby sit, so that was good news for me. By the time we moved in, it was obvious that we had another baby on the way. There were get acquainted coffees and very soon I really felt a part of this little community.

Mother really liked our new home, especially the large corner windows in the living room. The builder had constructed a cornice over the windows, which included florescent lighting. This accented the draperies and was very attractive. However, we found that sometimes it made a humming sound when we first turned on the lighting. Mother commented on this and asked what that sound was, and we explained that it was just the cornice lighting.

After several days of this, Mother asked, "Could we please drive by that grain elevator someday so that I can see where it is located?"

"The grain elevator? What do you mean?" I asked.

She responded, "Well, every time I ask about that sound, you say, that noise is just the corn a 'sliding. And I thought there must be a grain elevator nearby." We both had a good laugh about that!

Mother and I had lots of time to talk. She really disliked living alone but had been busy catching up. There was much she couldn't do while she was taking care of Dad. She told me more about Dad's family. I knew that he had three brothers and four sisters. The sisters we knew. There was Aunt Lena in Davenport, who was just younger than Dad. We had visited her fairly often and kept in regular contact with her, as we had Aunt Emma and Aunt Annie. Also there was Aunt Marie, who had always been frail and had died while we lived on the farm. I was about seven when she died and had no vivid memories of her.

We never had met any of his brothers. Otto had left Dixon as a young man following a disagreement he had with his parents. He had left a trunk with Dad, full of things that he wanted and told Dad that he would send for the trunk when he got settled. However, none of the family ever heard from him again. Dad had come to believe that he had met with difficulties, maybe could not find a job, had a serious accident, or maybe had been killed.

His youngest brother, John, had served in World War I. He had received injuries from being gassed during the war. He lived near Denver, as the high altitude was more comfortable for him. The family was in regular contact with him.

His oldest brother, Edward, had settled on a farm, which he had purchased near White Cloud, Michigan. They had kept in touch by mail, but the letters had been very infrequent of late. Mother knew his last address and suggested that we look him up. White Cloud was only about

35 or 40 miles East and North of us. We planned to drive over and visit him when John would have some time off during shift changes, and he could take care of the children.

It turned out to be quite an adventure. After checking at the court house in regard to the deed and the specific location of his property, we were given directions and drove there. He seemed very glad to meet us and asked many questions about Dad. Mother told him about our lives and especially the incident of Dad's vision of Otto, just before he died. He showed us about his property, but it was obvious that he lived very simply and was in poor circumstances. Essentially, he lived the life of a hermit but seemed happy and content. He spent much of his time carving wood into very remarkable pieces. We promised to keep in touch with him and he with us. It was a very interesting afternoon.

Mother stayed about a month, but then returned to Dixon. She needed to take care of some farm business but planned to return before the new baby would arrive in middle or late November. She called Aunt Emma and Aunt Annie and told them of our visit with Uncle Ed. So very shortly after that, Aunt Annie and Uncle Floyd called me and arranged to visit us, and also go and visit Uncle Ed, her brother.

What a fun visit that was. It was always lively when they were around, and we had a great time. Uncle Floyd liked our house but said that it would be a fairly easy task to put in a bathroom in our basement. I thought that was a great idea! When the children and I spent the morning in the basement, me doing laundry and them playing with their toys, it would be a great convenience. When Johnnie was off for a few days between shift changes, the deed was accomplished.

In September of 1957, Janet, now five in August, had entered kindergarten. Our first child to go to school—quite a landmark! There were other remarkable things that happened that fall. The Russians revealed that they had launched Sputnik, the first space ship to be launched into space from Earth. We all marveled at this new undertaking. We gazed at the nighttime skies and hoped to catch a glimpse of it going by. Predictions were made that the USA would soon begin plans for our first entry into the space race. Locally, the new bridge, which connected the lower and the upper peninsulas, was completed and dedicated with ceremonies over the Labor Day weekend. The Governor and other dignitaries walked across the bridge before it was opened for general traffic. This was to become an annual tradition. It certainly enhanced the State of Michigan for commerce and general travel.

By fall I was very busy planning for Christmas. I knew that when the baby arrived, I would have very little time to shop, so I had completed most of the shopping and was busy sewing. Now that Janet was in school a half day, I could complete the outfits for her Christmas doll, which included school clothes, a nurse's outfit, a wedding gown, and many other casual clothes. I found a trunk that would hold the doll and all of her clothes, so that would be ready soon and carefully tucked away. I had made brother and sister outfits for Janet and Jack. They consisted of short pants for him and a skirt for her, made out of the same wool plaid, with shirts and blouses to match.

Next I started addressing Christmas cards, so that after the baby came, I would write a brief note on them and maybe include a picture. This would facilitate getting the cards out on time. I was determined to get all this out of the way early, so I could enjoy the month between the baby's arrival and Christmas.

The baby arrived with a minimum of difficulties on November 23rd, a healthy, strong baby boy, whom we named, James David. What a blessing! Mother had arrived in plenty of time, and all my careful planning fell into place nicely. However, this was the year for Asian flu. It had been widely reported and greatly feared. There seemed to be very little anyone could do about it, except avoid contact with anyone that came down with it. Well, the day after I came home with the new baby, John came home from work with all the symptoms. That rearranged all of our sleeping plans. We isolated John in a bedroom by himself. The rest of us doubled up, which crowded our little three bedroom house, but it all worked out very well. No one else came down with the flu, so we all decided that the whole thing had been greatly over-rated or exaggerated. Looking back on it, I remember it as a cozy time, with all of us tucked in together enjoying the new baby.

This delayed plans for Jimmie's baptism, so it was rescheduled for later. I asked our good friends who lived about a block away to be his godparents. I was very happy to have made so many new friends in the neighborhood.

Mother had plans to spend the winter in California beginning in early January, as Lura had sent out a signal that she needed help with her family, and asked for Mother to come. Also, she wanted to spend time with both Anne and Lura's family. It was good for Mother to be needed, as she was very lonely living alone.

Mother and Dad Hanzel came up for Christmas with the car loaded with lovely Christmas presents for all of us. When they arrived, the tree was in place with all the packages wrapped and ready. It was a lovely Christmas with all three grandparents in attendance. All my early preparations paid off. But it came to an abrupt halt, as there was a prediction for a heavy snowstorm for the Midwest for a few days after Christmas. The three grandparents left together on December 27th. The Hanzel's drove Mother nearly to Chicago, where she could catch a bus to Dixon. It was just in time, as the weather prediction was correct. On the 29th, the snow came in huge amounts, and the roads were drifted shut for several days. Locally, John was able to get to and from work. But I remember watching the street in front of house disappear behind huge snow piles as the snow plows worked to keep our street open. I could tell when a car went by, because people attached little flags to their radio antennas. All you could see was an occasional little flag going by.

As the New Year approached, I was rested, and after all the excitement of the new baby and the holidays, I began to look forward to the New Year. In my prayer time, I continually thanked God for all the blessings of the past year. Much had happened that year: the move from Paris to the rental lake house, Daddy's passing, I found that I was pregnant, moving into our first newly built house, Janet starting school, the arrival of Jimmie, and our lovely Christmas. I felt settled at last, became well acquainted with my neighbors, the DuPont people, and played in a couple of bridge clubs. I wondered what the New Year would bring.

I could not visualize our living in such a small town with the long winters and short summers. The shift work schedule was taking its toll on our family life, so I included this in my prayers. I prayed that the Lord would help me to be content with this life style. Or, if there was to be a change in the New Year, help me to accept His will in all things. It was then that I began sensing that a change was coming.

Our calendar for the New Year was filled with bridge dates, John's bowling schedule, doctor's appointments, and Janet's kindergarten activities. One day John came home from work and said that someone from the main office in Wilmington was coming that week. He had been scheduled for an appointment with him for the next day, January 14th. The grapevine revealed transfers taking place in the future. The plant was running so well that perhaps there was a plan to reduce the extra staff the plant had needed during the start-up phase.

John was interviewed on January 14th, and about a week later, he was invited to Wilmington, Delaware for an interview. When he returned, he was excited about the offer of a new position. It would begin as soon as it could be arranged, if we agreed to the relocation. There was so much to discuss and consider. I approved of the move. However, there was no way I wanted to stay in snowy Michigan with all the children, waiting for our house to sell.

I said, "If you go, fine! But I want to go when you go!"

The whirl-wind began. We accepted the offer on February 4th. The plant surprised us with a going away party at the local hotel on Friday evening, the seventh. Jimmie was baptized that Sunday, the ninth, with our good friends, Bea and Bart serving as Godparents. Johnnie left the next day for a week in Wilmington to settle into his new job and house hunt for a rental for us. He called me on the fourteenth to tell me about the house he rented, and that the company would pick up all our moving and travel expenses. In addition they would carry our house expenses if our house did not sell within three months. He would fly home on Saturday, the fifteenth, the packers would come on Tuesday, the eighteenth. The van would load on Wednesday. Then the children and I would fly to Chicago to stay with Nickie and George until John could drive our car through to Wilmington. Then the children and I would fly out to Wilmington, Delaware to join him there, until the furniture could catch up with us. Wow! I was amazed that it all happened so quickly

It would be another new beginning for us. I knew no one in this part of the country, and I didn't know the area, or the house we would be living in. Until we could sell our Michigan house, we had to wait to buy another one. Once again, in faith we accepted this would be the right move for us. We had high hopes that it would work out well.

Wilmington

O ur plane was on time that Saturday afternoon, February 22, 1958, when the three children and I arrived in Wilmington. What a joyful reunion it was to be all together with Johnnie waiting there to greet us. We had only been apart since Wednesday afternoon, but it seemed like much longer than that. We had so much to tell each other. When I stepped off the plane into the warm sunshine of Delaware's early spring weather, it was like going from the frigid north to paradise. I liked it already!

Johnnie drove us directly to the Hotel Du Pont in downtown Wilmington, which would be our home for four nights until the moving van could catch up with us. I talked non-stop about Chicago and our visit with Nickie and George, where we stayed until we took the flight to Wilmington. The flights were a huge undertaking, flying alone with a five year old, a two year old, and a three month old baby. Thankfully, it had gone well. The Scheppach's had met our flight, and we had a great visit with them. But it was wonderful to finally be together again!

Johnnie reported that he had a sinking feeling when our plane took off from Muskegon. He thought, "There goes my whole life, my wife and the three children. Will they be safe until we are reunited?" He had gone back home and finished loading up the car with the rest of our things, including a few house plants and other items too precious to trust to the moving van. He had locked the house and had driven from Michigan to Delaware. His drive had gone well, even though some of the road had been snow covered and icy. He had made good time and had arrived on Friday afternoon. It had been a lonesome drive, but it would have been very difficult for our young family. In retrospect, it had been a good decision to go our separate ways, but it was wonderful to all be together again.

That first night in the hotel, we all got dressed up and went downstairs to the main dining room for an early dinner. What a treat! The dining room was very elegant, and the children were on their best behavior, perhaps a little awed by it all. The baby had been fed and he slept peacefully in his basket, while the rest of us enjoyed our dinner. We were quite a sensation to the other well-dressed diners out for a Saturday night. The waiters and others had stopped by to say hello and admire our little family. However, when we tried to dine there the next night, it was chaotic! The baby cried, the children were restless, and the whole incident was a disaster. For the rest of our hotel stay, we ordered room service, which was really much easier for all of us.

It was a pleasant interlude to rest up and get ready to move into our new home. On Wednesday, February 26th, John took the day off from work and was there to help direct things. We had toured the house on Sunday, so I had time to think through how I would arrange things. There would be plenty of room in this large two-story, four bedroom house with two and a half baths. It was spotlessly clean. John had been determined to find just the just the right rental for us after selecting the make shift summer cottage in Michigan that had become tedious after so many months of isolation on the lake. This house would be our home for at least six months until our Michigan house was sold and we could select and purchase our permanent home.

Moving day was exciting for all of us. It was a lovely warm spring day. The neighbors were friendly and stopped in to offer their help and support. The neighborhood was full of children of all ages, preschoolers to teenagers. It was a great first day in the house, which we would occupy for an indefinite period. Already I loved the nice warm weather of Delaware. It was wonderful to have all of our own furniture and things with us. It helped us all feel right at home.

The movers were great and helped unpack most of our things and place the furniture just where we wanted it. While Johnnie was there to take care of the baby and Jackie, Janet and I went to the local school to enroll her in Kindergarten. The school bus would pick her up in the morning. We learned exactly where the bus stop was, so things were falling into place very nicely.

John enjoyed his new job at Chestnut Run, about a fifteen minute drive from our home. He worked with other engineers, planning new products and designs for the Elastomers Division. He was meeting new people and soon we were making new friends and developing a busy social life, which included golf and bridge. One of the perks from DuPont was a membership in the two golf clubs, the club at Chestnut Run and the main club in Wilmington nearer the downtown area. We were living in the suburbs west of Wilmington nearer to Chestnut Run. Because of the young ages of our children, I was not ready to play much golf yet, but John enjoyed playing golf when the early spring weather permitted.

There was a Catholic Church about a mile from our home, so John registered in that parish. I started to look for a Lutheran Church, but I was still uneasy concerning our differences in religion. I wanted so much to be together in that important part of our lives, but how could we resolve this issue? I searched for a Brethren Church, but none was available, so I began attending a Lutheran Church nearby. Now my going alone to church did not feel right any more. I prayed in earnest for a solution. I longed for the feeling of deep worship, Christian fellowship, and service that I had experienced in the Brethren Church so many years ago. Also, I longed for both of us to share the reality of Christ together in the same church. Now that we had three beautiful children, how would I be able I teach our children about God if we were apart in regard to what we believed? I had many questions.

I embarked upon a study plan of spiritual readings and church history to search out what I truly believed, what scripture taught, and how that compared with Lutheran theology and Catholic theology, and what I had learned through my experiences with the Brethren Church. I borrowed books from the Lutheran Church Library and read the life story of Martin Luther. Then I looked for the history of the starting of the Church of the Brethren. It was all very interesting and enlightening, especially since I had recently learned a little more about what happens when we die.

In late May, we received an acceptable offer for our home in Whitehall, Michigan and were very happy to have it all confirmed and settled. The sale of our home there closed that chapter of our brief stay in Michigan. We were ready to put down more permanent roots, here. It was even more urgent that I reconcile the religious uneasiness I was feeling before we purchased another home and became permanently settled. I tried to talk about this to John, but he was not open to discussing this issue. In his mind this had been settled long ago, and he was not interested in sharing in my studies or searching, so I continued to read and study.

With summer's arrival, I was able to start playing golf again, as teenage baby sitters were readily available in the neighborhood. All during that summer while I was making friends, becoming involved in the neighborhood, playing golf, and taking care of the children, this issue was very much in the back of my mind. When Mother came to visit, I tried to discuss this with her, but she had a very different attitude toward religion. To her, there was very little difference between any of the Christian churches. It was how you honored God in your heart and in your actions that really mattered.

The summer flew by, and soon I was shopping for school clothes for Janet, who would enter first grade in the fall. In September John's parents drove to Wilmington for a visit and we had a nice time. All the children had grown since last Christmas, but Jimmie had changed the most. He was now crawling everywhere and making progress in trying to talk. Jack was all boy and followed Grandpa everywhere. Janet was a pal of Grandmother's. They had lots of fun enjoying the children and exploring our new location.

Things quieted down following the Hanzel's visit, as Janet was in school all day and Jack and Jim took naps every afternoon. My reading and studies were bearing fruit. I began to realize that there were two significant milestones that had changed my view of religion. One milestone was the revelation that I received in Dixon on Good Friday: "This day you shall be with me in Paradise." This incident had convinced me that there is life after death, and it begins at the moment of death, not at the "last trump". When the last trump is sounded that is the beginning of the final judgment. I had been studying this aspect in my reading. Now I could understand why the practice of asking the Saints to intercede for us is not so ridiculous. They are alive and well and alert in heaven. The other mile stone was the passing of my dad. His calling out to his long, lost brother just before his death made me realize that perhaps the idea that someone from our past who has gone before is sent to accompany us on our journey from this world to the next is real. The conclusion was that when you die, you aren't just asleep, waiting for the last trumpet, but you are alive and aware! It was all very life changing!

As I continued to ponder the truths in these experiences, I became more and more convinced that the Catholic Church taught the truth in this regard. Also, in my reading and studies, I came to realize that the Catholic Church was truly founded by Jesus Christ. The Holy Spirit had been sent to protect and guide the church through the clergy and especially the Popes. Yes, there had been abuses and sins committed by previous popes. After all, they are human and subject to errors and sin, but when they proclaim a premise as fact from the seat of Peter, they are protected from error by the Holy Spirit. Therefore, the Church teaches truth, as revealed in scripture and as revealed by the Holy Spirit.

When I joined the Brethren Church all those years ago, Dad had asked me what creed they believed in and taught. In the Lutheran Church they believe in the Apostles Creed. The Covers told me that they did not have a creed, per say, but taught the entire New Testament as their source of revelations by God. I had studied scripture faithfully all those years, but there were passages I did not fully understand. Now I came to believe that this was true. There had to be some source of interpretation to help students like myself. In my early days when I spent so much time at the parsonage with the Covers, many of the questions I had were answered by them. I needed an impeccable source for my future questions.

I had attended the Lutheran Church regularly for two years when we had moved back to Dixon in 1945 and regularly attending the Catholic Church in Whitehall during that past year in Michigan. I knew that both the Lutheran and Catholic Churches recited this creed at services every Sunday. I now knew that the liturgy was very similar in both churches and that Martin Luther had been taught, trained, and ordained as a Catholic priest before he left to establish the Lutheran Church. So it was not surprising that the two services were so much alike.

Then it occurred to me: that the real presence of Jesus in the Eucharist was stated as fact by Jesus at the last supper. The scriptures states emphatically that "This is My Body, This is My Blood!" As a result, when you really believe in the real presence, then all the pomp and circumstance surrounding it and the respect that it is given to the Eucharist is right and proper. Wow! Of course! It must be true! The Catholic Church had always taught this from the very beginning, that He is truly present. The Brethren Church taught that everything was true in the New Testament. Now, I came to really believe!!

But if that part was true, what about the need to re-enact the demonstration of serving others in the re-enactment of the washing of feet? That had been a basic part of the ceremony in remembrance of the Last Supper, as well as the distribution of the Body and Blood. This was taught in the Brethren Church. What about that? I still had many questions that had not been answered. As I pondered this, I came to realize that my previous concerns about the Catholic Church had been partially resolved.

I wondered what to do about it. I did not want to be disrespectful of my dad. I loved him and honored him. Then it occurred to me, "He is up there in heaven right now and knows the truth about all of this!" Dad's strong faith had brought him through all of his difficulties in this world, and now he was experiencing Heaven. Wow! Maybe he is cheering me on. Or at least maybe he won't be disappointed in me if I became a Catholic. He will understand that I am experiencing a leap of faith. Now I felt I had to act on my new found knowledge, and once again, change. What had been the basic tenants of faith had become a new, expanded experience with the tremendous powerful God.

I prayed about how I could change something so important. I did not want to turn my back on the authentic basic faith in God that I had experienced in the Brethren Church and reject what I knew was authentic Christian living that I had observed in that Church. The Covers had been so dear to me and so important in my Christian development. *Well*, I thought, *they've passed on, as well, so they too were in heaven. Maybe they would not be offended but understand that with this new found knowledge I had to take this next huge step.* It suddenly became clear to me that the right thing to do was to join the Catholic Church.

We had received the money from the sale of our Whitehall home. Now that Janet was in school full time, it was time to start shopping for our next home. John and I discussed looking into what was available, ruling out the unappealing homes, and in the process locate some real possibilities. We both wanted to get settled and start putting down permanent roots. Before I took action on becoming a Catholic, we needed to be settled in our new location. So I started researching Realtors and possible areas.

Nearly every day when I had the car, I took the children on a drive and started to look. I went through model homes when I found some open and read the ads in newspapers of available houses. Sometimes, on Saturdays we would get a baby sitter and tour around together. Soon we discovered the area that we both liked best, which was a little farther from the Chestnut Run facilities but was much more to our liking.

By December we had it narrowed down and began to look in earnest in a specific area North of Wilmington. It would be wonderful to be settled by Christmas. In the end, we located just what we wanted, made an offer which was accepted, so we were able to move right after New Year's.

My mother was spending the winter in California, splitting her time between Anne and Lura, who had both settled in the San Francisco area. But Mother and Dad Hanzel were planning to drive out to visit us for the holidays, arriving around December 22nd. They had an open ended schedule, so they decided to stay and help out during the move and see us settled in our brand new home on Ivydale Road. They were wonderful help, especially with the children, keeping them amused and safe, while I unpacked and settled in. It all worked out extremely well.

Our new home was a split level with a large welcoming foyer, just inside the front door. On that level was a large family room, two car garage, a half bath and laundry room. There was another half flight of steps that led down to the basement level where the furnace was. There was plenty of room for John's work shop and the children to play, so a lot of the toys were sent down there. To the right was a half flight of steps leading up to the living, dining room, and kitchen level.

I liked the new kitchen with a lot of built in appliances. There was a fireplace in the living room and large picture windows looking out over the street in front. Off of the living room and dining room, there was another half flight up to the top level, where we had four bedrooms and two bathrooms. One bathroom was off the hall, available for the three children's rooms. We had our own bathroom in the master bedroom. I put my sewing machine in the family room and planned to make or re-do a lot of the draperies and curtains in the next few weeks.

We had registered in the parish and had attended the holiday Masses in the Catholic Church, The Immaculate Heart of Mary Church, which included a grade school and was about two miles from our home. I called the office to tell them that I wanted to receive instructions with the intention of becoming a Catholic. They said that they would follow up on this after the holidays. By the time the Hanzel's left on January 9th, we were very well settled and established in our new home.

Janet had started first grade, so she continued the second half of first grade in the grade school which was nearby. It was an easy walk with no busy streets to cross, as the school was in the middle of our subdivision. We started to meet the neighbors that lived on our block, but it was slow getting really well acquainted. We realized that while people were friendly when we met them, they were slow to seek you out or call you. It is quite a difference from the Midwest.

One Sunday afternoon, we started a fire in the fireplace and hoped that some of our neighbor would drop by. My newly re-vamped draperies were hung and the house looked ready for company. Sure enough the doorbell rang, but it was only the paper boy collecting for the newspaper. Then a little later it rang again. This time it was a Lutheran Minister from the local church. He had tracked me down. I had told the pastor from the other Lutheran Church that I had briefly attended that we were moving away when I returned some books. When he asked where we were moving, not wanting to lie to him, I answered that we were moving to the North side of Wilmington. I wanting to end my association there, never thinking that he would follow up with the local pastor. I was a little embarrassed and tried to give him the brush off. But low and behold, before I could usher him out the door, the bell rang again, and it was the pastor of the Catholic Church, coming to call and sign me up for instructions. The Catholic priest knew and recognized the other minister and left with great haste, explaining that he didn't realize we had other company.

Well, talk about being embarrassed! What were the chances of them both arriving on the same afternoon? As a result, I had to call the church office and explain about the confusion. My instructions began, and Father Jennings began an extremely thorough study. Nothing was missing. We stared at the beginning and proceeded at a very slow pace. I felt like I had waited too long, and now I was pounding on the door of the Catholic Church, not sure that I would ever be admitted!

Sometime during that time when I was struggling with the thoughts of becoming a Catholic, I began to think about how much I would miss singing the familiar hymns and songs of praise, as I had always done. I had enjoyed singing in the choir and knew so many beautiful, inspirational hymns. Well, I thought, there is no reason that I can't sing them to myself. I had become used to the Latin Mass and used that quiet time to pray and meditate on the gospel. Now I looked forward to going to Mass, even though it was still a little strange to me. In fact, I had attended Mass for the year that we lived in Michigan and most of the time in Wilmington, except for a brief two or three times when I visited the Lutheran Church right after we moved to Delaware. It began to seem right for me to attend Mass, although I missed the music and singing.

One night I had a dream. In my dream I was before a huge staircase and at the top of the stairs was a huge throne, and on that throne was a very fat, old man all dressed in white, wearing a large, white peaked hat.

He spoke kindly to me and said, "Come forth, my daughter."

In my dream, I was only a little girl, about five or six years old. So I walked carefully up the stairs and when I got to the top, He said, "Come here and sit on my lap. Do not be afraid. I want to welcome you into my church. My church may seem a little strange to you at first, but in a very short time, I know that you will be very happy and comfortable in my church. Welcome!"

When I woke up, I wondered about the meaning of the dream. It was a very vivid dream. I had never visualized God, the Father, in this way. Surely, that was God the Father, on His throne of grace, or was it?

One day after I began my religious instructions, I picked up the newspaper from the front steps. There on the front page was a picture of exactly what I had seen: The very same man in the same costume on the same throne! Under the picture was the caption stating that Pope John the XXIII was our newly elected Pope. (I was so new to the ways of the Catholic Church that I had not recognized the Pope's garb.) It was true. Looking back, I now realize that it was under Pope John XXIII's direction that the liturgy of the church changed, so that everyone heard much of it in his or her own language and were encouraged to sing during the Mass. Eventually it was he who directed that the windows of the Vatican be open, in order to allow the wind of the Holy Spirit to blow in, which would usher in the Charismatic Renewal.

My instructions with Father Jennings seemed to go on and on. We covered everything very completely. I think he finally realized that I truly believed and was ready to take this very important step of entering the church.

The happy day was set for Saturday, July 18th, 1959. My next door neighbor served as my sponsor or godmother, and she presented me with a very beautiful crystal rosary. When Father Jennings blessed it, he remarked that he would give it a special blessing for "a happy death!" I was so surprised with that blessing. Now I realize what a special blessing that is, but at the time I was a little taken back. I was baptized conditionally and was confirmed. Then Father Jennings explained that he wanted to take me to a favorite church of his in downtown Wilmington for my first confession. He said he would drive me down and back, so John and the others returned home.

Well, Father Jennings turned out to be a very fast, somewhat daring, and erratic driver. I was quite frightened by his driving, and I wondered if I would live through it. Then I almost got the giggles thinking that at least I would have a very happy death! But the ride was worth it, as the church was really a lovely Italian church with many statues and beautiful, stained glass windows. The priest was kind and patient, hearing my first confession as I stumbled through it. It was difficult for me, but he made me feel at ease, so somehow, I completed it. What a relief to get that all done and be back with the family.

I was very happy to receive my first communion in the Catholic Church the next day. I prayed a long time and after that I had a happy thought that when Janet would receive her first communion the next year, I would be a regular Catholic. I felt badly that I had not been a Catholic when our children were baptized and wished that I could have one more child to experience that special occasion again with the new family member.

Sure enough, soon I realized that I was expecting! Joe was born almost exactly nine months later in April 1960.

I had a very easy pregnancy with no difficulties at all. I went to daily Mass as often as possible to make up for all those years when I could have been receiving the Eucharist and hadn't. It was possibly the most comfortable pregnancy and delivery of them all. The hospital in Wilmington was great! Finally, when I was settled in my room, I found a very compatible roommate and lovely room. But when my first meal arrived, it was meat instead of fish, so I requested that they bring me something else, as it was Friday. Well, when the tray came back, it contained a lovely lobster tail. What a surprise! I never thought that hospital food could be so nice.

Joey was a very good baby, healthy and strong. I remember being very comfortable in our lovely new home with our master bedroom and our own bathroom. We bought an extra bottle warmer to put in the upstairs bathroom and an ice bucket for the night time bottle so I didn't have to go downstairs in the night. I felt so pampered and happy. What a blessing!

Gradually, we became acquainted with all of our neighbors. There were many children the same ages as ours. We had children in and out of our home frequently. We were very happy in that neighborhood and made friends that we have kept in touch with all through the years that followed. Because of the ages of our children, I didn't have much time to get involved in volunteer work or serve on committees at the church. I longed to feel a part of the church community. I wanted to have that sense of common purpose and service that I had when I had been a part of the Brethren Church. I realized that time would come when the children were a little older.

One lovely summer day we decided to take the children to the Fourth of July Parade in downtown Wilmington. It was a great family outing; Janet was nine, Jack six, Jim four, and Joey fifteen months old. The bands played, there were marching veterans wearing colorful uniforms, and local dignitaries giving political speeches. We got ice cream treats. There was someone selling balloons, so of course everyone had to have one. The children were fascinated by the fact that the balloons floated up on their strings. We tied them on their wrists and explained what would happen if they let go. Indeed, we observed some of the other children losing theirs. John patiently explained that it was because they were gas filled-balloons, helium, and that's what made them fly. It was great fun for all.

A few days later I was sewing in the family room when suddenly I smelled the strong scent of gasoline. I rushed out in the garage to investigate, and there was Jack and his friends from the neighborhood with the gas cans for the lawnmower.

"What are you doing?" I screamed. "You know better than to play with the gas cans!"

They answered proudly, "We're making gas filled balloons!"

And sure enough they had gotten some balloons from somewhere and were attempting to fill them with gas! Well, I put a stop to that! I patiently explained that it was an entirely different kind of gas, helium, and that this would never work to make them air-borne, and besides it was very dangerous to get gasoline on their clothes and hands. I brought them in, cleaned them up, mixed up some lemonade and served cookies. I wanted to make sure that they would never try that again! It was a wonderful neighborhood, but you had to be forever on your toes to keep up with all their little projects and ideas.

We decided to enter both Jack and Janet into the Catholic school at Immaculate Heart of Mary Parish. They were bused there, and many of the children in the neighborhood attended that school. I felt that there was much that I still didn't know about the traditions of the Catholic Church and wanted them to have this experience. We were very pleased with their standards and high level of academics.

Janet had received the preparation for her First Communion during the spring of second grade and now in the fall of 1962 was entering fifth grade. Jack was starting second grade, and Jim was starting kindergarten. It seemed strange to only have one child at home in the morning. Jim went to kindergarten mornings, and with all that excitement, he was ready to take a nap in the afternoon, and Joey did, also, so it seemed that I had more free time for reading, sewing or whatever I wanted to do. Joey was only sixteen months but he was growing up quickly.

It was then that Johnnie came home with the news from the office "grapevine" that he was up for a promotion and transfer. Oh, no! I hated to think of moving away. We wondered where we would be sent. We liked Wilmington, and we had made many great friends there, but we were willing to accept a transfer. We were confident that this would be the right thing to do, to stay with DuPont. It was a wonderful, solid company and offered great opportunities for advancement. Company moves were not too difficult, as the movers did all the packing and preparation, but it might be more difficult for the children to be up rooted at this time. Well, we'd wait and see. We didn't want to tell the children just yet. We decided to wait until we really knew where and when.

It did change my long range planning. I had put in a rose garden in the back the previous spring and had plans for either a patio or adding a screened in porch to the dining room. Neither project would go forward now. In fact, there was no need to make new curtains or make any changes in the house until we learned more.

The big question mark was where would we be going? Of course I started praying about it and hoped it would work out. It was then that I had another dream. In my dream, someone said to me, "Oh, didn't they tell you? You're going to Oakland County, and you will be very happy there."

When I woke up I felt sure that this was a prophetic dream. It was so vivid and real, but where was Oakland County, I wondered. My first thought was that it would be somewhere in California. The Oakland Bay area was near San Francisco, and my sister was in that area. But I didn't know if that county had the same name. It would be nice to be near my sister, but I was not excited about moving to California, as the life style there was so different. I had heard about it from my mother, that the people there were very avantgarde, concerning family life and politics. I considered us more Midwest in our ways and more traditional in our approach to life. I puzzled about it and looked over some maps looking for an Oakland County but never really located one.

In November, Johnnie came home with the news that he was been transferred to the Detroit area. Oh, my! All I could think about was the terrible impression of Detroit during the race riots. This time when he went, I could go along as well to begin looking for a house. We made all the arrangements, and I called Mother and invited her over for Thanksgiving. Then she could stay while we made a quick trip to start looking for a house. We would plan to be gone about a week. The children were at an age that they were busy with school and wouldn't require a lot of work for her.

It was a nice little get away holiday for John and me. I was pleasantly surprised to find out that, while DuPont called it their Detroit office, it was actually located on the North end of Detroit on Seven Mile road. Most of the other employees seemed to have located in the Birmingham, Bloomfield area or in Farmington. After looking things over, we decided to concentrate on the Birmingham, Bloomfield area. One of our specifications was that we wanted to be able to enter our children in Catholic Schools. There seemed to be excellent schools in the area.

In a few days I had narrowed it down to two houses, one was an older, rambling home in Queen of Martyr's parish, and a new, just being built four bedroom colonial in St. Hugo's parish. There were advantages and disadvantages to each. The older home had lots of things already in place, like a finished basement, established lawn, and landscaping, but the closets were smaller, and some of the carpeting needed replacing. The brand new house was appealing, as it was fresh and new, but still lacked things like drapery rods, painting and finishing. The builder assured us that the lawn would be seeded as soon as spring arrived, as well as the basic shrubs in the front. We wondered if it would take a couple of months to get this house finished, having experienced the long delay in our Whitehall house.

Flying home we discussed the options and decided to make on offer on the older home. At first all was well, but there was an extra lot that we did not want, and the seller refused to sell just the house without the other lot. We prayed and prayed and eventually, we were convinced that the right house for us was the one on Millington in Bloomfield Hills. When I checked on availability for our fifth grader and second grader, it was St. Hugo for us. There was space for both Janet and Jack if we were living in the parish. We would be able to get the other two into school when the time came. The Queen of Martyr's school could not assure us that there would be space for both Janet and Jack. We both realized we felt uneasy about the whole project there.

After trying to make the Birmingham house work for several weeks, we finally gave up and we flew back a week before Christmas to see if the Millington house was still available. It was and the builder had gone ahead and finished out the bathroom and kitchen with all the tile and cabinet colors I had tentatively picked out that day when I was there, just in case we decided on it. The builder said he liked my selections and decided to finish it just the way I had chosen. We both realized that the Lord was directing us to St. Hugo's, so we confidently signed the purchase agreement. It was then that I noticed that we were going to be living in Oakland County!

The closing could be as soon as two weeks, since we had already been approved for a mortgage. We flew home to celebrate Christmas and settled on moving and packing plans for the first week in January. It was goodbye to Wilmington and hello to our new life in Michigan.

Life on Millington

We arrived at the house on a clear but very cold day, Saturday, the 12th of January, 1963. I had forgotten how cold it can get in Michigan after living in the very mild climate of Delaware for the last five years. The house was just as nice as I had remembered it. The builder had been true to his word, and everything had been cleaned and finished just as we had requested.

The children were delighted with the house and began to explore and pick their rooms. There were four bedrooms and two baths upstairs with large closets for each room. On the first floor, there was a large front to back family room with fireplace. The large kitchen and dining area was nearby. There was a half bath next to the kitchen with the living room on the front and dining room on the back, next to the kitchen. We all knew that we would be very comfortable here.

Janet and Jack had been enrolled in St. Hugo's School and would start on Monday. Jim would start kindergarten in public school, as there was no kindergarten offered at St. Hugo's. Joey would be three in April, so he was our only stay at home child now. Very quickly, we were all settled and established in our new location. Everyone in the neighborhood had only recently moved there, and there were several more houses being built, so everyone was very interested in getting acquainted. The neighbors were so friendly and welcoming. There were lots of children in the sub-division, and so very quickly, our children found playmates of their own ages.

There was a dinner party a few weeks after we moved in, so that we could meet all of our neighbors. Bridge clubs were being formed, and soon we knew nearly all of our neighbors. It seemed that most of the people in our area had moved there, so that their children could attend St.

Hugo's School. We fit right in, as most of the families were Catholic. It was indeed a very good choice of neighborhoods. .

My mother flew over to visit us right after we moved in. She was planning to spend the winter in California but wanted to see that we were settled before she left. We had a great visit, but it had turned very cold. One day we planned to go shopping at the Mall, but we watched the thermometer, hoping that the temperature would be above zero. It didn't that day, but the next day was a little warmer, all of ten above, so we went out for a few hours while Jimmie was in kindergarten, taking Joey with us. It was great fun to begin to find my way about this new area. Bloomfield Hills is a lovely area, so we had lots of places to explore. By the time Mother left, we were pretty well settled. She helped me unpack the rest of the dishes and all the "odds and ends" boxes. She was satisfied that we were fine and continued her trip to California.

I had a sense that we were finally where we belonged. It was great to be back in the Midwest. We were near our roots and our parents' homes, about the same distance to both Dixon and Danville. But most of all, I was very thankful that we were together in the same church; finally back where we belonged, both geographically and liturgically. Hurray!

John was very happy at work in the Detroit office of DuPont. It was only about twenty minutes away. But the great news for me was that John was assigned a company car, so now, for the first time, we were a two car family! What a delight that was! There were plenty of projects to do around the house. Some of the draperies and curtains had to be re-made to adapt to our new house, but all things in good time. Wintery days are great for doing such things. It was just wonderful to feel at home again.

When spring arrived and the snow had melted, I realized that the lawn was a sorry sight. Our contract called for sodding the front yard and seeding the back, but it was not scheduled until much better weather would arrive. In the meantime there was no place for the children to play, as there was nowhere in the yard that was not muddy. What a mess! As time went on we decided to have the back yard sodded too, so it would be a quick fix, once the time came to do it.

We decided to put in a concrete patio, just outside the sliding doors from the family room in the back. That was more quickly scheduled within a few weeks. Then, at least, there would be a place for Jim and Joe to ride their tricycles on the patio and driveway. Mother and Dad Hanzel had returned from Florida and arrived for Easter weekend, April 14th, for their first visit to our new home, loaded down with wonderful starts of flowers and shrubs from his abundant garden. How thoughtful, timely and welcome! We had a great visit with them. It turned out the construction crew came to pour the concrete patio on Saturday before Easter, so finally the yard was taking shape.

Another crew came to lay the sod, arriving on May 22nd, but wouldn't you know it? A late snow storm arrived that afternoon, so they went home and came back a day later to complete the project. Of course the snow melted as fast as it came down, but it proved to me that in Michigan you never knew what the weather would bring. It was wonderful to have the yard finally done!

We were very involved with the neighborhood. I was playing in a once a week girls evening bridge club, and both John and I played in once a month couples duplicate bridge club. John was playing in a once a month guys duplicate bridge club. There were activities at the parish and with the office group, so we were as busy socially as we wanted to be.

By summer, we heard about a swim club, the Surf Club. It was located only a few blocks away. We looked into it and decided to join. That really made our summer. The older three were signed up for swimming lessons, and eventually they all learned to swim. Some of our children spent some time swimming on the Surf Club Swim Team. I loved it, too. I always enjoyed swimming, and it was a great way to spend a summer afternoon: reading a book and visiting with the other moms, while watching the children have fun in the pool. The adults had a brief cool-off swim every hour. In addition, there were parties and cookouts at the Surf club. So it was great fun for all.

When school started again that fall there were three Hanzels to ride the school bus to St. Hugo's School: Janet in sixth grade, Jack in third grade and Jim in first grade, with only Joey, age three, at home with me. Then I became more active at St. Hugo's Parish. I attended the meetings of the Altar Guild and decided to help with Janet's Girl Scout troop and became a Den Mother for Jack's Cub Scouts group, as well as attending the social events of the parish.

Jim would be six that November, so we planned to have a birthday party for him. We had made a rule that when you were six, you could have six guests attend. His birthday would be on Saturday, so I decided to have a theme that would include all of the siblings. The theme was a circus. I decided to make circus seats, like riding on the backs of circus animals, seven in all, one for each of his guests and Jim. I made each seat from large cardboard boxes of various sizes. The heads and necks were made of paper Mache and appropriate tails were attached to the other end. Each was painted like a circus animal: elephants, tigers, lions, circus horses and giraffes. Janet and Jack would be the food vendors, with Joey as a helper, "Get your popcorn here!" We planned to serve popcorn, lemonade and hot dogs, and later, birthday cake, and ice cream,

The nice thing about this Saturday Birthday Party was that John would be home from work and be available to help herd everyone about. I had great fun planning and making all of the circus animals. Everything was ready, but on Friday, November 22, our president, John F. Kennedy, was assassinated in Texas! As a result, all regular TV programing had been canceled. It was a terrible time of mourning. We were undecided as to whether or not to cancel the party. In the end, I called all the parents and said we had decided not to cancel the party, as the children could hardly understand the gravity of this terrible event. The party went off as planned and was a huge success.

It all took place inside. When each child arrived, he was invited to select his animal. When all were there, we had the parade of animals, ending in the family room. John presided in describing the events that were going on under the "big tent", as our children had a great time serving the various refreshments. Before cake and ice cream, Jim opened all his presents. When it was time to leave, each guest was given his animal to take home as a party favor. We were so glad that we went ahead with the party. It was so much fun. Many years later, to my great surprise, one of "our circus animals" showed up at a St. Hugo Rummage Sale!

My focus was really on St. Hugo's Parish. I wanted to serve the parish in any way that I could. I remembered how wonderfully well everyone worked together and served one another at the Brethren Church, giving support in any way that they were able. I wanted to truly serve the Lord in this place with that same spirit of unity and joy. I wanted church to be the number one priority in our family life.

About this time we became interested in joining a country club so that John and I could play and our children could learn to play golf. We looked into the club that was right across the road from St. Hugo's, Stonycroft

Golf Club, and eventually joined. It was a great experience for all of us. They had a wonderful Juniors Program that provided lessons and taught the etiquette for golf. Eventually all our children took these lessons and learned to play golf very well. It was only a nine-hole golf club, but it worked out to be just right for all of us. We were all busy, but we could squeeze in time for a round of nine holes, sometimes twilight golf, and on weekends, we could play more if we wanted to do so. Eventually all the children became very competent players, and they still enjoy playing as adults.

By the time Joey was ready for first grade, I was asked to be chairman of some committees, and eventually, I became President of St. Hugo's Altar Guild after serving my apprenticeship in many different capacities in that organization. I really enjoyed it and made many life-long friends there.

After Joey started first grade in 1966, one of my dear friends invited me to join her in volunteering at Lourdes, a Catholic Nursing Home nearby. I was happy to do so, as about that time, Mother Hanzel had entered a nursing home in Danville. She had experienced severe memory loss and was unable to function as usual. At that time the doctors called it "hardening of the arteries", but now it is called Alzheimer's.

We were all very sad about it, especially Dad Hanzel. It was really tragic for him. We visited her whenever we could, but I wished that I could do more for her. This volunteer work provided a way for me to bring a little cheer to somebody else's Mom or Dad, so I hoped this would help in the whole scheme of things. I was feeling very comfortable in the Catholic Church now and was so thankful that I had been guided to become a member, but changes were in the wind for the Catholic Church.

In 1959, Pope John the XXIII announced his intention to summon a council. That council, the Second Vatican Ecumenical Council, officially opened in Rome on October 11, 1962. I want to include here, the Prayer of Pope John XXIII to the Holy Spirit for the success of the Ecumenical Council, as the Council opened.

"O Holy Spirit, sent by the Father in the name of Jesus, who art present in the Church, and does infallibly guide it, pour forth, we pray, the fullness of thy gifts upon the Ecumenical Council.

"Enlighten, O most gracious Teacher and Comforter, the minds of our prelates, who in prompt response to the Supreme Roman Pontiff, will carry on the sessions of the Sacred Council.

"Grant that from this Council abundant fruit may ripen; that the light and strength of the gospel may be extended more and more in human society; that the Catholic religion and its active missionary works may flourish with vigor; with the happy results that knowledge of the Church's teaching may spread and Christian morality have a salutary increase.

"O sweet Guest of the soul, strengthen our minds in the truth and dispose our heart to pay reverential heed, that we may accept with sincere submission those things which shall be decided in the council and fulfill them with ready will.

"We pray also for those sheep, who are not now of the one fold of Jesus Christ, that even they glory in the name of Christians, they may come at last to unity under the governance of the one Shepherd.

"Renew thy wonders in this day, as by a new Pentecost. Grant to Thy Church that, being of one mind and steadfast in prayer with Mary, the Mother of Jesus, and following the lead of blessed Peter, it may advance the reign of our Divine Savior, the reign of truth and justice, the reign of love and peace. Amen."

From The Documents of Vatican II, by Walter M. Abbott, S.J.

This was a monumental beginning. This council had a huge task before it, but they worked diligently to complete this task. Word of the council and its activities trickled down from time to time, but, for the most part, we the people in the pews were not aware of what was happening so far away in Rome

We learned of Pope John the XXIII's death on June 3, 1963. Sadly, he would not be there to see all the results of this council. We knew that the next pope, Pope Paul the VI, was elected shortly afterward and agreed to continue the work of the council.

It was only after the official closing of the Second Vatican Council on December 8, 1965, that we began to hear more and more about all that had happen during the council. Very serious discussions had taken place and decisions were made, but the responsibility of implementing these decisions was huge! We began hearing of synods being formed and meetings that would take place in every diocese of our country and around the world. It would take several years for all this to be translated into all the languages of the world and passed down to all of us.

We had to make an important decision in 1966. Should we continue Catholic education for our children beyond eighth grade? We paid tuition at St. Hugo's but the high school tuitions were quite a bit more and very likely to rise in the future. These were turbulent times in the sixties, and as a result, we decided that religious influence was even more important now during their teenage years. We made the decision to continue Catholic education for all four of our children. Janet entered Marian High School in the fall of 1966.

About that time, Father Esper was sent to St Hugo's to serve as our Pastor. He was a wonderful priest and we soon realized what a holy, devoted person he was. After getting acquainted with our parish, he began making subtle changes in our parish, which gave more responsibility to the laity. First, he established a parent teachers association and appointed its first board. Later he established a parish council for the parish. Both organizations were under his direct supervision but really had a positive impact to the parish.

I had completed my year as President of St. Hugo's Altar Guild in 1968. Following that, I was appointed first secretary of the Parent Teacher's Guild. Our task was to write the By Laws for this organization. It was quite a task. He had appointed a lawyer, a member of our parish, as president, so we were under very capable direction in this project. I really enjoyed the time spent with this organization and the Altar guild.

When Jack graduated eighth grade at St. Hugo's in 1969, it was already decided that he would go on to Brother Rice High School. Jack had been a paper boy for several years, so it was then that he gave his route to Jim and began caddying at Bloomfield Country Club. This was a great summer job. He was familiar with golf, so it was especially enjoyable for him. This turned out to be the pattern for all three boys, first a paper boy for the Detroit news, then a caddy at Bloomfield Country Club.

During this time, parish meetings were held through-out our diocese, called Speaker-Up Meetings, providing the parish members the opportunity to discuss the impact of the changes that were taking place as the result of Vatican II. The Altars had been turned around. Now the priests would be facing the congregation during Mass. Most parts of the Mass were now said in the native language of that country, in our case English. The singing of hymns at Mass by the congregation was encouraged. Later meetings were held in homes in small groups, so that these discussions could continue, and suggestions were submitted to the local Synods that were taking place throughout the country. It was truly a time of great change in the church. As a result, I was feeling more and more at home in the Catholic Church.

About this time, John heard rumors that he was up for a transfer. Oh, no! We hesitated to interrupt the children's school situation by moving to a new area. We were so happy right where we were. We prayed about it, and John decided to do a "little trolling" to see if there was a job opportunity locally that would be right for him. Bingo! John heard that The Cooper Tire and Rubber Co. wanted to expand their sales department, so he checked into it. It turned out to be just what he was looking for and he accepted the offer enthusiastically. It would be quite a change, as Cooper was a much smaller company. He would be a direct salesman and would be on salary plus commission. It was like jumping out of a huge, stable ship to the unfamiliar, cabin cruiser. He had been employed with DuPont for about twenty years. After much discussion, he decided to accept the offer and began working with Cooper in 1970.

The decision to send our children to Catholic High School, Marian and Brother Rice, increased our educational costs significantly. These costs would continue to increase when our children would enter college. It was necessary to do a little forward planning. Now that John had a new job, we wondered if the extra commission checks would be sufficient to cover all of these expenses. And college expenses loomed in the future.

At this time there was a teacher's shortage. I had always hoped to finish my degree, so it looked like this was the time for me to go back to school and complete my degree in elementary education. Then I would be qualified to teach full time, and the extra income would help with the rising educational costs. So, I applied at Wayne State University and began taking daytime courses there in the fall of 1970. The family was not greatly impacted by my attendance at the University, but eventually, it might make quite a change in our family life. Although, when I would begin teaching full time, I would still be able to be home when the children came home from school, and our vacation times would be compatible. I hoped that this would all work out well.

It occurred to me that in each decade of our lives there was a theme or common characteristic about each one. We had been married in May, 1950. The first decade was about becoming established as a married couple and becoming parents. All of our children were born during this decade, Joey, the youngest, being born in April, 1960. The next decade had been about raising our children, learning that each one has his or her individual personality and talents and how to nurture each one. Now we were in the 70's. It seemed that this was going to be the decade about letting go and sending them out into the world to try their wings but being ever watchful and caring in this process of launching and sending forth.

Janet had graduated from Marian High School in June 1970 and had decided on Central Michigan University. Plans were made for her to enter that University in the fall. It was a real wrench to let her go. It was the end of family life with all four children living together at home. It was great seeing her growing up and getting ready to enter an adult world, but we were finding this change to be difficult.

The Year That Was, 1971

●──●

After the holidays in early January, everyone got back to their school schedules. Janet was a freshman at the Central Michigan University, Jack was a junior at Brother Rice High School, Jim was in eighth Grade and Joe was in fifth grade at St. Hugo School, and I was starting my second semester at Wayne State University. We were all off to a good start, so I thought. But soon it was all about to come to a crashing halt.

January progressed with the usual busy schedule for me, consisting of Altar Guild Meetings, bridge clubs, PTG Meetings, Brother Rice Mothers Club Meetings, and cafeteria duty at St. Hugo's, as well as my classes and homework from Wayne State. But on January 28th, Joe came home from school very ill. I took him to the doctor immediately, as it looked like it was another attack of Stevens Johnston Syndrome. He had episodes like this several times before, but this time he was very ill. Stevens Johnston is a syndrome in which all the mucous membranes in the body swell as the result of an allergic reaction to some substance as yet unknown. But this was by far the most serious reaction to date. He was given complete bed rest and we hoped he would soon be better, but by Wednesday, February 3, he was admitted to the hospital. We were terribly worried about him.

I had a paper due at Wayne State on Friday, but it was completed, so I decided to drop it off Thursday morning and give notice that I would skip all other classes that week so that I could spend my time at the Beaumont Hospital with Joe. There was a nasty snow storm overnight on Thursday, but I was determined to go out anyway, even though I knew the roads were bad because I wanted to clear myself at Wayne State and see Joe, so off I went.

I was returning from Wayne State and on my way up Woodward Ave, heading to the hospital, when I skidded on a snowy, icy patch on Seven Mile and hit a truck head on! I was so frightened, but I really could not control the car! Even though I wasn't going very fast, we still collided. What an impact! I was wearing my seat belt, but, at that time, there was no shoulder harness, only a lap belt. I was thrown up and back down again hard and was crushed against the steering wheel.

My immediate thought was. *Oh! I can't get my breath! This is why they say the person was killed instantly! They couldn't breathe! Well, unless you can inflate your lungs, you are going to be listed as that, too! Fight! Get your lungs inflated!*

It seemed like forever before I could breathe, and when I drew my first breath, I thought, *Oh, good! I'm going to live, but Oh! Ouch! I think my back is broken. Now what am I going to do?*

When I looked about, I saw another driver who was knocking on my window and motioning to me. I rolled down the window and he said, "Are you alright? Quick, turn off your engine!"

So I did. Then I asked him, "Are the police here yet?"

Another driver, a lady driving a sandwich truck appeared on the other side, and asked if she could help, and I said, "Yes! Please call my husband's office. Tell them I've been in an accident and they are taking me to Beaumont Hospital."

About that time the police arrived. I was delighted to see them, but they were not very glad to see me. They questioned me and said, "You'll have to get out of the car! NOW! I will need your ID so bring your purse! A tow truck is on its way to haul your car away. Get out of this car now! You are blocking traffic!"

"But I can't get out." I explained. "I think my back is broken. And I shouldn't be moved until the ambulance gets here. Is there one on the way?"

"OH! Alright! I will call one, but you have to get out of the car now!"

"I need the ambulance to take me to Beaumont Hospital on Twelve Mile Road." I said, trying to be patient.

"Look, lady! You're blocking traffic and you're in the city of Detroit, and they'll be taking you to Receiving Hospital in downtown Detroit. Get out now, or we are going to haul you away! I will be back to have you sign some forms."

So I got out gingerly, hoping nothing bad would happen and stood in the snow on the side of the road, wondering what to do next. Well, the sandwich truck lady came back and reported that she had made the phone call and asked if she could help me with anything else.

I said, "Thank you so much. I really appreciate it! Thank you, thank you." Then I explained that they wanted to take me to Receiving Hospital, but my son was a patient at Beaumont Hospital. "It is going to be so difficult for my husband, for us to be in two different hospitals. Is that your truck? Do you think you could drive me to Beaumont?"

"I will be glad to!" She said, "I'll bring it around."

About that time the police came back. We exchanged cards and information, and he gave me a ticket. I told him I had made other arrangements and to please cancel the ambulance. I found out where they were taking my smashed car. With that all cleared away, I was free to go. The sandwich lady arrived on my side of the street and I was ready to go. I explained to her that I thought my back was broken and did not want to sit down. I was afraid to move much at all. So I ended up standing, holding on to the grab bar in the front of the truck all the way.

As I stood in the truck, I was so thankful that she had done so much for me, but I was in so much pain that if I tried to talk, I was afraid that I would break down and cry. So off we went. When we arrived at Emergency, I thanked her again and asked for her card. It was such a blessing! It was snowing quite hard by that time, so she handed me her card and drove off after leaving me with the attendant who promptly proceeded to load me into a wheel chair. Ugh! It was a wooden slated wheel chair, and I was afraid that I would never get out of it alone without doing more damage to my back.

Once inside, the attendant pushed me up to the line and left me. *What now!* I thought, as I clutched my purse. *I will not cry! Surely, someone will appear and help me. I am not done yet.*

When I saw a pink uniform go by, I recognized her as a volunteer, so I waved to her. "Would you please help me? I am here alone, and there is no one here to help me!" I pleaded.

"Well, do you suppose it's your attitude? You'll just have to wait your turn like everyone else," and she stalked off.

I sat there and took stock of myself. I realized that all through this ordeal, I had tried to keep my cool and not think about what really had happened. I guess I have been too demanding and controlling. I didn't want to think about what a mess I was in, and it was, really, my own fault for going out on such a day like this. I should have waited to go out until the roads had been cleared and visited Joey in the afternoon. I started to pray and ask God to forgive me for wanting to do things my way.

I thought, *I probably don't look very injured. I am wearing my good winter coat. I am not visibly bleeding. That volunteer had no idea I was in such pain.* I tried to relax and take it all in my stride.

After all, they were very busy. Maybe the people that are ahead of me have more urgent needs than I have. I have come this far, I won't give up now. Thank goodness for the lunch truck lady! When it's my turn, I thought, *I will get the help I need. At least I'm out of the cold and snow! I know I can't move without help, but at least I am closer to getting the help that I need.* As I prayed, I began to feel much more peaceful.

Eventually it was my turn and I explained what happened. When they took me back to an examining room and took my clothes off, they saw all the bruising on my abdomen, and now they realized how much pain I was really in. About that time, in came Johnnie and with him was Father Esper. *Oh! Maybe it's worse than I thought. They have called a priest to give me the last rights!*

It turned out the Father Esper had seen John, as they both came into the hospital at the same time. When John explained that I had been in a car accident and was in emergency, he had offered to see me as well. It was so wonderful to have them both with me. They prayed with me, and soon I began to feel much more positive about everything.

Eventually, an orthopedic doctor was called in and he ordered a series of x-rays. As there was a bump on my forehead, where I had hit the steering wheel, they wanted to check on that, as well as my spine.

Yes, I was right. I had fractured vertebrae, the fifth lumbar vertebrae, but no damage to my skull, just a headache. So I was admitted. Poor John! Now he had two of us in the same hospital, so he went up to see Joey while I was getting settled in my room.

The orders stated that I was to have complete bed rest. I was not allowed to get out of bed for any reason until I could be fitted with a back brace. One had been ordered, and it would take several days for it to come. I wanted very much to go and visit Joe, but that was not possible. I had to stay where I was. I knew that Pediatrics did not allow bed-side phones so I couldn't call him. I was stuck here for the next few days. It was a pleasant room, so I had much for which to be thankful. I began to pray for Joey and me.

Pretty soon Johnnie arrived. What a day it had been for him. I felt so sorry for him. He had so much to do and would have to get home soon, as Jack and Jim would be coming home from school. Oh dear, and dinner to get. Well, I could not help in any way, except to try to be as little trouble as possible.

The days dragged by for me. It is amazing what the effects are when you are required to lay flat on your back nonstop for three days. Boredom sets in fast. It isn't easy to read or watch TV. Although your body is at rest, your mind goes on nonstop. Soon, I realized that the best thing to do was to stop trying to plan or to consider the "what ifs." The most consoling thing I did during those three days was to pray, and that I did. I prayed for forgiveness for my accident, for being so determined to go out on such a bad day. I prayed for Joey. I prayed for John. He had his work to do and mine, as well as visiting us in the hospital. I prayed for the doctors and nurses.

It occurred to me that I really needed this time flat on my back with nothing to distract me to consider where I was, what mistakes I had made, what I should change, what I should do next, and what God was calling me to change and to do in the future. This time was not something I would ever have chosen for myself. But in retrospect, it was a time well spent. Yes, painful, lonely, and difficult, but, in some weird kind of way, I realized that this was what I was called to do at this time. I prayed almost nonstop.

My doctor made rounds very early every morning. He explained to me that the fracture was a jagged break, and it was rubbing against my spinal cord. This had caused some nerve damage and numbness in my left leg. He thought that this would gradually go away, or, if not, it would not get worse. Therefore, it was very important to avoid further damage to my spinal cord. It was something that could not be corrected surgically. It would just require time to heal. It was very important to protect further damage by wearing a back brace which would keep the spine in proper position.

On Monday, the eighth of February, my back brace arrived! It looked like a corset. It extended from my ribs to below my tail bone. It was carefully laced up into the proper configuration. It could be hooked or unhooked, so that I could get in and out of it by myself. It was difficult to get on. I would have to wear it whenever I was out of bed. I had to take it on and off while sitting up in bed, not an easy thing to do. But, surprisingly, it was quite comfortable once I had accomplished the feat of putting it on or off. I was encouraged to walk about a little and get use to wearing it.

At last I could see Joey, who was on a different floor of the hospital. A volunteer was recruited to go with me. It was great to see him. Joe was much better, and we talked about how wonderful it would be to both be home.

Both Joe's doctor and my doctor conferred, and agreed that we would both be released on Wednesday, February 10th. I had been in the hospital for exactly a week and Joe a week and a day. All the arrangements and follow up appointments were made, and it was wonderful to both be going home at last!

There were lots of things to do once we got home. Both of us felt weak but quite well. I did have some back pain. In a few days, Joe was able to go back to school. I found I was able to do most things well. But I was much slower. It was arranged for the car to be towed to the dealer, and they determined that it was a total loss, and the insurance company confirmed this,

John took me to my first appointment with my doctor. He said he would tell me later how long I would have to wear the back brace, as we would have to wait and see how fast the bones would heal. It was very important that I ride in the car as little as possible, as any sort of jarring could aggravate my back, slow down healing, and possibly do further damage to the spinal cord. He said I could not drive during this time.

I said, "Don't worry about that! I will never drive again!"

He replied, "Indeed you won't! You won't drive, until I say you can drive."

Life had really changed for us all, and that was not all that changed. About this time we got a call from Dad's neighbors in Danville. Dad Hanzel had gotten lost and had been found by a neighbor. It seemed that now John's dad was getting "hardening of the arteries", too! John and I had been wondering about it, as sometimes, when we talked to him on the phone, he seemed confused and mixed up. We decided that it was time for Dad to come and live with us. So John made plans to take the train down and drive him back to Michigan in his car, bringing his dog and all of his clothes and maybe his favorite chair, so that he would feel more at home with us. We would wait until spring, until everyone was feeling better, to decide what to do about selling their home on Poland Road.

While Johnnie was gone to Danville, I got the boys to help me. I prepared Janet's room for Dad Hanzel, and put all of Janet's things in an extra closet. When Janet would come home from school, the three boys could bunk together for the summer, and Janet would be in Jack's room. We would make it work. Next summer we will all go down and see Mother Hanzel. John had visited with her, while he was down there. So Dad came to live with us on February 24th.

What a change! It was a huge adjustment for all of us.

Dad's little Sheltie dog, Chip, adjusted very well to his new surroundings. It was clear that he was Dad's dog, and they were great company for each other. He was no trouble at all. He slept in Dad's room and was never far from him. When they walked around the block, people would ask me, "And how old is the dog?" He walked in step with Dad and seemed like he was an old dog, but he really was only about three years old. They soon became friends with a friend of mine's father, who was living with my friend and her husband. They lived just around the corner from us, so the two men became good friends, as they both had dogs. They were often seen together, walking their dogs. Sometimes they came over and visited together on our patio on nice days. It really helped Dad to have a friend like that.

But Dad really missed Danville and had trouble realizing that he should not be living alone again. He had always been very competent and independent, and of course, he missed visiting his wife. We knew that we had done the right thing by bringing him here to live with us, but we couldn't help but re-examine the situation, because Dad couldn't remember from day to day why he was living with us. Almost every day he would ask me, "When does John get home from work?"

And when I would tell him, he would say, "Good. When John gets home, I want him to put me on the train, so I can go back home to Danville. I have stayed here long enough,"

It bothered him that there was so much activity at our house. The boys would come and go, and he couldn't keep track of what was going on at our house. If he lost something, like once he misplaced a pair of shoes; he would accuse the boys of stealing his shoes and selling them. He always wore expensive shoes and he was very protective of them. Fortunately, he slept well, so we could go out in the evening, and the boys were responsible enough to handle things while we were away.

We had not replaced my car, but we had received the insurance money. Dad's car was here, but he did not seem to be interested in driving. He seemed to realize that he did not know how to get about in our area. He did not seem to mind if the boys used his car. Jack had his driver's license, so he drove the car pool back and forth to Brother Rice and drove Jim and Joe to piano lessons. I still was not driving, but my back was a little more comfortable now, so things were getting back to normal. Except it was a new normal. When I went out in the day time, someone needed to pick me up for meetings. John would usually take me grocery shopping on Saturday. I scheduled any doctor's appointments for after school, so Jack could drive us. We managed, but it was difficult.

About that time, I was notified that I had a court date to settle the ticket that I had received on that February day when my accident occurred. I wondered what would happen. John took the day off from work and we went together. It turned out that the arresting officer did not show up, and the judge informed me not to say anything! The case was dropped without prejudice, because he had not appeared. What a relief!

But that was not the end of it. The insurance company informed us that the driver of the truck that I had run into had begun a law suit to recover damages to himself and to his truck and all sorts of things, which all added up to a lot of money. Finally, months later, that, too, was settled out of court and the insurance covered everything. At last we could put all of it behind us!

On April 2, about five weeks after Dad Hanzel had moved in, we received a phone call from the nursing home where Mother Hanzel was and they informed us that she had died, unexpectedly and peacefully, in her sleep! We left as soon we could and arranged for Janet to join us.

It was a very sad time for all of us. The funeral arrangements were made. They were well known in the community, so it turned out to be a very lovely, well-attended funeral, with burial at Gundy Cemetery, near the farm where Jeffery was buried. It was Easter Week, as Easter was April 11th, and her funeral Mass was on April 6th. As a result, the children all had time off from school, so we stayed a few extra days to attend to things regarding the farm and the house on Poland Road. We realized that it was time to sell the house. We decided we would come back when school was out, have a sale of the household goods, and get things in order to put it on the market. We hated the thought of putting an end to that era, but it was time.

Dad held up very well during all of it, but we could see that he had lost weight and was not doing well. I took him to the doctor, but he found nothing of concern, except we knew he was very unhappy. We began to realize that he felt he was not financially able to support himself. That was why he minded living with us. He asked if he had any money left. Over and over, he would say, "Well, my life is over now, (since his wife was gone), and when I am gone, make sure you send some money to my sister in Yugoslavia."

When I asked him how much he wanted to send, it was always a different amount. Sometimes it was five thousand dollars, other times he would say fifty thousand dollars. He really had no idea what he had.

I told John, "We really have a problem here." So, John sat down with him one Saturday and explained that he did have plenty of money. He still owned the farm and had money in the bank. The money from the Poland road house had been invested with his broker, and he had Social Security. He was glad to know that, but it seemed to him that, if he had plenty of money, why did he live with us?

We talked it over. Finally we decided that it was time to start to look for a place for him to live, so that he would feel in charge, yet his needs would be met. He would be paying his own way. After much searching and asking about, we found such a place at Briarbank, a lovely home about three or four miles from our house, right there in Bloomfield Hills. It was run by an order of nuns. There was a chapel there and there was Mass every day. They served three meals a day. They had about two acres of land, lovely grounds with some other houses on the grounds. They served both men and women. He would be safe and secure there, as they really looked out for all their residents. There was a waiting list, so we put Dad's name on the waiting list. I felt sure that he would be much more contented there, living on his own, yet with all his needs met. It was close by, so we could visit him often.

It seemed that there was always something more to deal with. Jim and Jack were caddying at Bloomfield Hills Country Club that summer, so now it was Joe's turn to deliver the Detroit News. Jim had graduated from St. Hugo's Grade School and was scheduled to enter Brother Rice High School in the fall. I had been elected President of The Brother Rice Mother's Club. I began to realize that God had other plans for me. And that I was not going to be returning to Wayne State University anytime soon, if ever. I had come to realize that I had never really prayed about that decision. I had just thought it was a great idea and had acted on it. It had not been God's plan for me. I had much to learn.

Janet was home for the summer from Central Michigan University and she had a summer job in Birmingham, so it was turning out to be a very busy summer. My back was healing nicely, but I was still in my brace. Things seemed to be going along normally, but it was the lull before the storm.

On August 25th, Jim had finished caddying. He had called from Wilson's Drug Store, as was their habit, to ask for someone to come and pick him up. Jack answered the phone and said Janet had taken Joe to his piano lesson, and there was no car at home. Someone would be there after a bit. Fortunately, John arrived home early for a change, so we left right after that, to pick up Jim at Wilson's Drug Store. Well, when we got closer to the intersection of Woodward and Long Lake, we could see that the traffic was backed up all the way for blocks.

I was anxious and said to John, "Let's turn into this parking lot and go west, and it will come out, right by Wilson's Drug store. Then we can pick up Jim, and it won't matter how long the traffic is tied up."

Well, John didn't want to do that, but I insisted, so we did. When we got there, Jim was not there! We parked the car and walked to see if Jim had gone to look at the accident. Then we discovered that it was Jim lying there on the street, and he had been hit by a car! I ran to kneel down beside him and put his head in my lap. There was a huge crowd of people gathered.

Someone came out of the crowd and asked me if we were the Hanzel's, and I said yes. Then he asked if Dr. Bookmaker was our Doctor, and I said yes. About that time the ambulance arrived, and they started loading Jim on a stretcher. They would be taking us to St. Joe's Hospital. A man came out of the crowd and said he was a doctor. He volunteered to assist them, when they placed Jim on the stretcher. He said it was obvious that this leg had a compound fracture, maybe the other leg, also. They took great care in placing him on the stretcher. John said he would meet us at St. Joe's, and I should ride with Jim in the ambulance.

When we were alone in the ambulance, I prayed, right out loud, the Our Father and the Hail Mary over and over again, while I stroked Jim's head. He was not responding but was crying like a new born baby. I knew he was in terrible pain, but it seemed to comfort him. From time to time I told Jim that we would soon be in the hospital and everything would be okay.

When we unloaded at emergency, Dr. Bookmaker's assistant was there to meet us. Evidently the man on the street had called the doctor's office with the message that we were on our way to St. Joe's. Since his assistant was already there making rounds at St. Joe's, he was alerted and went down to help us. It was very reassuring to have him there to call all the shots. They all seemed very concerned about Jim's condition.

I said, "Let me stay, as I think it is calming for him." So I stood out of the way, at his head, and tried to be as inconspicuous as possible.

I heard everything that was said. The doctor remarked, "Note the infantile cry. It is obvious that there is extensive brain damage."

The nurse took the scissors and cut his pants all the way up to his waist.

Oh! I thought. *Those are his new school pants to start Brother Rice High School! Oh, well. It doesn't matter. We'll do anything to help him.*

With his pants cut open, a huge gash on his thigh was revealed, sliced open like a piece of meat. It wasn't bleeding very much. Evidently no arteries had been cut. They looked at his legs and the doctor said, "It looks like there are compound fractures in this leg and possibly both legs. But with so much obvious brain damage, it will not be possible to have him receive an anesthetic at this time, in order to properly set them. Have them x-rays the legs for now, so that we can see what we are dealing with."

I could see that his legs were twisted way out of shape. They covered him with a sheet, and an orderly came to escort us up to x-ray.

When we were on the elevator, I prayed silently to the Lord. *Lord, You heard what they said about his having an anesthetic at this time. Please! You will have to do something now, quickly! Then surgery will not be necessary!*

Now, remember, I had seen his legs on the street and in emergency. When they uncovered him in x-ray, they looked entirely different. They did several x-rays, but every time they moved him, he would moan, so they decided that was enough for now. The x-rays were sent back to emergency with us. When we got back to emergency, the doctors looked them over very carefully and were amazed to see that there were no fractures in either leg. Then they re-examined Jim's legs. Incredible!

"Well, we will have to admit him to intensive care for now, and a neurologist will be called in to evaluate his condition," the doctor ordered.

"Oh, before we go, Doctor, can you please suture his thigh tonight?" I asked.

He looked shocked and turned pale. I really thought he was going to pass out. I think he had forgotten all about the gash on his thigh!

"Oh!" He said, "I couldn't possibly do that! We will have to call in a surgeon to do it." All the arrangements were made, and soon we were up in ICU.

John tracked us down there and we conferred. I told him everything that had happened, and I said I would like to stay all night in the hospital with Jim. The nurses were very nice and said it would be alright. I thought he might wake up and would like to have family with him. John said he would go home and tell everyone what had happened and pick up something for dinner. Then, in the evening, he would come back and see us. I asked him to please bring me a couple of things that I would like to have from home.

About a half hour later, a surgeon did arrive. He turned down the sheet and when he saw Jim's leg, he swore and said crossly to the nurse, "Give it a good disinfectant soak and I will be back in twenty minutes to suture it!" And then he stalked out of the room.

Well! I thought. *He must be having a really bad day, but mine hasn't been too great, either!*

In about twenty minutes he came back, and turned to me and said, "You, get out!"

But I said, "Everyone else let me stay."

"I don't need a fainting mother or an audience present. Step out in the hall!"

So I did. I leaned against the wall, covered my eyes with my hands and prayed as hard as I could. After quite a long interval, he came out and was all smiles, much calmer, and actually pleasant!

"I couldn't believe it," he said. "There were no major nerves, muscles or tendons severed. It went together like a piece of cake. I am sorry I was so short with you. But sometimes I think they bring me these cases of young people all broken and expect me to put Humpty Dumpty back together again. Sometimes it just can't be done. But, in this case, he will be just fine."

"Oh, thank you!" I replied. "Oh, doctor, how many stitches did he have? His brothers will be asking about it, but this time, I think he has the record!"

He laughed and said, "I have no idea how many there are. I just kept stitching and stitching, and it all came together. There are too many to count. There are about sixteen or eighteen on the outside, but I have no idea how many there are inside! I surely hope he has the record and that no one else comes even close!"

I returned to Jim's bed side, and he was breathing easier now and seemed to be resting. The nurse said, "Why don't you go and have a bite to eat and rest a little. I will keep a close watch on him."

When I returned, they had arranged a quiet little space where I could rest and still be near Jim in case he woke up and needed something. Later John and Janet came in, brought the things I had asked for, and updated me on how things were at home. They didn't stay long.

Somehow we got through the night. There was very little change until morning. Then Jim stirred and tried to talk. I told him what had happened and that he was going to be okay. He seemed satisfied with that but really had trouble forming words. I wanted to ask him more about how it all happened, but I guessed he really didn't remember much about it all.

I said, "Now don't try too hard. You have been through a lot and we will just have to give it time to come back."

About mid-morning the Neurologist came in and introduced himself to me. We talked briefly. Then he asked me to step out and he would conduct his examination.

When he returned he said, "Yes, there is extensive brain damage, but it is all temporary, and it will all go away. Eventually he will return to normal."

I was so relieved! I asked, "How can you be sure that it is just temporary?"

"My dear, when I say it is temporary, it is temporary! This is my field! In my experience, it is my opinion that in time he will make a full recovery."

Then he went on to explain that his brain was like a bruised apple, but with the body's wonderful repair system that after a time, all the bruised connections would be repaired and he would be fine again.

That little verbal exchange did help me feel much more optimistic and hopeful about Jim's situation. What a wonderful thing our bodies are! We are truly wonderfully made! But it was very difficult to watch him try to eat. He couldn't hold a glass well or use a spoon. He would miss his mouth if he tried to eat a potato chip. Or he would search for a word and not be able to come up with it. These were some of the things I observed during the next few days and weeks.

"I just have to believe that it will all end well, and he will make a full recovery like the doctor had predicted," I told myself. .

I stayed another day and night, and when they admitted him to a regular hospital room and Jim was communicating better, I decided that it was time for me to return home with the promise to Jim that we would visit him during visiting hours every day from now on.

We all took turns visiting him. John and I went to see him once each day. Still he complained that his legs really hurt him. On about the third day after he was out of ICU, he was sent down for more x-rays. They showed that there were small fractures in each knee joint. The Orthopedic Doctor was called in and he cast both legs from the ankle to hip, which immobilized both knees. These casts would have to be in place for about five to six weeks. Then when they were removed, he would need physical therapy to regain normal use of his legs again.

Meanwhile, Jack had returned to caddying at Bloomfield, and all the caddies and club members wanted to hear how Jim was getting along, as they had all heard about his accident.

That weekend Jack Nicklaus, the famous pro golfer, was scheduled by GM Corporation for an appearance with all the GM dealers in this district. Jack Nicklaus would play one hole with each foursome. Then wait at that tee and play with the next foursome all the way around. He had heard about Jim, the caddy, who had met with such a terrible accident. Later, when the play was completed, he asked the Caddy Master how Jim was doing and where he was. When he found out he was still in the hospital, he said that he would go and visit Jim and sign his casts! We were all excited about his coming to see Jim.

Actually it made the papers. There was a nice article about his appearance at the hospital with a picture of Jim with Jack Nicklaus. Jim was thrilled by that experience! He had visited him after visiting hours, so no one else from our family saw him. Jim had much to tell us and his friends when they visited, and they all signed his cast, as well.

I would like to add a little foot note here. About a year later, this event with Jack Nicklaus was repeated. When he returned to Bloomfield, he asked about the young boy who had broken both legs. He was told that Jim had made a wonderful recovery, and that he was there, that day, on the caddy bench. Then Jack said, "Well, bring him over, and he will be my caddy for today."

When they finished the round, he gave Jim a nice tip and took off the glove he had worn that day. He gave it to Jim, signed it, and told Jim that he had worn that glove only once before when he had played and won the tournament that he had played the week before. It is amazing that such a famous person would be so kind and caring. He is truly a gentleman. Our family had always been fans of his, but now we were really avid fans after this experience!

After it had been a little over a week since Jim's accident, the doctor said, that if I was willing, he thought Jim would be better off back at home, and I agreed. If he were home, there would be more normal activity around him, and it would be much better for his recovery. Perhaps his friends would stop by to visit him more often, and that would help to keep him up to date with school and family. The difficulty was that I did not think that we could manage to get him in our car, as his legs did not bend. He was now fitted with crutches and could walk a little by swinging his legs forward. He was not allowed to put much weight on his feet, but of course his knees did not bend. It would be much better, all the way around, for him to be home. I thought I could rent a hospital bed and would place it in the dining room. Then he would be in the middle of the action going on at home. He could use the bathroom, which was on the first floor. Going up and down stairs seemed impossible at this time.

I called the insurance company to see if they would pay for the hospital bed rental and ambulance ride home. After all, it would save the insurance company the hospital expenses and, emotionally and psychologically, we thought he would recover much more quickly in the home situation.

When I called the insurance company, she said, "We never pay for the ambulance to take them home from the hospital, only when the person is admitted."

"Let me talk to your supervisor, please." I said.

When she came on the line, I said, "Look, if you will help me to get him home, I will be glad to do the work of taking care of him for the next five weeks or so until Jim can have his casts removed. Consider the cost of the rental of the hospital bed and ambulance ride home versus the cost of keeping him in the hospital for five more weeks."

"Hmm, I will talk this over with my supervisor, and I will get back to you," She replied.

A few hours later, she called and told me, "We will be very happy to provide the things you asked for, and we have arranged for the delivery of the equipment: a hospital bed, bedside table, and portable commode. Yes, under these circumstances, we will pay for an ambulance to bring him home. Would there be anything else you would need?"

"Thank you so much. I really appreciate this. It will be much better for Jim and all of us." And soon all the arrangements were made.

So Jim arrived home on September 8th, just two weeks after his terrible accident. We hooked up a long cord to the kitchen telephone so that Jim could talk on that phone. We began having all our meals in the dining room, so Jim would be at the dinner table with us, rolled up into a sitting position in his bed. Friends dropped by after school and kept him up to date on all the things happening at school. It was much better for everyone to try to get back to normal somewhat.

I called Brother Rice High School and explained the situation. It was arranged that a tutor would come in twice a week, so that he could keep up with his school work. Dad Hanzel was there, too, so he popped in and visited with Jim and with his dog, Chip. The doctor had encouraged him to exercise as much as possible. Before long, Jim got quite good at propelling himself out of bed and about the house and yard on his two crutches.

Mother was home in Dixon for the summer and she decided to come over for a visit to help us out. I knew it would be crowded, but I agreed and indeed it was wonderful to have her with us for a few days. She was a big help, just by keeping both Jim and Dad Hanzel amused and happy.

After a few days, she took me aside and told me that Dad Hanzel had opened up to her. She said that she thought we ought to make other plans for him, as he felt out of the loop and in the way. I realized that with everything happening I had not spent much time with him. Mother and I talked about the situation. I realized that he could not keep track of what was going on from day to day. He needed some place of his own that had a more regular schedule, some place with more peace and quiet, geared to his needs.

I checked with Briarbank, an assisted living facility nearby, about vacancies. But they still had nothing available for Dad. It was a deep concern for all of us.

Mother stayed only about a week, as she was assured that Jim and I were doing well. My back was healing, but I was still wearing my back brace. Jim was doing well and trying hard to keep up with his school work. He had a few weeks to go before his casts were scheduled to be removed. Things were on the mend, so she went back to Dixon and she tried not to worry about us.

It was time for me to be checked by my doctor. By now, I felt that I was ready to drive again. We had talked about it before, but now I was ready to really plead my case. It would be much easier for everyone for me to be able to drive. At my next appointment I asked. But he still said no. Not yet.

My next appointment was for a month later, at which time the x-rays would be repeated. Maybe then he would approve my driving again. It was frustrating. I could drive again, I knew I could. And it would be better for everyone. Oh, well, surely he would let me do it next month.

On October 5th Jim was taken to see his doctor, and his braces were removed. I was very glad for Jim, but it was quite a jolt for him. His legs were weak, and the muscles were unready to function properly. The doctor decided that his legs should be wrapped, with half of the shell of the cast in place. It would take time for Jim to get used to this new feeling. Physical therapy was scheduled for him at St. Joe's Hospital,

When I had my October visit with my doctor, I explained how difficult it was with all the trips to therapy, and the doctor finally agreed to let me drive again, but only in the daytime and only for short trips. So, at last I felt like myself again, but it would be another month before I could stop wearing the brace. *One step at a time*, I thought. At least I could drive again!

Poor Jim! He had been so good about it all, but now the therapy was extremely painful. His knees had to learn to bend all over again. Stretching the muscles and getting things working normally was a huge task. Jim started back at Brother Rice. He had missed all of September and three weeks in October. His schedule was adjusted so that he could attend classes in the morning with therapy every afternoon. Eventually, his schedule was changed so that he went to therapy after school and could attend school all day. He used crutches, so that he would be more stable. But it was still a very painful experience.

In November two things happened. Finally, I was allowed to stop wearing my back brace. But if my back started to be painful, I was to wear it again for a few days. What a relief! It had been nine months, like a very long pregnancy.

About this time, they called to inform us that there was an opening at Briarbank, so Dad Hanzel was admitted. It was amazing how quickly he adjusted to their schedule. I realized that our schedule had been anything but regular, so no wonder he liked it better.

At Briarbank there was a wake-up call then Mass in the chapel, followed by breakfast every day. Meals were served at a regular time in the main dining room. He was surrounded by people of his own age, so there was lots of talking and getting acquainted time. The residents looked out for each other, and of course the staff was very helpful. He had his own room and shared the bathroom with one other man. The bathroom was located between their two rooms, so they could enter without going out in the hall. It was all working out very nicely. It was a happy arrangement for all of us. We picked him up every Sunday afternoon and he came over for a visit.

Jim continued to go to therapy from mid-October until Christmas time. It was a very painful and difficult time, but it really worked, as it got him walking well again. Amazingly, he kept up with all his class work, and at the end of his first semester, he had attained very good grades, considering all of the difficulties he had. We had lots to celebrate that Christmas. We had come through quite a year, with much sadness, adjustments and painful difficulties. All of us were ready to put 1971 behind us and to begin a New Year!

In looking back over this whole experience, I realized that the healing power of God had been with us all along the way. Joe and Jim had made wonderful recoveries. My back was still achy at times but okay. My doctor had used psychology with me. He would not let me drive again, until I really begged for permission to do so. It looked ridiculous when I looked back on all this. Now I realized that my confidence was returning. I knew I would be very hesitant to drive on snowy days again. But that's alright. It would be foolish if I didn't, and I would be extra careful from now on.

Year Of Change, 1972

●————————————————————————————————————●

School started promptly after the start of the New Year with Janet returning to Central Michigan University, Jack and Jim to complete their junior and freshman year at Brother Rice High School, respectfully, and Joe in the middle of fifth grade at St. Hugo School. I was busy as ever. I was Vice President of the Brother Rice Mother's Club, as this was my learning year, and next year I would be president. Dad Hanzel was settled comfortably at Briarbank. John's job was going very well at Cooper. We all hoped that the troubles of the past year were far behind us and that this would be smooth going. But it was not to be.

It seemed that there were left over things that had to be addressed and a few new wrinkles to deal with, reinforcing any thoughts that I could not return to the University or hope to have a career outside the home. It was quite clear to me that I was still needed right where I was, full time.

For Valentine's Day, John surprised me with a new Monte Carlo. We had been using Dad Hanzel's old Buick. It was still in very good condition, so the new car was to be for me exclusively, and the boys could use the Buick as their car. How lovely. No more worries about going out or finding the gas tank on "E". It was Jack's responsibility to buy gas and take care of the Buick, as he was the only driver, now that Janet was back at the University.

In April, both John and I were scheduled for our annual physicals. His doctor decided that now was the time to repair a hernia that John had for years, but recently it had become more and more of a problem. As a result, John was scheduled to be admitted to St. Joe's Hospital on Monday, April 17, and for surgery the next day. It seemed that our string of hospital stays was going to continuing on, into 1972.

It all turned out very well, and John came home on Friday of that week. He had dreaded it, as he had never had any experience with being a patient in a hospital since he had his tonsils removed many years before. It was my turn to take care of him.

By the next Friday, John was experiencing a bad case of cabin fever, so I agreed to drive him to the office for a short pop in visit and to pick up his mail and messages. He was not allowed to drive for another week or so. Just before we planned to leave, I received a phone call from Brother Rice saying that Jack was ill and could I please come and pick him up? So I did that errand first.

It seemed that Jack had been feeling pains in his tummy during the night, but he had decided he really didn't want to miss school, so the car pool picked him up as usual. He went off without reporting it, although he had refused to eat any breakfast. By noon he was really sick. When I checked him out at home, I felt sure that he was having an appendicitis attack. I called the doctor and scheduled an appointment for 3:00. I cautioned him not to eat anything, and we would be back in an hour. Then I would take him to his appointment.

At the doctor's office, I asked Jack if he wanted me to come in with him, but Jack, now sixteen, said he was old enough to go by himself. So I waited in the waiting room. In a few minutes, I was called to come in, as the doctor wanted to talk with me. Dr. Bookmyer met me in the hall. He said, "I want you to go in and talk to your son! In my opinion he has a very hot appendix, and he should go to surgery, as soon as it can be arranged, but I will not do surgery, unless he agrees that it is necessary! Your son tells me that he wants to wait and see, as sometimes it subsides!"

So I went in to talk with Jack. "Honey, the doctor says that you do, indeed, have appendicitis!" I said. "Why do you object to having surgery?"

"Mom, I don't want to have surgery now! I am running for Student Council, and the election is next week. I don't want to miss it! And besides, while you and Dad were at the office, I looked it up in the World Book, and it said that sometimes it subsides. Well, let's wait and see. Maybe I won't have to have surgery at all!"

We talked further. "Really, Jack, I have great confidence in Dr. Bookmyer's opinion. If he says it should come out, we should do it. Let's not be foolish and risk that it bursts. That could really be trouble if that happened. I think it is great that you thought to look it up, but you really have had no experience with these things. I don't blame you for wishing it had not happened at this time. But, if you have it taken care of now, I think you may have a very quick recovery. Maybe you'll be home in a few days. And before you know it, you'll be back in school. If it bursts, you may get a bad infection, and who knows how long it will take to recover from all of that."

Finally, Jack agreed that it was best to have it taken care of now. But in talking with him, I found out that while we were gone to John's office, he was feeling a little hungry and thought that if he ate something, he might feel better, so he had eaten a piece of cake and a glass of milk. It was not sitting very well, and he felt nauseous.

I called the nurse and Dr. Bookmeyer returned. He wasn't pleased that Jack had eaten, as it would delay surgery for a few hours. We all agreed that it would be best to admit Jack to Beaumont Hospital now. His surgery was scheduled for 7:00 that evening.

Jack got along just fine and was home in a few days and was back to school in about ten days. He did win his election, even though he was absent. However, Jack and Dad were not model patients. Perhaps it was because they were so seldom sick.

While Jack was in the hospital, he was full of complaints. He objected mightily of being placed in pediatrics. Indeed, he was the only patient in that area that had to shave every day. But hospital rules are hospital rules and not likely to be changed. But his real objection was that he didn't have a bed-side phone. He missed calling his friends at all hours. His friends came to see him often, but they were reminded that visiting hours were limited, and the hours had to be respected. More rules!

When Jack was discharged from the hospital, he thought he would be well. But it wasn't true, as he had to be careful, so that he would not disturb his stitches. He did not feel all that well and was disappointed that there were still restrictions on his activities. There would be several more days before he could return to school. He was restless and wanted to be well immediately! Oh well, youth and their tremendous energy. All things in good time we reassured him. Actually, he had recovered very well.

John was anxious to get back to the office, also. He kept up with work somewhat by talking to the office daily and reading the mail. Eventually, they were both back at work and school. Then our life settled down again.

But it left me feeling uneasy. What will happen next? I wondered. Many things had happened in just a year and a few months! Almost ever
yone of our immediate family had been hospitalized. Mother Hanzel had passed, and Dad Hanzel had come to live with us and all the difficulties surrounding that situation. I found myself feeling apprehensive and discouraged.

The joke at John's office was that The Hanzel's were really testing Cooper's Health Insurance Policy. We had only been with them a little over two years, and the policies had graciously covered our family very well. It was such a blessing that John had found such a good job. We felt confident that he would probably work for Cooper until he wanted to retire. He had spent twenty years with DuPont, so he qualified for a small pension from them eventually. His education with an engineering degree plus his experience with DuPont had prepared him very well for his current position as a sales representative of Cooper Tire and Rubber Products. His commission checks were coming in nicely. John was a people person and really enjoyed his new job.

Dad Hanzel was adjusting very well at Briarbank. I was very thankful that it was working out so well. He was becoming well acquainted with the other residents and even seemed to be best friends with a woman in another building. When I stopped in to see him one day, he was playing cards with her in the sitting room. I watched them for a while, as they played, and for the life of me, I could not figure out how the game was played. They chatted along and then would state that one of them had won and a few pennies were exchanged. They seemed to be having a marvelous time, so that was the main thing. They were having fun.

I had plenty to do, as I was involved with projects at St. Hugo's and Brother Rice High School, but still I felt uneasy. It felt like I was waiting for another shoe to drop, like more illnesses or more difficulties with the family would turn up at any moment. I felt that I had to be on guard all the time. What was coming next? Much had happened in a relatively short span of time.

I prayed about it, thanking Him for all the blessings that had been showered upon us. Although there were terrible difficulties and problems, all was well now. I asked Him to help me get over this funk. What should I do about it? It felt like the time when we moved to Michigan, from Paris, Illinois, and I was so depressed. How should I deal with this?

I decided that beginning this very day, I would set aside some time every day to pray. I was sure that He would guide me and help me recover my confidence and sense of direction for my life. I thought of those quiet days that I had been hospitalized, which had been filled with so much time in prayer. I knew in my heart that it had been His Power and Love which helped us get through all the past difficulties.

About a week later, a good friend called to chat for a while on the phone. She told me that their parish was having regular prayer meetings every Wednesday night. She and her husband were thinking of attending. She asked if we would like to join them. So I talked it over with John, and we decided to go. It would be fun to go out in the middle of the week, a nice little distraction for us. We had gotten to know them through work, as her husband was one of the engineers that John called on at Fisher Body. The plans were made and we picked them up the following Wednesday night, and we went together to our first prayer meeting.

This was our first introduction to the Charismatic Renewal. There was lots of singing, prayer, and praise. There was also praying in tongues. That had been explained to us before the meeting started, telling us that this might happen. But I felt uneasy about it. I had read those passages in the Bible about praying in tongues. But I did not expect to experience it in our modern world. The meeting lasted about an hour and a half, closing with a final song and prayer.

I couldn't wait to get out of there, as I wanted to discuss all of this with our friends. They invited us in for a drink. It was quite an experience for all of us. Was this approved by the church? It must be, as it was in the church facility. We all had many questions about it. They said they would ask their priest about it, and I hoped to speak to Father Esper about it, also. We all agreed that we would like to go again next week.

This was the beginning of our regular attendance at these prayer meetings. It was fun to go out in the middle of the week, and we returned to talk it over at their house each evening. Father Esper was aware of this movement in the church, and he approved. He had mentioned it to us before, but we had not connected the two. He had suggested that sometime, perhaps, we could arrange to go to Ann Arbor to a prayer meeting there led by Ralph Martin. Father Esper loaned us a book written by Ralph Martin, and it did answer some of the questions we had about the Charismatic Renewal. It was very different. I did not want to become involved with something like an occult, so it was a relief to obtain more information. We were drawn to it and wanted to continue to attend. However, summer loomed and with both of our families' busy schedules, our attendance during the summer was irregular.

Janet came home for the summer on May 12th. She had completed two years at Central Michigan University. She surprised us with the news that she and Tom were talking about getting married. He had graduated at the end of this semester, and as soon as he got a job, they hoped to get married. It was a shock to me! I had not expected this. She wanted to drop out of school, work for a time and be ready to marry, maybe as soon as next spring. We had met him, but we did not realize that she was really serious about this young man.

In talking about it, she said that she was undecided about what she wanted to do, in regard to a major and a degree. Why continue to go on with school with such an indefinite goal? She had considered a teaching degree, but ultimately decided against it. It would be good to take some time off to consider what she really wanted to do. She thought that she might like to work in an office, and maybe she could find a job like that for now, locally, and maybe she and Tom would have more definite wedding plans and dates in the future.

This hit me like a ton of bricks. I had been so preoccupied with everything that had been going on at home during the last couple of years. I had just assumed that Janet would continue at the University and graduate. We talked further about her plans. It was evident that she had done a lot of thinking about everything. She had some money saved and still had her birthday bonds that her Hanzel grandparents had given her. With this, she planned to shop for and buy her own car, which would give her transportation to get to work. She thought she might live at home for perhaps a year.

It was a well thought out plan. It would be wonderful to have her back at home for a while. Ultimately, it was her decision to make. We just wanted her to know that we were very willing to continue to support two more years at the university. We wanted her to be really sure of what she wanted to do. We would be supportive of whatever she decided. And I wanted her to take plenty of time in considering marriage, as this is such an important step. I pointed out that she is so very young to be taking this step.

She countered by reminding me that I was twenty when we got married. She would be twenty coming up in August.

It hardly seemed possible that she was nearly twenty! Where had the years gone? It was a reality session for me to come to grips with this situation, as it was so unexpected.

John went car shopping with her, and she bought a darling little, bright green, two door car, used but in very good condition. She soon landed a very nice office job in Birmingham. So her life was going along, just as she had planned.

Soon school was out for the boys and they were busy caddying, and doing the paper route, so the summer was in full swing with time to play golf at Stonycroft. Our caddying sons played every Monday morning at Bloomfield Country Club, as the course was closed to members, so that the greens keepers could catch up on course maintenance. Jack and Jim and their caddying friends had lots of fun playing this beautiful course with which they were so familiar.

Near the end of the season before school started, a Caddy Tournament was held over a few Monday's of play. It was hotly contested, and the winners were honored at the caddy banquet in the fall.

Dad Hanzel had not given up talking about his sister in Yugoslavia. He wanted to reward her for taking such good care of their mother and father. She was the youngest daughter, and it was she that really looked after them as they grew older. She lived in the family home and took care of them until they passed. Dad wanted to help her financially. It seemed to be heavy on his mind. I suggested that he leave some money in his will, but he said no, he thought that would be cumbersome to execute. He wanted to see that it was taken care of in his life time.

I talked about it to John. I felt that this was something that we should take seriously. The question was how to do it? And how much did he really want to give her? What would be the appropriate thing to do? If we sent it by mail, could we be assured that she really received it? Yugoslavia was behind the iron curtain, controlled by Russia and Tito. The people there were under the tight control of the government to a great extent, according to all that we could find out about the country. If we hired a currier, what assurances would we have that he really delivered the money, or did he just pocket it or give it to the wrong person?

Finally I said, "Johnnie, why don't you and your Dad fly over there, locate her, and present it to her in person? Then, we would be sure that she really got it."

It seemed Dad had always wanted to go back. They had attempted to do it a couple of times by going by ship and train, but it never worked out. Later they had talked about flying over, but Mother Hanzel was terribly afraid of flying. Then when she got sick, any travel was out of the question, and Dad did not want to leave her and go alone. Now the planning was up to us.

Finally Johnnie said, "Look, I am so busy at work right now that I really don't have the time to look into it. Why don't you call the travel agent that the office uses and find out about the feasibility of travel within the country of Yugoslavia? You do the research on it to see if it would be possible."

So I did. I called the travel agency and set the wheels in motion. They agreed that they would call me when they had some information about possibilities. This was becoming a very busy summer for me. I was busy planning for my year as President of the Brother Rice Mother's Club. My year would start in the fall. It was great to have Janet with us, but she was working full time, and the two older boys were busy with caddying at Bloomfield. Joe was doing the paper route, so there was lots of coming and going.

Between all our activities, it seemed I never had enough time to keep up with the house work, laundry and cooking. The boys had ferocious appetites. Baked goods disappeared like magic. I was baking every day and still, it seemed there was never enough, yet no one seemed to gain weight. Life was good but very busy!

We were all planning to take a weekend off and go over to Dixon and visit Mother, and the plan jelled when I received the invitation to attend my twenty-fifth High School Reunion. How could it be that I had been out of high school for that many years! We had a lovely weekend in Illinois and a nice visit with Mother.

When we returned, there was a message from the travel agent, so I made an appointment to go and see about the possibilities. Much to my surprise, there was a wonderful package going to Yugoslavia in October! It included a flight from Detroit directly into Dubrovnic. It included six days at a hotel in Dubrovnic, meals included. We would need to fly up to the northern part on our own, rent a car and drive out to visit the family. We thought perhaps a three day weekend visit would be the right amount of time to spend with them. We could rest up before and after the family visit in this hotel and visit the many points of interest in that famous walled city on the Adriatic Sea.

The travel agency put together maps of the area. I knew that the area that Dad Hanzel had lived in as a boy was Austria, but after World War II, it had been incorporated into Yugoslavia. I could not wait to show all of this to Johnnie. That evening we both poured over all the information. It was so exciting to think about attempting such a great trip, and it was relatively inexpensive.

I said, "Wow! Maybe I'll go with you! And you might be really glad I was along, as I could look after Dad if you were busy getting the luggage or making the arrangements at hotels."

Johnnie thought that was a great idea. He thought it would be a wonderful trip, but also, it could be a little risky to travel behind the Iron Curtain. Neither of us had traveled out of the country. John had been stationed briefly in Hawaii, but the Navy had been the travel agent and everything was arranged for him. We felt quite daring to be thinking of undertaking such a trip!

That Sunday when Dad came over for his usual Sunday visit, we showed him the trip information. Dad was very excited about the possibility of actually going back after all those years. He had come to this country after the First World War. He located his home village on the map. It looked like we should fly into Zagreb, the nearest large city, and rent the car there and drive over. Dad suggested that we get in touch with his niece and her husband, who lived in Cleveland. They had visited Mother and Dad Hanzel several years ago, and they had kept in touch by letters back and forth.

I called them that very afternoon and invited them to come over and visit us and help us plan our visit. It was really beginning to come together. Would we really be going there? How exciting and wonderful!

The Glavans came over for a weekend in July. They were a great help. They had been back a couple of times and assured us that we needed to be cautious, but travel was safe, as long as we knew where to go. It was through them that we were able to make the arrangements by letters back and forth as to where to go and where to stay. So it was all arranged.

We were to go Tuesday evening, October 10th and return Wednesday. October 18th. We were all booked, and the reservation made. We were really going!

Our Trip

There were many things to do now that we knew we would be going in October. We all needed to get our passports. We decided that John would get his sometime during the week when it would be convenient for him. I would arrange to pick up Dad and the two of us would get our pictures taken, fill out all the forms and take care of setting the wheels in motion to order ours. John arranged to obtain a European Driver's License, as we planned to rent a car and drive to see the family. We had plenty of time, but we wanted to order them promptly.

Now that Janet was living at home, she would be very capable of supervising the boys while we were gone. I started planning meals and putting a few meals in the freezer to help her with this. Next, I had to finish getting ready to start my year as President of Brother Rice Mother's Club. I had recruited all of the chairmen for the various board positions. Actually, the October dates were very compatible with our travel schedule. There were several events in late August and early September, such as my first board meeting, the opening Mother Club event of the year, and monthly board meetings. But, there was a little lull in the middle of October, before planning for the Christmas events, so it was the perfect time to get away.

I wanted to go shopping with each of the boys and get their new school clothes purchased. They each had definite ideas about what clothes they needed. It was wonderful that they all wore school uniforms to class. The Brother Rice boys wore white shirts, navy ties, and navy blue pants, and each needed a navy sport coat. But it wasn't a big problem, as we already had a collection of sizes of shirts and pants.

As far as my clothes for the trip, I didn't need much in regard to clothes, but the one thing that I did shop for was a language guide. When Dad and I got our passport applications, I showed him a couple of language guides

I had found at the book store, and he helped me decide which one was the dialect that seemed right to him. I poured over it all and made some notes. We were all excited about our upcoming trip!

This was a very special year for Jack, as he was starting his senior year. It was too early to start going to colleges and thinking about next year when he would be starting college. My, how could it be that in just a year from now he would be away at school? As for Jim, he would be starting his sophomore year and knew his way about and had made friends at school. Joey would still be at St. Hugo's, starting sixth grade. So, all the things to do to prepare for the start of school were in progress.

In mid-August Jack and Jim played in the caddy tournament at Bloomfield Country Club. It was quite an event, as this year Jack was the winner of the tournament! He was so surprised and pleased. He would be honored at the caddy banquet in November.

We were all busy with our projects, and in no time the three boys were settled in school, and things fell into a routine. Janet was happy with her job in Birmingham. Tom came down to visit us again that fall. He was still unsettled as to what he would do about a permanent job, but they were talking of eventually getting married. There were many changes in the wind. John and I and Dad were now counting the weeks before we were to leave for Yugoslavia on Tuesday, October 10th.

Finally the day arrived. John took Tuesday off from work and went over after lunch to help his Dad pack for this trip, bringing him back to our house for the rest of the afternoon. We were all together when everyone assembled after school and work to share in the excitement over an early supper. Our flight to New York left at 8:00 pm. After lots of hugs, kisses, and good wishes for safe travel, we left for the airport at 6:30.

Our schedule called for the flight to New York, which took about an hour and a half, followed by a non-stop flight to Dubrovnik, Yugoslavia. We had to change terminals to get to the gate for our overseas flight, but we had plenty time, as our overseas flight was somewhat delayed. We actually took off about 11:30 pm. We were more than ready to settle in and take a little snooze. It was a very comfortable flight, and we awoke a few hours later in time to see daylight over the Alps. What a sight and a thrill that was to see those mountain peaks at sunrise! Our first glimpse! We were served a light breakfast before arrival at Dubrovnik about mid-morning, local time.

There were lots of formalities and waiting in line at the airport. We had to go through customs and then claim our luggage before locating our tour guide to escort us to our hotel. Of course we had to wait until all of the passengers on our tour were identified and counted before we could board the buses to the hotel. It was then that we realized that we knew another couple traveling on the same trip as ours. They lived in West Bloomfield and we had played bridge with them a few times! They were Greek by heritage, and it was their plan to stay for a few days to rest up in Dubrovnik before flying on to Greece to meet their family. It was fun to know that we were sharing this experience with an acquaintance of ours.

Eventually all the necessary things were taken care of at the airport and off we went to our hotel. The hotel was very nice. We were shown to our rooms and had a little time to rest and unpack before our get acquainted meeting, which was scheduled for the hotel ball room on the main floor. We were very pleased with our accommodations. We had requested adjourning rooms, but we were shown a very nice suite with a little sitting room, two bedrooms and bath, with lovely windows looking out over a back garden and lawn area. We were happily surprised with our suite.

At the meeting, we were given lots of information about our schedules, time and places for meals, and services of the hotel, like a beauty shop and gift shop. In addition we were told how to get about in the city, what tours were available, such as tours of the walled city, and answers to any questions. It was all very friendly and complete. After that we were ushered into the dining room for our lunch. Then we were on our own.

After lunch John went to check on our flight arrangements for our flight to Zagreb, which we had booked for Friday, returning on Sunday. Then we went up to our rooms to rest and re-group. We realized that we had just one day to explore the city, before taking off to see the family, but we would have several days after the family visit, to go about this area, so we decided we should just take it easy for the rest of the day. In the morning, we would decide what we would do on Thursday. Dad seemed to be holding up very well, but it was best to get thoroughly rested before embarking on the next leg of our trip.

The next morning Dad got up when it got light and seemed to be adjusting very well. Then he asked John, "Where are we? Are we staying in a hotel in Detroit?"

When we explained that we were in Dubrovnik, Yugoslavia, he could hardly believe it! He seemed really happy that we were all going to visit his sister. He was rested and ready to see the sights. He heard about this famous, walled city, when he was living in Austria as young man, but never had been able to visit.

We had breakfast, and while Dad and I lingered at the table, Johnnie went to the hotel office to change some money into local currency and arranged for a brief tour of the area for that morning. Our guide spoke English very well and gave us a driving and talking trip to show us where the best shopping areas were, took us to view the Adriatic Sea, and pointed out where the old walled city was located and other points of interest. It really helped us to get acquainted with this area. He showed us where to get the bus for the shopping center that he had pointed out to us and the bus to take to go to the walled city.

After lunch, we decided to take the city bus to the department store, which the guide had pointed out to us. We walked around a bit and began to think about what we would like to buy to bring home as a remembrance from this area. There was a park in the back of this shopping center that bordered on an inlet to the Adriatic Sea, so we went out and walked around a little. There, we spotted a very large, imposing Russian battleship, which was docked nearby. It made us feel very uneasy to be so close to one, but we strolled along and tried to be inconspicuous, even stopping to rest a bit on one of the park benches and to enjoy the view and lovely fall weather. Then we caught the bus and returned to our hotel to rest before dinner. We were very pleased with our first full day in Yugoslavia, a day well spent. At dinner the other tourists in our group talked about what they had done and shared information about their excursions.

After dinner we returned to our rooms and packed for our weekend to visit the family. The hotel had assured us that it was alright for us to leave our big pieces of luggage and some of our things in our suite while we were gone. We carefully packed the things we needed in two smaller bags. It would be much easier than taking everything with us. We retired early, as we wanted to get off to the airport in plenty of time the next day.

The next morning right after breakfast, we took a cab to the airport. Our flight was scheduled to leave for Zagreb at about 10:30 am. Zagreb was a fairly large city, about 250 miles north of Dubrovnik. Our flight left promptly, and we arrived at the Zagreb Airport in the early afternoon. We had reserved a car for this time and place while we were in Detroit. I stayed with Dad and the luggage while Johnnie checked on the car and made all the necessary arrangements. At this time he cashed enough traveler's checks so that we could give Aunt Liza the amount of money which he and Dad had decided upon in the local currency. That way we did not have as long to carry this larger amount of cash with us. When everything was in order, we got into the rental car, armed with the local maps of the area, and embarked upon the next step of our adventure.

According to our maps it wasn't that far to Maribor, maybe about seventy or seventy-five miles north. The roads were two lane highways, nicely paved but full of curves and hills, so we found it slow going. It was difficult to tell if we were headed in the right direction. It was a nice, sunny day, so that helped us to determine the general direction. At intersections, there were no signs to guide us as to whether we should turn or not. Sometimes we guessed wrong and found that we were going around and heading east or south again. Then we retraced our trip and got back on the road going north. We were driving through lovely farm land and from time to time we would see local people in their fields or on the roads, and they always waved to us vigorously.

"This must be a very friendly, welcoming country," I remarked. "Look how they all wave to us." We waved back and drove on.

After a while we arrived at a small village that had a gas station, so we stopped there to ask for directions. It was then when Johnnie got out of the car that we realized we had our trouble lights on. At the airport, John had inspected the car and had checked all the various knobs to familiarize himself with this car. It must have been then that he turned on the emergency lights by mistake, so we had been driving through the countryside all this time with our red lights flashing. No wonder they all waved to us so vigorously.

They were very helpful at the gas station. We pointed to the map and showed them where we wanted to go, so they marked the map to indicate the best route. The rest of the trip was uneventful.

When we arrived in Maribor, it turned out to be a much larger city than we had imagined. It seemed to be a bustling city of about 80,000 or more. Our instructions from the Glavans were that we were to ask the way to the old train station. The niece that was to be our hostess for that weekend lived two houses down from the train station. That sounded easy enough to locate. Wrong! We drove all around and found three or four streets that crossed the railroad tracks, but there was no station anywhere. Everyone we asked about this replied no. According to my language guide, they were telling us that the trains no longer stopped at the station, and if we wanted to take the train, we would have to go to Ljubljana.

Well, we had no interest in going clear over to that city. It was the old train station that we wanted to identify, so it was back in the car again to investigate on our own. Finally, we decided that we would have to abandon the idea of finding the train station and headed to the small village of Cezanjeveio where John's dad had been born, as that was where Aunt Liza still lived in the original family home. By this time it was getting late in the day. I thought that when the sun went down behind those mountains, it would get dark early and we had better locate the family before that happened.

We took the road that seemed to lead us to Cezanjevieio. We had been told that it was a very small village of about forty or fifty houses. We knew that it had a village church there, as John's dad had told us many times about how he would walk down the street a short way from their home to ring the church bells on Sunday mornings.

Shortly we came upon a village that seemed to fit the bill. It did have a village church and was about the right size and distance from Maribor. We asked Dad if it looked like his old home village, but he said no, it didn't look quite like it. There were no signs to indicate the name of the village. Yet, according to our map, it had to be right. Just then a hay wagon, fully loaded with hay pulled by a team of huge, horned oxen came into view. This was driven by two men. We waved to them and they stopped. Johnnie got out of the car to ask them if this was, indeed, Cezanjeveio. And he pointed to the village.

The men replied, "Yah! Yah!" But shook their heads "Nie! Nie!" And shrugged when we asked if this was where Elizabeth Lipowich lived.

I rolled down the window and said, "John, ask for Liza Hangel?" (Dad had told us their name was pronounced "Han-jail" in Yugoslavia with the accent on the second syllable. He had changed the g to z when he moved to the USA, to simplify his name.) John did that, and they both broke out with big smiles, and replied with a vigorous "Yah! Yah!"

Then John pointed to the village and again they nodded. Using sign language and eventually counting in German, they indicated that her house was five houses past the church. Hurray! John indicated a big thank you, thank you, by bowing and giving a happy, high five to them. We all waved happily to them as they continued on their way.

Dad explained that Liza had been married briefly just before the war, but when the Nazi's came to that part of the country, they had killed her husband right before Liza. It was terrible for her. Then she had moved back home to live with her mother and father and took care of them for the rest of their lives. These men probably knew her only by her maiden name.

We drove on into the village, and when we drove into the driveway of the fifth house, there was Aunt Liza, standing on the porch, watching for us. I would have known her anywhere as Dad's sister. It was the same face as Dad's, peaking out of the kerchief head scarf she was wearing. When we got out of the car, she rushed out to meet us. She and Dad embraced each other in tears. It was a wonderful, warm greeting. Immediately, they were chatting together like magpies. The language seemed to come back to Dad instantly. It was wonderful the see them so happily communicating with each other.

Eventually, we entered her little house, the one that Dad had lived in as a boy. It was a small, thatched cottage, very strongly built, with thick, stone walls covered with a stucco-like finish. Evidently, it had not changed much since Dad had been there. We entered the living room, which was quite large and seemed to function as the common room or main room in the house. It was heated by a large fireplace with a cooking space on the kitchen side which was in back of the living room. There wasn't much furniture, just a few chests of drawers, a table and a few chairs. Around the walls were built-in benches for extra seating, built with a seat that would lift up with the box below, serving as storage areas. It was a very humble home, clean and serviceable, with windows on all sides. I noticed that Aunt Liza was wearing a dress that I recognized as having belonged to Mother Hanzel. I remembered that Dad had planned to send Aunt Liza many of the clothes that were left after she passed. They had been sending her boxes of things from time to time over the years.

It was rather a cool day here, about 300 miles north of Dubrovnik, and less than a mile from the Austrian border. There was a fire lit in the fireplace. I noticed a few pictures, snap shots that Dad had sent her years ago, showing Johnnie and me with Janet and Jack, taken when they were very young in the yard of their Danville home, and some pictures of Dad and Mother Hanzel. She had obviously treasured them all these years. They were not framed but fastened to the walls with small nails. It was a very simple home. It did not have in-door plumbing. It was amazing to realize that his parents had raised all of their rather large family in this home. By seeing the pictures, I knew then that she knew who we were, so we relaxed and enjoyed watching the brother and sister, chatting together so lovingly, catching up with all that had happened.

At one point, when she left the room briefly to bring back something for us to drink, I asked Dad, "What did she say?"

He looked confused and replied, "I didn't quite get it all myself."

When she returned, I said to Dad, "Tell her that we couldn't find the home of your niece in Maribor, so we had decided to come here."

And Dad repeated all this, exactly as I had said it, but said it in English. Then I realized that his mind was not agile enough to translate back and forth, from one language to another. So I indicated to him to just skip it. It was all right.

After a bit, all of us were ushered outside to be shown her backyard. There were the remains of a garden, now pretty well harvested and put to bed for the winter, as it was October. There was a shed, which contained a small pen just big enough for the very large pig that it contained. Later Dad told us that Aunt Liza was too old to chase pigs, so they had arranged for the pig to live in this very small pen. Indeed it could not turn around in it. Obviously, it was fed at one end, and the pen was cleaned from the other end. I supposed that it would be very tender meat, when it was butchered, as it really did not have much exercise, and hence very little muscle.

Later, a nephew arrived by car, evidently to bring Aunt Liza to Maribor for the festivities, and he was surprised to find us here. Johnnie tried to explain that we had been unable to find the house in Maribor, so we had decided to come here. He seemed to understand a little English. In the end, he indicated that he was late in picking up Aunt Liza to take her to Maribor. It was determined that all of us should go now, and we were instructed to follow his car, with Aunt Liza riding in our rental car. We then realized that it was this nephew she had been expecting and was watching for when we arrived.

It was only a short distance to Maribor and to the cousin's home, as he knew of all the short cuts. When we all arrived, we were all very warmly greeted. I guess they had been expecting us much earlier and were very happy that we had finally arrived. More relatives arrived, and we were introduced around. What a wonderful experience to meet all these relatives. It was a once in a lifetime occasion!

It seemed that the original plan was for us to stay in Maribor, with the cousins, and that Dad would stay with Aunt Liza in her home. Johnnie and I talked about this. We wondered, if perhaps Dad would be confused and might wake in the middle of the night and not know where he was and where we were. We wondered what to do and how to explain all of this. At one point, I made a funny comment to John, and one of the nearby nephews laughed. I turned to him and said, delightedly, "You understand English!"

He replied, "Little bit." And he indicated a small distance with his fingers.

So Johnnie took him aside and tried to explain the situation to him, that Dad had a short term memory loss, and we did not want him to be staying apart from us. We did not want to make extra work for any one or upset their plans. Eventually he understood our situation, and he informed our hostess.

Later, she took me aside and showed us our accommodations. She ushered me into a lovely bedroom on the first floor. Evidently a cot had been made up quickly and was placed in the same room. She indicated the cot and said the word that I knew that was the word for "Uncle", and then she indicated the double bed and pointed to me and said, "You and Yonnas." I hugged her and nodded enthusiastically. But at the foot of the double bed was a lovely, antique baby's cradle. I pointed to it and indicated by pantomine a sleeping baby, "Who is going to sleep there?" The house was full of company, and I wondered where they would all stay.

She laughed, tossed her head, and said "You and Yonnas make!" She indicated all of this by pantomine as well, pointing to me and then rocking a baby in her arms.

We began laughing. I realized there are definitely ways to communicate, even with just a few words and sign language! We did not know each other very well or each other's language, yet we understood each other perfectly. She had made us feel very welcome.

It was a lovely evening. They explained to us that they had arranged for an English teacher who taught English in the local schools to be with us for tomorrow. He would show us about and answer all of our questions and show us the points of interest. Even more relatives would come to see us tomorrow evening and on Sunday. How thoughtfully plans had been made for our visit. A local wine was served to all of us and then a lovely supper. After dinner it was clear that Dad was really exhausted with all the travel and excitement, so we all decided it was time to retire. I wondered if all these people would stay here tonight or if would they come back the next day.

We slept well. Our bed was beautifully made up with gorgeous embroidered linens. I hated to sleep on them, they were so lovely. We all woke up when it was light. It was only our hostess and her husband that had stayed there that night. After breakfast, they took us to their cemetery where Dad's Mother and Father were buried. It was different from our cemeteries. Each grave site was elevated, to about two feet high. Each was small, about four by ten feet, and had a simple head stone. Stones and bricks outlined each, and it was covered with beautiful, freshly planted pansies. There were small pathways, so that people could get about their grave sites without stepping on the graves. There was no lawn or mowed grass; all the graves were flower gardens and very well cared for. Each family took care of their own. It was explained that they changed the flowers seasonally. It appeared that these pansies might last through the winter and into spring in this climate.

We returned to the house then, as the English teacher was due to arrive. It was interesting to see the change in them when he arrived. They became very closed and formal, like they were almost afraid of him. They had been so friendly and chatty with us all morning. Our hostess stayed at home, but her husband put on a jacket and followed along, a pace or two behind us, rarely saying a word. Indeed, the teacher was fluent in English. He took us to a viewing point where we could see into Austria. He told us about the changes in the borders after the war and had maps to indicate where the original borderlines had been. When we told him about our difficulties in Maribor, he said that if only we had asked any of the young people in the area, they could have talked with us, as he had instructed most of them in English at school. We never thought of doing that but had asked only adults. He spent about two hours with us, but it was very stiff and formal. Actually, we were glad to go back to the house and say goodbye to him. In retrospect, we realized that he was probably a government employee, and we sensed they had not trusted him.

When he left, the cousins were visibly relieved, like we had all passed a test, and it was over. Next the cousins wanted to take us to visit Dad's oldest brother's wife. His brother had passed on many years before this. She was living nearby with one of her daughters. This brother was a year or two older than Dad and Liza was just younger than Dad in the family line.

They had a rather large vineyard, and they took us out to see it. It was very well kept. She seemed much older than Dad and quite frail. She was dressed all in black and covered in a large black, wool shawl. Dad was able to communicate with her. In fact, they all said he spoke very well, even though it had been years since he had used this language this much.

That evening even more relatives arrived with their families. It was Saturday, and evidently they had finished work for the week and were now able to come and see us. We were quite a novelty to them all. They closed the draperies and we all settled in for an evening of visiting and exchange of ideas.

They asked us what our country was trying to do in Vietnam. They were very much against our presence there. It was difficult for us to respond to this, as we were also concerned that the war was dragging on, and as parents of three young boys, we did not want to see them going off to war with such indefinitely defined goals. But we wanted to explain that our country did not have imperialistic plans to take over there. It was clear that they were repeating the communist lines that their country was supporting. I knew that we were missing a lot that was said because of the language barrier. The younger people understood English and acted as translators for us. The wine flowed and it made for lively conversations.

Later in the evening, Johnnie pointed out to me that they were generously giving us the best wine, but they were diluting theirs with water, so we asked for ours to be diluted, also.

It was difficult to sort out who was who and to know how they were all related. Everyone there was directly related to John's dad. They were all nieces and nephews of his, their wives or husbands and children, and of course, there was his sister, Aunt Liza. There was a young boy, about the same age as our Jim and could have been his twin brother, he resembled

Jim so much. I wanted to capture him and bring him back to the states, so that he could really know us and how we lived. It made me homesick for our own family. If only it were possible for all of us to get well acquainted.

The conversation turned to the plans for tomorrow. It seemed that there was a concern about all of them coming to Mass with us. We had indicated that we thought it would be nice if we could go to Mass at Dad's old village church. It seemed that their concern was mostly about what impact it would be to the government officials with such a large group of us. Eventually it was decided that it would be best to limit the size of the group that would go to Mass. It was decided that it would be Aunt Liza and only a few of the cousins and nephews. They did not want to call undo attention to us.

Another family gathering was planned for after Mass at the cousin's home in Maribor where we were staying. They said that Dad's only other living sister, who lived a distance away, would be there on Sunday. She was much younger and Dad did not remember much about her, as she was just a baby when he went to Graz for his apprenticeship to learn shoemaking. This had happened when he was about twelve years old.

The family was concerned about our safety when driving back to Zagreb. They wondered if it was safe for us to drive alone all that way, as we might be going through very sensitive, political areas. They suggested that they form a family caravan of several family cars, to protect us on the way back. We showed them the maps and the route we used to come. They showed us a supposedly better and safer way to return, but warned us to be extremely cautious of any government officials at the airport. In the end it was decided that it would be safe for us to travel back alone, as it might call too much attention to us to be traveling in a caravan. They were Slovenians, and as long as we were in the Slovenian Province, they thought we were safer.

Much later when we were in bed, Johnnie told me that one of the nephews had taken him aside and told him that his father, one of Dad's brothers, had recently passed away in the last year. He missed his father very much. He said that John's dad looked exactly like his father and wanted to know if we would allow Dad to stay for a year with them? They would so enjoy having him and taking him about. He explained that he was very much able to take good care of him, since he owned three cars. Evidently, that was a mark of great wealth in that area, having three cars. I asked Johnnie what he had told him. John said, "I just told him, I was very sorry, but I could not give my father to them to replace their dad."

I thought that was a very wise answer, as it must have been a very awkward and emotional moment for both of them. It was all going by so rapidly with so much to take in. It was truly a once in a life time experience. How wonderful to get to know them. It was the right decision to take Dad over here. John told me that Dad had already given the money to Aunt Liza, and she indicated she would put it away safely, and only use it a bit at a time, so as not to attract attention to herself. It had been wise to give it to her in the local currency.

The next morning we had a light breakfast and drove over to Cezjanjevio in our car, following their son and his wife, who were the ones that had been designated to go to the Mass. We stopped for Aunt Liza and all walked down the street, as the church bells were ringing. It seemed that the priest had been forewarned that we would be there, as there were several folding chairs in the front set up for us. All the others stood.

It was a wonderful experience attending this Mass, the first time for us to be attending a Church so far from our country. The altar had been turned around, so that the priest faced the congregation. Most of the Mass was in their language, but some parts were said in Latin. We felt honored to be there and we were able to follow along and to recognize the various parts of the Mass. Truly our church is a universal church. When it came to the homily, the priest obviously made reference to us, as we heard the words American and America several times, and everyone strained to see us. At the offertory time, instead of passing the basket, we all got up and proceeded to the altar. Behind the large wall, which was behind the altar, there was a place designated to deposit our donation. It was a slot, like a mail slot, into which we put in our donation. We had some local currency with us, so we used that. If we had put American money in there, it would have been too obvious where it had come from. Then we filed out the other side of the altar.

I knew that we would soon be to the Eucharistic part of the Mass, so I whispered to the son of our hostess, who I knew spoke very good English, that we would like very much to receive the Eucharist.

He looked horrified and whispered back, "Oh, no! You can't!"

And I whispered back, "Well, why not?"

He whispered, "You have eaten!"

I thought about it and responded, "We think it is alright." I knew that in the states the requirement was an hour's fast, and not from midnight as it had been previously.

He shook his head no again. "You didn't see the priest the night before!"

I was silent for a minute. Then I said, "We think it is alright for us."

He just shrugged, as if to say, "What can you do about these people."

At the proper time we all went, Dad, Aunt Liza, John and me. It was so wonderful to be here that it seemed disrespectful not to receive. We were so thankful and joyful.

After Mass, some of the parishioners came over to speak with Aunt Liza and Dad. He seemed to be getting acquainted with old friends and neighbors that he had known years ago. We found ourselves being led about the neighborhood and introduced to more people from his youth. Eventually, we all went back to Aunt Liza's home, and then we returned to Maribor.

Many of the relatives were back and some new ones, too, like his younger sister whom we had not met before. What a festive occasion this was! We had brought with us our new Polaroid camera that instantly produces a picture developed right before us. It was a huge fascination for all of them, as they never had seen anything like it. Fortunately, we had brought lots of film with us, as we gave away almost all the pictures we took, but we did bring many great ones back with us.

It was a cool morning, so when Johnnie would be developing the picture, he would tuck the camera under his arm, so that the warmth would speed up the development time. They all laughed about that. One of the men playfully pretended to take a picture with his old box camera. Then he also tucked his camera under his arm. We all had a good laugh about that.

It was fast approaching the time when we needed to leave to go to Zagreb. Then our hostess presented me with a lovely bouquet of fresh flowers as a goodbye gift. I felt tears coming to my eyes. They had all been so wonderful to us. We were all herded together in order to take a large, group picture with all of the relatives and us together. After instruction from John, one of the nephews took several pictures of the entire group on our camera, so that we could share copies with them of this great day, and John would be in those pictures, too.

It was a tearful goodbye all around. We felt certain that we would never all be together like this again. Then we were off to drive back to the airport in Zagreb. It turned out to be a pleasant, uneventful trip, which was accomplished much faster, due to the instructions of the cousins. We got there well before dusk, turned in our rental car, checked on our flight, and settled in to await its arrival. We were filled with lovely food and beautiful memories of our time in Slovenia. And I was still lovingly carrying the bouquet of flowers with me.

It was dark when we got to Dubrovnik, but there were cabs available, so it was easy to return to our hotel. We all decided we would sleep well that night! What an adventure it had been!

The next day was Monday and we had two whole days before our early morning departure on Wednesday. I decided to have my hair done in the hotel beauty shop and went to make the arrangements after breakfast. Then we took a city bus to the shopping center to do a little shopping. We wanted to take some things back to Michigan with us. Dad said he wanted to take a small gift to his lady friend that he played cards with. I admired the lovely glassware that was displayed in the department store. We purchased a set of lovely glass pitchers of several different sizes and also some wine glasses. We thought these glasses would remind us of drinking the new wine while we were in Yugoslavia. Dad picked out a lovely covered candy dish. We all thought that we had made very appropriate purchases to take back to Michigan. Later we found some wooden hand carved plates, which were made locally, so we bought those, as well.

On Tuesday we decided to take the escorted trip around the old walled city of Dubrovnik. The guide was great, spoke well, and told us stories about the buildings we saw. At one point we all walked up the steep steps leading to the top of the wall. The view was wonderful from there. We walked along until we got to the seaside, and there we had a marvelous view of the Adriatic Sea. We realized that just over there, several hundred miles away, was Rome. Wouldn't it be marvelous if we could ever go there! It was a wonderful experience. We made a visit to a lovely, very old church. Later we stopped for lunch at a place recommended by our guide before we all returned to our hotel.

The two days had flown by, and now it was time to start packing up our things in preparation for our return flight. We wanted to be fully rested before we got on that plane for our long flight back. Dad Hanzel seemed very happy and contented.

Our friends who had gone to Greece had returned. We had great fun sharing the experiences of both our trips. There were many tales to tell about all of our adventures

Our flight was to leave in mid-morning, so we left for the airport in the early morning. When we boarded our return flight, the cabin overhead storage areas were soon packed, as everyone had many things to bring back. The popular item for many seemed to be comforters filled with goose feathers. They were very nice, beautifully made, and a wonderful buy, but they really took up a lot of space, so some of them had to send theirs to the luggage compartments down below. It was a quiet flight back, as the passengers dozed, talked softly, and rested. We were served two meals, so that added distractions to the trip. We arrived in Detroit, about 6:00 p m. there, past midnight in Yugoslavia. It was a tired group that got off the plane. All of us were experiencing jet lag. It was not so difficult going over, but coming back, it really hit us.

Our family was all there to meet us when we got home. Janet and the boys had made a huge sign and posted it on the garage door: "WELCOME HOME SLOVS". In our tiredness, we first thought they were calling us slaves! Then we realized they were correct. We felt as if we had become recently initiated Slovenians. We were so glad to be back and had lots of things to show and tell, pictures, maps, and small gifts, but mostly many, many stories of all of our travels. It was a wonderful homecoming! We decided that John's dad would stay with us that night, and we would bring him back to Briarbank mid-morning the next day. He wanted to go right to bed.

The next morning I washed Dad's travel clothes, so they would be fresh and clean to take back when Dad returned to Briarbank. John took him back in mid-morning on his way into work. Now it was back to business as usual, for all of us, but it was difficult to get back to our normal routine, after this marvelous experience!

There was the usual heavy schedule of car pools, trips to the store, bridge clubs, Brother Rice meetings, phone calls from friends, and in addition, there were college meetings to go to with Jack. That first weekend when we returned, the three of us went to a college night that included representatives from Notre Dame. We were very interested in this one but wondered if Jack would qualify and could be accepted there. It was turning out to be a very busy fall, and Christmas was just around the corner. There was much to do and many things to think about before the start of the New Year of 1973.

Changes in the Family

Tom came down for a visit over the holidays and it became official. Janet received an engagement ring for Christmas and plans for a spring wedding were beginning to take place. We invited his parents to visit us, as we had never met them, but it ended up that we went up to visit them in their northern Michigan home in the middle of January. We were very fortunate, as we had wonderful driving weather that weekend, very little snow and the roads were great. It turned out to be a very pleasant visit. They were very friendly, down to earth people. They had two children, Tom and a younger daughter just younger than Joe. They lived very close to Portage Lake, which flows into Lake Michigan, really lovely, beautiful country.

Now things were beginning to take shape for the wedding. Janet and I could begin working on wedding plans, bridesmaids selections, place and date for the wedding and reception, invitations, and planning what we all would wear. In addition to this, I was busy with finishing my year as Brother Rice Mother's Club President and helping Jack with filling out college admission forms and deciding on the college for next fall. We spent several weekends taking Jack about to look over campuses.

Final plans began to fall into place by late February. It had been determined that the wedding date would be May 26, and Jack had been accepted at Notre Dame University! So now we could fill in all the dots and finalize all these plans. The bridesmaids' dresses were ordered and Janet and I started shopping for Janet's dress and mine and planning the invitations and guest lists. It was lots of fun but extremely time consuming!

We were still attending the prayer group in Royal Oak, and indeed lots of prayers were needed all around. We were shocked when it was announced that abortions had been legalized in our country! Groups were being formed to object to this and the Right to Life Organization was formed. I wanted to be a part of all of this, but first I had to complete our family plans for this spring.

The next few months went by in a blur. There were so many things to do and last minute details to complete. Anne, my sister, was planning to fly in from California, and of course the grandparents, my mother and John's dad, as well as our good friends from near and far were making plans to come to the wedding. It was all very wonderful and terribly exciting. For me, the wedding went by in a flash. The weekend before the wedding had been Jack's graduation from Brother Rice, so when everything was all over, I felt like going into hiding and just loafing for a week until I could catch my breath.

The summer was fast upon us now, and the golf course beckoned. The boys were busy with their summer jobs. Jim had decided to take driver's education that summer so that he could get his license as soon as he turned sixteen that fall. As was our custom, John and I started to make plans for our annual summer vacation at a cottage somewhere in Northern Michigan just before school started in the fall. This year we chose to make plans for a cottage somewhere near Janet and Tom. With Janet's help, we decided upon a cottage on Portage Lake. We were all looking forward to this vacation and visiting Janet and Tom.

The week after we returned from the lake was a busy time for all of us. I helped Jack get ready to go to Notre Dame and Joe and Jim ready for the start of school. Jack was busy with last minute parties with his Brother Rice buddies. The last weekend in August, John and I drove Jack to Notre Dame and we all attended Freshman Parents Weekend. It was a lovely affair, and we were very pleased that Jack was actually going there, but it hit me like a ton of bricks afterward. Our family had suddenly shrunk from four children at home to only two. I began to realize this was just the beginning of the "Empty Nest Syndrome", and I didn't like it one bit!

I was still on the board at Brother Rice Mother's Club for one more year, but it was really just an advisory position with no real responsibilities. I began to feel a little useless after such a busy year before this. What was I to do with all this spare time?

I didn't want to go off and start something that was not in His plan, as I had done when I decided to go back to school at the University. It was clear to me that He had taken care of all our needs. With John's new job, his commission checks were providing very well for the tuition bills, for the wedding costs, and even showing us what to do to take care of Dad Hanzel and helping him find peace. He was very contented at Briarbank, and the trip to Yugoslavian was such a blessing for all of us. So I prayed that God would show me what it was that I was to do next. I hoped very much that He would show me what I should be involved with at this point in my life.

But I didn't need to worry; the Lord did have plans for me. One of my friends from Brother Rice Mother's Club told me about Birthright, a pro-life group that had opened in Royal Oak. This organization was formed to help women who found themselves pregnant and needed help to continue their pregnancies. I received this news with joy. I didn't really feel comfortable with political action groups, such as marching in the streets to protest the decision to legalize abortion. But with Birthright, I could do something in a positive way, to try to prevent people from choosing abortion as a solution to their problems. I felt certain that if these people could get the support and encouragement that they needed, they would not choose an abortion. I remembered how sad I had felt when I had a miscarriage and when I lost Jeffery. I knew that I had not done anything to harm him. It would have been terrible to live with the knowledge that I had deliberately terminated my pregnancies.

I prayed about it and received confirmation, so I made an appointment to check it out. In a short time, I had received training and began working a day or two a week in this office. At this time the office was staffed entirely by volunteers. Pregnancy tests were done by nurses in our office. I was trained to talk with the girls or women that came to our office to determine if they were really pregnant, and if so, what choices they had. A manual had been prepared with the names, addresses and phone numbers of various places where these girls could go to receive medical help, financial aid, or places to live. Girls could continue to go to school while in the later months of pregnancy and receive counseling and direction to adjust to the responsibility of caring for a new baby. In addition they could receive information in regards to how to go about releasing her baby for adoption, if this was what she chose. We could refer them to places where they could receive the help they needed.

Every situation was different and their needs varied. Most importantly, they needed a place to talk out their feelings and think through their problems, before they were forced to do something in haste and later regret their decisions. We helped them think it through, what action they really wanted to take and how to go about it. It was important to talk with them when they first received the results of the pregnancy test, helping them not to panic, to run away from the reality of their situation, and to receive help to find solutions to their problems.

Many of the girls were teenagers living at home and were afraid to tell their parents. As a parent of teenagers, I tried to help them see that in the end, their parents were the right people to talk with, reveal their situation and talk out the solutions with them. We offered to be with them and their parents, to talk about the help available to them. The most important thing in helping them discover what to do was to take plenty of time to review the options available to them, so that they were not making rash decisions that were not thought through carefully, because these decisions were something that they had to live with for the rest of their lives. Also, we encouraged them to include the father of the baby, so that he could share in the decision making process.

The office was open from 9:00 a.m. to 4:00 p.m. Monday through Saturday, except Saturday when we closed about 3:00 p.m., so there were many time slots to fill. But the word spread and we had an adequate supply of volunteers. There were monthly meetings in our homes, in the evening to discuss how we could improve the quality of our services. In addition we needed financial donations, (to pay the rent, telephone bills, and office supplies), as well as recruit volunteers to serve in the office. I was involved with Birthright for many years and found it to be very interesting and rewarding work.

We had been attending the prayer group in Royal Oak, but with the wedding, Jack's graduation and his start of college at Notre Dame, and our plans to travel to Yugoslavia, our attendance at prayer group had been interrupted by our busy schedule. Now that things had settled down with only two children at home, Jim a junior at Brother Rice and Joey in eighth grade at St. Hugo's, our schedule was not as hectic or demanding as it had been. In the fall, it was announced that there would be a Life in the Spirit Seminar starting in October and lasting for seven weeks, finishing just before Thanksgiving. We decided it was about time for us to really investigate what this was all about, instead of just being on the fringe of things and not really being knowledgeable about the significance of it all.

What an experience this was for both of us! In the beginning we had some doubts about what was being taught, such as what was "tongues" and "prophecy"? Had this been just a onetime happening at the first Pentecost or could we really expect that this would occur in our society today? Also, was this approved by the church or was this some kind of false teaching, or worst yet, was it really a "cult" of some sort that would undermine or change our religious beliefs?

As we were going through the seven weeks of teaching, we continued to compare all of this with scripture passages and think carefully about the validity of these teachings. We read the booklet and followed the scripture passages and prayed about it every step of the way. When the evening came that we were to be prayed with for the "Baptism of the Holy Spirit", we were confident that this was in line with scripture and the teachings of the church, so we eagerly awaited this evening. We really didn't know what to expect. It was a wonderful prayerful experience with the leaders and other members of the prayer group laying hands on us and praying that we would receive the Gifts that the Holy Spirit had for each of us.

Indeed this was a life changing experience for both of us. It filled in the answers of a lot of questions we had. Before, I think I had a pretty clear idea of who God, the Father was: the creator, the great designer of everything. We knew who Jesus, His Son, was; our Teacher, Role Model, and Savior, who paid the price (by His death on the cross) for our sins and paved the way for us to be re-united with God the Father. Jesus opened the gates of heaven for us, something that was impossible for us to do for ourselves. But I did not have a clear idea or picture of who the Holy Spirit was. At that time in the Lutheran Church, He was referred to as the Holy Ghost and also in the Catholic Church. This didn't help me understand just who He was. I remembered that in the Brethren Church, they talked about the concept that we were to be temples of the Holy Spirit, because He came to live in our hearts at Baptism. Therefore, since He lived within us, we were to avoid all sin, especially sins of impurity.

Now I realized that at the first Pentecost, the Holy Spirit came upon the Church and empowered its members, so that each individual was able, or empowered, to know and do the will of God. It was through the Holy Spirit that the power came to do His Will, as it said in John 14:26-27: Jesus said, "The Advocate, the Holy Spirit, whom the Father will send in my name, will teach you everything!" So it is right and proper to pray to the Holy Spirit for guidance and direction, as the power of God comes to us through the Holy Spirit. This was a new revelation, a new concept, and a wonderful, powerful one!

During my prayer time I had a recurring thought or vision. Baptism is like dyeing a cloth. When I was baptized as an infant in the Lutheran Church, I came out a soft pink. Then when I was baptized in the Church of the Brethren, I came out a light red. Later when I was baptized in the Catholic Church, I turned crimson. And then, when I was prayed with for the Baptism of the Holy Spirit, I became a deep scarlet. I think He was showing me that we are permanently changed as we experience a closer relationship with God and each person in the Holy Trinity.

John and I discussed and shared our thoughts, as it was a new concept for both of us. It was wonderful to talk about our feelings in regard to our faith. It brought us to a new place of closeness in our relationship. We had talked about everything else, but for so long religion was not a topic that we discussed. This was agreed upon before we married. It was understood that we would each go our own way in this regard. We now prayed together when we had a problem or question to be resolved and discovered that it was a wonderful, powerful experience to pray in union and with confidence, asking the Holy Spirit to guide us and show us His way!

Now we looked forward to going to Prayer Group, since we had a better understanding. Neither of us felt we had been changed or "received gifts" but, in looking back, I see that this was just the beginning. The first step was a huge growth in faith, which is the primary foundation for everything and certainly the gift of the Holy Spirit. In addition, we came to a new understanding of scripture. After this "Baptism", every time I read a scripture passage, new meaning and understanding jumped into my mind. It became alive, as now I prayed first to the Holy Spirit, for wisdom and understanding to help me grasp what the real content of this passage was. That was why it is called the Living Word, because each time we might be in a new situation, the meaning would be revealed in a slightly different way to reflect our needs at that time. Also, when we went to Mass, the liturgy took on a deeper, more powerful significance to us both. We both talked about our progress in this regard.

We each set aside a daily private prayer time and were faithful to it. John used the time he was in the car driving to and from work as his private prayer time. I set aside a space of time right after Jim and Joe left for school. I left the dishes in the sink or any other important thing I had to do to wait until I had my prayer time. I really looked forward to this special time each day. About this time we had replaced the sofa in the family room and added a lovely red leather chair and ottoman for this room. I gravitated to this chair as my "prayer chair" and still have it and use it for this to this day. (It is in my Florida home in the office. When I am in Michigan, I pray in one of the flowered chairs in the living room or in my chair and ottoman in my bedroom.)

Of course during all of this, family activities and our regular social life continued, but there was a new closeness between John and me, as we shared our thoughts and discoveries in scripture and in our prayer time. I was more involved with Birthright now, instead of school activities which had dominated my volunteer time previously.

About this time, John's dad had a serious decline in regard to his health. He had fallen and broken a hip, which was severely damaged. It was not healing well, so soon he would require the services of a full care nursing home. Of course John and I prayed about this. We knew about Lourdes Nursing home, the one in which I had done volunteer work years ago. I knew that they usually had a long waiting list, but we decided to check it out first and get his name on the list, as it was such a wonderful place. We went out one Sunday afternoon. We were talking with the secretary about the possibilities of admittance, which seemed very unlikely because of the long waiting list, when the director, Sister Benedicta, happened to come by and remembered me. She asked if it was my mother who needed care, and I explained that it was John's dad that needed admittance. She kindly took us aside, into her office, and it was all arranged. He would be admitted, as soon as the paper work was completed and when he was discharged from the hospital. What a huge blessing! We knew he would receive the best of care and would be so comforted, as there was daily Mass in the chapel.

From time to time, I wondered if our increase in income would continue and if it would be enough to provide for all of the college bills and the bills at Brother Rice. Soon we would have two in college, Jim and Jack, and Joe would be at Rice. But I continued to trust in the Lord, it was all in His hands. Look what wonderful care Dad Hanzel would be receiving at Lourdes. It was all His doing! We were so thankful. Lourdes was only about twenty-five minutes away, so it would be convenient to visit him. I felt that He was guiding us in everything for which we prayed.

In my daily prayer time, I experienced something unusual. After I praised and thanked Him for all the blessings and sought answers for the things we were seeking, it was my habit to take some time to listen, in case He wanted to tell me something. When I was in deep thought, all of a sudden the image of a very good looking, red radish appeared in my mind's eye. When it first happened I said, "Oh, I am sorry, I must have dozed off or lost my concentration." But lately almost every time I was be in deep meditation that image of the radish would appear. One day after this had happened again, I said, in exasperation, "Oh, that radish again! What's with this radish anyway?!" I am not especially fond of them and could not imagine why this radish kept appearing.

Immediately, I heard he Lord's answer, internally. He said, *I thought you'd never ask! I want to tell you about this radish. This radish represents you. I am very pleased with the white stuff that is growing inside of you. I want you to know that this is covered with My Precious Blood. When you are plucked from this earth, the green stuff that the world sees will be cut off and discarded, but what I treasure, the White Stuff inside of you, will be taken up to heaven with you."*

Needless to say I was overwhelmed. I pondered this over and over again. I had been given books about prophecy, but I had never expected to experience it. In fact I was a little afraid and very uncertain about how I would know if I heard His voice, and, if I did, what I should do about it? The books I read said that if you thought you were receiving prophecy, you should weigh it carefully, considering: "Is this real? Did I make it up? Was it from 'the other guy' or was it from God?" If it was from God, was it meant just for me or for the whole prayer group community? Now I realized that I was afraid that I would not recognize the true source. How could I be sure that it was really from God? Or was it something I made up? I realized He understood my uncertainty and because of this, He was speaking to me first in pictures, to remove all doubt that it was He, who was speaking to me. And because of the personal nature of the "prophecy" and the way it had come to me, I knew it was just for me and not to be shared. (Now, in writing this book, I feel sure that He wanted me to share this experience in this way.)

Being a farm girl, of course I recognized a radish but never in the world would have thought of such a thing! I had taken many art courses as part of the Occupational Therapy curriculum at University of Illinois. I enjoyed painting and so it seemed natural that He would show me pictures, as it was easy for me to visualize things. And because of the circumstances in which I received this, I knew it was just for me. Wow! This opened the flood gates of prophecy, and over the years, I received many beautiful thoughts from Him in this way. I was taught that prophecy was always to build up our faith, not to scold or chastise us, which would definitely be from "the other guy." Certainly this vision had a positive affect for me. I stopped worrying about money, the "green stuff", and tried to concentrate on what He wanted me focused on and what He wanted me to do.

Later, in 1975 at the prayer meeting in Royal Oak, the leadership announced that we should all pray about new leadership. One of the leaders had been transferred, so the Core Group had decided this was a good time to expand. We were asked to pray, first that God would speak to us and show us whom He wanted to serve this group. Second, that each of us should carefully consider if He was calling us personally to serve in this way. John and I took this very seriously, and we did pray.

Much to my great surprise, He did speak to me about this. He said, "Yes! I am calling you and John to be leaders, but not in this prayer group. You are very weak, but I will build you up. I intend to use you both in a powerful way to develop a prayer group at St. Hugo's Parish. From this day forward, I want you to stop attending this prayer group and to turn your attention to begin planning for this."

We talked it over together. I shared what I had heard, and John reported that he had heard a very similar thing. We talked about how we should proceed. We decided that we should talk to Father Esper first. When we did he was very supportive and said he would like this very much, and he would lend his support and his help.

We decided to set up a meeting at St. Hugo's to begin plans for starting a prayer group in our parish. We talked about who to invite to this first planning session. In the end, we decided to call together some of our best friends, those with whom we had worked and trusted, and to set the wheels in motion. Well, we laid a big egg! They had no interest in this, had no idea what we were talking about and it was a big flop!

In retrospect, we realized that we tried to do this by ourselves, in our own power. We knew He was calling us, but we had not carefully considered just how to go about it. We should have heeded His warning when He said, "You are very weak!" Of course! We tried to do it on our own strength, not on His. Now we were in a real mess. We felt cut off from the previous prayer group, so now we were stumped. What to do next? We had no recourse but to pray, pray, pray, and to seek His will in everything. We would wait until He showed us what to do next. We were so sorry and regretted our haste. There is a saying, "Act in haste and repent in leisure", so that was what we did. And we did wait and wait and wait and pray and pray and pray. We missed the other prayer group: the singing, praising, and fellowship. We prayed together and were faithful to our usual private prayer times, but there was silence, no word about what we were to do next in this regard.

But life goes on. We had many things to do with our family. Jack was home for the summer. Janet had a new job working at a marina, and she loved it. Mother came back from California and came to visit us. It was a lovely visit, and, in the course of our many conversations, she asked if we had made any plans for our anniversary, as we would be married 25 years in May. It hardly seemed possible! I shared that we had enjoyed our trip to Yugoslavia so much that we discussed taking another trip to Europe, maybe Italy and Rome this time. Our previous trip was like eating potato chips; you can't stop by eating just one!

"Well," Mother said. "I have no interest in Italy! But if you decide to go to England, I would love to go along. I will pay my own way, of course."

That really took me by surprise. I had no idea that she was thinking about anything of the sort! In thinking it over, I realized that since we took John's dad to Yugoslavia, perhaps she felt it would be her turn, and we would take her to her family roots in England. She had always wanted to travel there and see it for herself.

I responded, "Well, we haven't made plans yet. John and I will talk it over."

Well, talk it over we did, and we really prayed about it. The result was: "Yes! Go!" We had hopes of going back to Europe several times, and it would be lovely to take Mother to England. She had never been out of the country before. Why not go now when Mother was in good health and wanted so much to see it. This was something to look forward to and to plan for this year.

In making plans for our trip, we decided that there was no way we could be gone during May, as Jim would be graduating from Brother Rice at that time. Then there would be all those events, such as the end of the school programs and the selection of a college for Jim. We decided to wait until fall after school started. With Jim away at college, there would just be Joe to arrange for while we were gone. Before when we took trips, we had counted on Mother or Janet to fill in for us. Joe, who would be starting his sophomore year at Brother Rice, suggested that he could stay with a buddy from school during that time, which turned out to be just the right idea. We began checking out trips to London for September. Also, we were still managing Dad's farms, and by fall most of the expenses would be paid and decisions made. We would be back in time to see the harvest taking place as it usually was not completed until late October. Of course we prayed about everything, and it seemed that the lull in middle of September was the perfect time to be away. The fall weather in England and Scotland would be mild at that time.

Jim chose the University of Dayton, a very well thought of Catholic University in Ohio about a four hour drive away. We were pleased with this choice. After establishing the three boys in school, Joe at Rice, Jim at Dayton, and Jack at Notre Dame, it was time for us to pack for our trip. Mother flew over a few days before and we left for our adventure on September 21st.

We took an early evening flight to London, arriving there about 8:00 a.m. their time. We took a cab directly to our hotel, where we checked in, rested and then decided to take an afternoon escorted trip for a get acquainted overview of London. Our plan was to see as much of London as we could in five days then take an afternoon trip to Edinburgh, Scotland, where we would pick up our rental car and progress about from there, while learning to drive on the left side of the road! Oh, yes, and learning to negotiate the round-a-bouts!

The public transportation system in London was very functional and easy to use. With a little help from the hotel and a map of the area, we soon learned our way around and saw many of the famous sights we had heard so much about: St. James Cathedral, Big Ben, the Tower of London, Westminster Abbey, Buckingham Palace, and even out to Windsor Castle.

It was fun discovering how to travel using the double-decker buses and trains. Mother really knew English history and we were thrilled to actually be there. Also, there was time to rest and get adjusted to the time zone.

The train ride to Edinburgh was delightful and gave us a chance to view the country-side. When we arrived, we found there were people meeting the train that wanted to advertise their bed & breakfast accommodations, so we decided to avail ourselves of this and found them very comfortable. We really enjoyed visiting the points of interest in Edinburgh. Mother told us about her grandfather who had migrated from this city many years before. He had been a publisher there and had come to America through Canada. Mother told us that she still had the captain's chair that he brought over with him on the ship. I found that I really liked the food in Scotland, more than the fare in London. We stayed there a few days and, when we left the Bed and Breakfast, they asked where we were going next. They put us in touch with other B&B's along our way, so we traveled all around from one to another.

From there we went north and west to see St. Andrew's, the famous golf course. After all, Scotland is the birth place of golf. It turned out to be very cold and somewhat rainy. There was a cold breeze off the North Sea. Mother settled in at the club house there and had lunch while we hiked about to see what the course was like. We decided not to play it, as it was just too cold!

From there we went on to Innsbruck, where there was a boom to their economy because of oil explorations, and John wanted to see this. It was really quite interesting up in the northern tip of Scotland. From there we made our way down the west coast. There was much to see, and we really enjoyed our stay in Scotland, visiting the many places Mother had read about and was very pleased to finally see them first hand. We had guide books that helped us locate the points of interest.

Usually in the B&B we visited, we were able to get rooms near or next door to Mother, but in one quite large one, her room was located on the other side of the stairs, so we decided on the time that we would go down to breakfast and that we would meet in the hall above the stairs, instead of tapping on her door. The next morning she was waiting for us there when we came out, sitting on a chest which was like a bench. She smiled and said, "I'll bet you can't guess what is in this chest?"

Well, we would never have guessed it, but it was almost filled with small pieces of used guest soap! We decided that they probably had experienced shortages of many things during WWII, among them soap, and next time they would be prepared. Perhaps all the stories of the Scots being so thrifty are not exaggerated.

Somewhere along the way back to England, we found Hadrian's Wall, the northern most point of the penetration of the Roman Empire and other evidences of their presence here in British Columbia. We located the Roman Baths at Bathe and other Roman landmarks. When we arrived back in England, we stopped at a small village for lunch. There was a sporting good shop there, so I decided to buy a soccer ball for the boys. In the conversation with the shop keeper, he asked if we were from the United States and wanted to know where we had traveled.

I proceeded to tell him all about our trip to Scotland and how much we had enjoyed it, probably going overboard on how lovely it was! Then he asked, "Tell me, do they still eat their young?" This is a fine example of the dry English humor and how they like to project themselves as a little bit more civilized than anyone else. We enjoyed a good laugh.

We did locate and visit the boyhood home of Winston Churchill and the village. This was really one of the highlights of the trip for me. I had always admired him, and it made all the stories of Churchill come alive.

Somewhere along our travels, Mother began ordering a very substantial lunch. We were a little surprised when this first happened, but later, when we checked into the B&B, she said she decided to eat her main meal at noon and ordered in a light supper in her room for evening. This way we could go out for dinner and stay as long as we wanted. She could have a quiet time of rest and we could do as we pleased. It really worked out very well for all of us. We had great conversations with people that we met along the way at the little pubs we visited. It didn't matter if we stayed out a little late, as Mother would be snug in bed and resting for the next day of travel.

We found our way back to London, where we turned in our rental car and stayed a night or two there in preparation for our trip home. We did a little shopping at Harrods, bought tickets for a play on the last night we were in London, and returned home Oct. 5th, joyfully filled with lovely memories of our trip. Now it was time to catch up with our family and begin planning for the holidays.

Hammond Lake

●──●

After the holidays and all the excitement of our family being together again, things settled back to the normal routine of Birthright, bridge clubs, writing letters to Mother in California, Janet in Northern Michigan, Jack at Notre Dame, and Jim at Dayton, driving the car pool to Rice for Joe, plus the usual work about the house. And of course my prayer times where I continued to seek His will for us. We continued to wonder when He wanted us to become involved with a prayer group again. We really missed this, but we did not want to go ahead of Him and His plans for us this time. However, waiting was difficult.

At this time, at the beginning of 1976, the idea of living on a lake was a recurring thought that came up in my prayer time. I wondered about this. It had been our habit to rent a cottage in north Michigan for a week or two in the summer, as well as spending a few days or a week in the Islands of the Bahamas or the Caribbean in the winter months. Now, John had four weeks of vacation time. I shared this thought with John and we talked about this idea.

John said it might be a good investment to buy a summer cottage on a lake. We could afford it now, as our house was almost paid off, but how much would we use it with the boys with summer jobs? He did not want the family to be up there all summer when he could join us only on weekends. Maybe we should begin to think about the idea of having a home on a lake here in Bloomfield. We decided to pray about this. In the end we both felt that He was guiding us in this direction, so we decided to look into another home. John suggested that I select a Realtor and begin checking out the possibilities, and if I found something really interesting, we would make an appointment for both of us to see it.

I found a Realtor, and before long he was keeping me really busy, viewing almost everything on the market in our area. Most of them were impossible, either too small, in bad repair, or basically not my idea of something we would like. Finally I said, "Please, don't call me about everything that is available. This is what we are looking for." And I outlined our requirements: not too far from St. Hugo's, at least four bedrooms, two car garage, right on the lake (not across the street), and in fairly good repair, with a nice, well equipped kitchen. Well, I didn't hear from him for a good three weeks. I began to put it all behind me. I prayed about it and felt sure that if we were to do this, the right thing would come along.

When I least expected it, the Realtor called me, and the one he showed me was just wonderful! I fell in love with it at first sight and made an appointment to have John see it, too, at the earliest opportunity. It was a contemporary and spread out over many different levels. The entrance from the driveway was across an eight or ten foot narrow bridge over a deeply recessed ground area. From the front door, it was three steps down into the living room. The living room was huge with high ceilings and about thirty by twenty feet in size with the dining room twenty by eighteen with a sky light over the spot where the dining room table would be. Both rooms had a lovely view of the lake through floor to ceiling windows. The galley kitchen was at the front of the house overlooking the circular driveway with lots of cupboards, built in stove, ovens and dishwasher. Up a level were three bedrooms and two baths. Down a level was a large family room, laundry room, and a full bath, with a bedroom and another room, which I dubbed as a hobby room, located under the living room level.

It had a two car garage up a level from the living room level, and way below, under the garage, was unexpectedly a bomb shelter! The house had been built during the "Bay of Pigs Era", and many homes that were built then included something of this sort. This one was very inclusive with a half bath, bunk beds, and shower. Just outside the entrance from the basement was the shower to shower off any nuclear dust before entering with an auxiliary exit, in case the stairway was blocked by a ladder and a push-up area above that provided a way out through the flower beds near the patio. The water supply was from our own private well. Would it have worked if there was no electricity? Oh well, we did not expect to have an emergency, or the need to try it out. It might make a great dark room, if ever someone was interested in photography.

The down side of the house was that the decorating needed up-dating and new carpeting was needed here and there. But the floor plan was wonderful and the view was perfect! The lot was shady and had many trees with one hundred and sixty-five feet of sandy beach along the lake in the back. The lake was very deep, clear and clean, no powerboats allowed, so it would be quiet and peaceful. It came with a rowboat, a sailboat, and a float to swim to when anchored out in the lake. I couldn't wait to swim in the lake. The lake was spring fed and about a half to three quarters of a mile across. Oh, and yes, it was only a couple of miles from St. Hugo's and Stonycroft.

Both of us were excited but tried to be casual about it to the Realtor until we were alone and could talk it over. I think we both knew that this was the one. John wanted to investigate financing, and we talked it over in detail. We both loved it and thought it would be just great, providing we could sell our Millington house at the right time. Maybe we could get settled there by spring or early summer. But of course we prayed about it, and wanted to do it, only if this was what He wanted us to do.

We both felt so sure about this house that by the fourteenth day of March, our offer was accepted and our Millington home was placed on the market. We placed it all in His hands and hoped it would all come together by closing, which was scheduled for May 12th.

When we called Janet, Jim and Jack, it was a big surprise to all of them. Joe was at home at the time, so he was the first to know and visited the house with us, so he was in on the project from the beginning. We heard later that Jack had called Jim at school to talk about this new development. Both were upset that we would sell their home while they were away at school and wondered what it would be like not living in Millington!

Despite their concerns it all came together nicely. Our Millington house was sold quite promptly, and the two closings were scheduled for the same day. It worked out perfectly. Now it was time to plan and begin the huge project of packing, discarding, sorting, and deciding what would go where. Our projected moving day was May 14th, and both Jim and Jack would be home from their universities and be on hand to help with the actual moving. They could help with the extra trips that we would make with our cars loaded with small odds and ends. That would be a big help.

Several weeks before the moving day, I stopped by the church office to tell Father Esper that we were moving and invite him to come for dinner in our new home and bless it. We were still very involved with the parish. We had been serving as lay ministers of the Eucharist, and I had been appointed to serve on the planning committee for the celebration of the fiftieth anniversary of our parish, which was scheduled for later the next summer.

When I told him we were moving, he said, "Oh, no!"

But I quickly explained that we would like to remain members of St. Hugo's and wanted him to have our new address. I invited him and the assistant pastor to come to dinner in our new home and bless it. The moving date was May 14th, so I suggested perhaps a week or so later, and we began consulting our calendars. It seemed that with one thing and another, the only date available was May 15, the day after we moved! The rectory was without a cook on Saturday and this was the best time for them, so I said it would be fine but to remember that we would have moved the day before, and there was bound to be unopened boxes sitting around. He promised that would not matter, so it was set for then.

Both Jack and Jim were home from school before the moving day. Joe had school that day, so he missed out on all the excitement. They were a big help, and it went very smoothly. "Many hands make light work," as my mother always said. Jim and Jack were delighted with the house on the lake. Their doubts and concerns evaporated as soon as they inspected the house for the first time. We closed on both houses on May 12th, moved quite a few things by car on May 13th with everybody pitching in to help and with many trips back and forth. The van moved everything else on May 14th. That day I stayed at the new house to direct where everything would go, John stayed at the Millington house to supervise that end with the boys helping out by making trips with the cars to bring what they could.

By the end of the day, everything was in place, the beds made up, clothes hanging in the closets, towels in the linen closet, and things looking very well settled. I had unpacked most of the dishes, pots and pans, so the kitchen was up and functioning. We were blessed with a nice, sunny moving day, so we grilled hamburgers and had a picnic supper on the deck. I felt like the day had gone extremely well.

The next day, Saturday, the main thing I had to do was cook and set the table. Indeed there were only a few unpacked boxes, but, by and large, things looked quite settled and in place. The boys had already checked out the lake by rowing the row boat across the lake. John promised that soon, he would ready the sailboat and teach them how to sail.

Of course, it being Saturday night, the boys all had places to go and things to do, so I was cooking for four of us, John and I and the two priests, as the boys had eaten earlier and had left by the time the priests arrived. I felt sure that they would bring holy water, just give the living room a few sprinkles, and maybe the dining room and kitchen, and that would do it.

Well, Father Esper and "Sarge", the assistant pastor, as we fondly called him since he spent many years in military service as a chaplain, arrived right on time. They said they would like to bless our house first and proceeded to walk through every room, sprinkling the holy water as they walked through, saying appropriate blessings in every room. I explained, again, that we had only moved in the day before and had plans to make some changes and redecorate soon. I was embarrassed when they came to our master bedroom, as the previous owners had decorated this room in shades of purple, deep purple draperies, pale orchid carpeting and wallpaper, and mirrored square tiles on the ceiling above the bed! But, if they noticed, they made no comment and proceeded on. They even went downstairs, so we decided to show them the bomb shelter. The entrance was through a steel door, concealed behind the sliding closet doors in the hobby room. It led down some steps, which then turned and led into the bomb shelter. "Sarge" was very impressed with all of this and thought it was a great idea!

With that accomplished, they all settled in the living room, where John served them a glass of wine, and I prepared to take up dinner preparations. It turned out to be a lovely evening, and it was truly a blessing to have them with us to celebrate this occasion as our first guests in our new home.

The summer flew by like the wind. I loved swimming in the lake and the boys all learned to sail. Shortly after we moved, Janet and Tom came for a visit, and before long, Mother arrived as well. Most of my cousins came by to see our new home. I was gradually getting the redecorating done and starting to hang pictures to make it all feel like our home. Eventually we re-carpeted all the rooms, had some painting done and purchased some new furniture. Of course we had the mirrors on the ceiling removed as fast as we could and that room re-decorated first without all the purple! We continued to really enjoy our new home.

I had become very involved with Birthright and really enjoyed it. In addition to "counseling" or talking and listening to the girls, I was asked to speak at various high schools in our area to explain about Birthright and the services available to everyone. This helped to advertise our presence. I was also asked to speak at the other offices in the Detroit area that provided similar services. One office was in the beginning stages of development, so I went there several times to help them with the training of their staff and ideas for funding and advertising. A little later I was elected president of our Birthright office, so that increased my commitment there.

John and I still missed going to prayer meetings and continued to pray for discernment in this regard. We searched for books about Charismatic Renewal and read as much as we could about it. It was like looking in the window and wishing we could be inside and participating. We were waiting for guidance and direction before attempting another beginning. But we were both busy with our various activities and with our children.

There had been many changes in our family. Jack would soon be graduating from Notre Dame, Joe would be finishing his junior year at Brother Rice. Jim was finishing his sophomore year at the University of Dayton. Janet was in Onekama, but we were concerned about their marriage situation. They were living apart now, and we could sense the unhappiness there, but Janet did not seem willing to discuss it. It seemed that things were always changing, and it was likely that this trend would continue.

I had been very healthy, but, at a recent checkup, the doctor discovered that I was developing symptoms of gall bladder illness. I had suspected this for a long time but didn't want to complain about it, but once it was diagnosed, I knew that it was time to do something about it. He assured me that it was not too a difficult a surgery. I would probably be in the hospital three to five days, and in a couple of weeks I would be back to normal. I decided to wait until after the Christmas holiday season was over and the boys would be back at school, so it was scheduled for January 4, 1978. I was not anxious about the surgery, as I knew that I had serious indigestion at times and was glad that it would soon be corrected.

I had experienced receiving anesthetics many times before, so when the time came when I was taken into surgery and they asked me to count backward from a hundred, I did and fully expected that, next, I would wake up in recovery with no memory in between. Well, that is not the way it was this time! My next memory was that I was on my way up, very fast! Up and up! At a terrific speed! I looked down and I could see the world rapidly disappearing from view below me! Now it looked like a very large, colorful globe of the world, like they have in school.

Oh, no! I thought. *Please, Lord, I don't want to go yet! I don't want to leave Johnnie and the children yet. I want to stay and help finish raising them. No! Please!*

Immediately that terrible feeling of terrific speed left me as it stopped. I felt I was floating and was feeling like I was covered with a warm blanket; as I heard His loving voice say, *Don't be afraid. You are going back! But when you go back, I want you to tell everyone that the message is JOY!*

As soon as I heard His voice, all fear left me, and I felt calm and serene, like I was bathed in lovely warm water. Actually, this whole incident takes much longer to tell about it than when it was really happening. I remember that as soon as I heard His voice, I felt wonderful. I was able to think fast and perceive things in a flash! It was wonderful to be set free from my body, as now, everything worked perfectly. My mind was clear. I could think and understand instantly. I was no longer hampered, by the limitations of my body. We communicated in a flash!

When I heard the word, "Joy!" I felt that terrible feeling of extreme speed again and felt I was being propelled down, down, down with the words echoing inside of me, like church bells ringing on Christmas day, saying "Joy! Joy! Joy!" When I opened my eyes, I was in the recovery room. I looked around for a clock. I realized that a good deal of time had passed. Everything seemed normal.

The nurse must have seen that I opened my eyes, as she said, "Oh, she's coming to now." She manually lifted my eye lid, and said, "No, it will be quite a while yet." And she resumed talking to the nurse on the other stool.

I struggled to tell her about my experience! It had been wonderful, and I wanted to tell her that the message was JOY, but nothing worked right. My lips were fat and swollen, and I could not talk or make a sound. But I knew where I was and wanted very much to tell her that I could hear very well and heard every word she was saying. I couldn't move my hands or head to get her attention. But she continued to talk to the other girl about the things they had done with their boyfriends! All these years later, I still remember! No one should be talking like that, especially when a patient is in their care.

Then I heard the Lord say, *Don't be worried. I will show you just whom you are to tell about JOY, because not everyone is ready to receive this message. Just rest now.* So I relaxed and dozed.

Later when I was back in my room and Johnnie was with me, I asked him what the doctor reported about my surgery. He said, "Oh, the doctor said everything is just fine, that you had a little trouble on the table, but you were fine now and he had every reason to believe that you would recovery nicely. He said the surgery was necessary, since the Gall Bladder was really badly inflamed."

I wanted to tell Johnnie about what really happened, and I checked inside myself, if I was to tell Johnnie about my experience. Then, in my mind's eye, I saw the stop sign, like the hand of a policeman, when he tells you to stop! And He said, *Wait until you are home and tell everyone at home the story at the same time.* That is what I did.

Janet came to help me for a few days when I came home from the hospital. She had fixed a lovely dinner for my homecoming. It was so good to be home with Janet, Joe, and John that evening. After dinner I announced that I wanted to tell everyone about something that had happened while I was in the hospital, and I proceeded to tell them about my experience when I was under the anesthetic. At first they were a little afraid that I had such a chose call with death. But I explained that it really wasn't a bad experience, because God was certainly there. At first I was afraid, but God showed me that He was in charge. Everything is really in His hands, and we are to trust in Him for everything. When we really believe, then we become secure and become joyful people. That is really the message! All through scripture there are examples. When the angel first appeared to Mary, the first thing that He said was, "Don't be afraid. I bring you tidings of great JOY, which will be for all people."

I have shared this experience with many people, always first asking the Lord to be sure that I should tell them and that they are ready to hear this message. Once, when I told someone about it they said, "Oh! You are one of those people who have had an out of body experience."

I thought about it for a minute and replied, "No, it didn't really feel like that. I call it an out of this world experience."

This experience I'm sharing is for each of you. God wants to take away any fear of death and erase any doubt. He wants His people to depend on Him entirely. He will prepare the time and way in which we are to leave this earth, and always, He will do what is best for us. Just place your trust in Him. When you do, you have nothing to worry about. Then, you too can have this JOY, this confidence, that ultimately everything will be wonderful, as He is in charge!

Later that night Johnnie said that he had checked with the doctor in order to determine when I would be able to travel, and he had booked a trip for us to go to Guadeloupe in six weeks, the first week in March. It was so thoughtful of him to do this, and we had a great time there, as I recovered.

I was happy to return and continue my work at Birthright. I was now president and doing "counseling", as well as many speaking engagements. I had thought about taking classes again at a university in counseling, so that I would be better equipped to do this work in a more effective and proper way. This time, I had prayed about it, and had gotten His approval first! After investigating the courses that were available, I found that I could get the courses I wanted at Oakland University in Rochester. It was a very convenient location, so I registered for my first class in counseling and effective listening, which was scheduled to begin soon after our return.

One morning on a lovely spring day in 1978, the phone rang and the person identified herself as Marge. She said she had just registered in the parish. When she asked Father Esper if there was a prayer group in the parish, he had told her that there wasn't one yet but to call me, as we had talked about establishing one.

I said that we would like very much to start a prayer group, but I wanted nothing to do with it, unless the Holy Spirit was fully behind it every step of the way. She said that she felt the same way about it. In the end, I invited her to come over that morning for coffee, so that we could get acquainted and share some of our experiences.

She arrived shortly and we spent the rest of the day together until I had to go to Brother Rice to pick up Joe. We shared our experiences with Charismatic Renewal. We had both been prayed over for the baptism of the Holy Spirit. We both missed going to prayer meeting. We prayed together, and through this time of sharing, it became apparent to both of us that we were being guided by the Holy Spirit, and now was the time that we had been waiting for, to begin again. We decided to pray about all of this and set up a time to get together with our husbands to talk further about this.

When the four of us got together, we prayed together, sharing the scripture that had been revealed to us. We came to the conclusion that it would be best to meet in our homes in the beginning while the prayer group was developing. Then when the group had grown and was larger, we could move to a facility in the parish. We decided to talk about the idea of a prayer group to others and see who might really be interested in this. When we had identified some people, then we would have our first meeting.

Also, we decided to set up a planning meeting with a few people that we knew who had been involved with other prayer groups and invite Father Esper to come to start us off in the right direction. We set the dates, first for our planning meeting and then a target date for a possible first meeting when we would begin inviting others who had expressed an interest in this. Marge said that their home was really not large enough to host this, as she had young children all in the lower grades in school, so it might be better for all the meetings to be at our home, as we had plenty of room. Also, it might be easier for people to always know where the meeting would be, instead of going back and forth between two locations. So it was decided that for now, all the meetings would be held at our house.

We invited the couple with whom we had been attending the Royal Oak Prayer Group to come to the planning meeting. They were delighted to come, as they had stopped going about the same time as we had. When John and I were out with friends or at meetings, we would pray about it and try to identify a few people who might be interested in this prayer group.

When the first meeting date arrived, Father Esper came, bringing with him a Nun, Sister Lucille, whom we had never met. She was new in our parish and had been active in a prayer group at her previous parish. At the first meeting we had about eight people in attendance. We conducted it like a mini-prayer meeting, starting with opening prayers, songs of praise, and scripture readings. Then John described what we were all about with a brief history of Charismatic Renewal and the scriptural basis for it. We discussed our thoughts and how to begin. Sister Lucile was delighted with the idea, and we knew she would be very helpful in establishing this. We all contributed in this discussion. Near the close of the meeting, Father Esper said that he felt we were off to a very good start. He explained that he had many parish responsibilities, and he felt that he would not have time to attend regularly, and also, that basically the Charismatic Renewal was a movement of the Holy Spirit among lay people. However, he was very happy to see that we were off to a good start, and he would like to give us his blessing. So he did, and that was how it began.

In the beginning, we started out having our prayer meetings on Thursday nights, and our core group, or planning meetings, on Monday nights. At the first prayer meetings on Thursday night, there were about twelve or fourteen people. The next week some of them brought their friends, and before long we had between fifteen-to-twenty attending. On Monday nights, we discussed the events and how we could improve our meetings. Eventually we all found our places where it seemed we were best suited to serve. John and Don, our friend who had first introduced us to the prayer meetings in Royal Oak, became the leaders. Sister Lucille, Marge and I were the teachers at our meetings. We all helped in any way that we could, and the Holy Spirit was always with us, inspiring us and helping us along the way.

We were very careful to plan any trips or times when we would be away, so that we were there when the prayer meetings were scheduled. We didn't want to interfere with the cycle, as things were going very well.

At one of our early core groups meetings, we prayed about the name for our prayer group, and it was decided that it would be called, "The Light of God." In John 8:12, John quotes Jesus as saying, "I am the light of the world, anyone who follows me will not be walking in the dark; he will have the light of life." Our little core group meetings were very powerful. We learned so much when we were together in our small group, in our living room. It was like a beacon, lighting our path and revealing His plan and His way for all of us.

One rainy Monday night in spring, only a small number assembled for Core Group Meeting. I think the weather had something to do with that, but we had our meeting anyway. After our time of singing and praying, Sister Lucille said, "Tonight, I want to read a passage from the Bible. Soon it will be Pentecost. This is from Acts, beginning with Chapter 2." She began reading, but when she got to verse 2, "and they heard what sounded like wind from heaven" at that very moment the red tulip that was in a small vase on the little table next to her burst with an audible, popping sound and the petals exploded from the stem and fell to the table!

Sister stopped and we all gasped. "Look," she said. "They are like little tongues of fire. And there are just enough for each of us to have one, and there is one left over. That one must be for all the others, the new people that will be coming to us!" It was an amazing experience! We each took a petal and decided to press it and place it in our Bibles, so that we would always remember this event. We felt it was a confirmation of our group that we were on the right path.

Eventually the prayer meetings size seemed to settle at about eighteen-to-twenty members. Some of us had been prayed with for the in-filling of the Holy Spirit, but most had not experienced going through the seven week "Life in the Spirit Seminar." We talked about this at our core group meetings. We decided that it was time that the whole group experienced this. I said that I did not feel that I was prepared to teach this, and I wanted to go through it all again myself. We prayed about it, and finally we decided to ask if someone from the Shrine Prayer Group could come to teach and lead the seminar so that everyone would be going through it together. They graciously provided a leader and he did a wonderful job, but he told us that this was only a one time gift. When there would be a need for another Life in the Spirit Seminar, we would have to teach it ourselves. We happily agreed to this condition.

His teaching was wonderful, just what we all needed. It was a good decision to go through this experience with all of us together. When it came to the night when we would all be prayed with for the Baptism of the Holy Spirit, the teacher brought two other people with him for extra prayer support. It was a very moving spirit filled experience for all of us. Now we were all on the same page and were experiencing new gifts and insights.

The group grew, and before long there were as many as twenty-eight to thirty-five people coming every week. Our living room was really crowded. It was clearly time to move to St. Hugo's. Father Esper was agreeable, and he suggested that we start meeting on Monday nights in the choir rehearsal room at St. Walter's Chapel. The meeting room was large enough for this group. There was another small room near the door, which became our prayer room, where we prayed with those that wanted to be prayed with privately. It was also where we met and prayed together before every meeting. Sometimes it was so packed with people waiting to be prayed with that we felt we were all crowed together in a phone booth. And in a way, it was similar, as we were calling to the Lord and the Holy Spirit to guide us and teach us and grant His peace and gifts to His people.

It was a special time of blessings and growth for all of us. Since our meetings were now held on Monday nights, we scheduled our core group meetings in our home on Thursday nights. As time went by, we found that we could meet every other Thursday, and eventually we met only once a month on Thursdays, for our core group meetings.

As I'm recalling this special time of grace, it occurs to me that, really, we had needed all that waiting time, so that we could grow in faith and learn that it is all His Power, not our power, and that we needed to pray about everything first. Also, it was wonderful having those early meetings in our Hammond Lake home for about a full year. I realized that if we had been meeting in our home on Millington, it would have been much more difficult. In that neighborhood, the homes were closer together, parking would have been a problem, and everybody was very aware of what was going on in each other's homes, who had guests or large meetings, and who came and went. The neighbors would have been very curious about our many meetings, while on Hammond Lake, the houses were much farther apart. Our driveway was large, circular, and below the street level, so there was plenty of parking, and all those cars were not so obvious. Anyway, we were new in that neighborhood, so they just ignored all that coming and going. No one questioned us about what was going on or what all those meetings were about.

After we began meeting at the parish, we heard about the First All Michigan Catholic Charismatic Conference, which was scheduled for April 20 to 22, 1979, in Muskegon, Michigan. At our core group meeting we decided that we would all make reservations to go and invite others in the group. It turned out that there was quite a large group going up for the weekend for this event. The speakers included Mother Angelica, Sister Briege McKenna, Father Francis McNutt, and Father Michael Scanlon. It was wonderful! The talks were so inspiring, and the music ministry was outstanding, as it was led by Father Carey, who had written many charismatic songs!

On the first night, we arrived shortly before it started, but the auditorium was packed, so we were seated way up in the balcony. We could see everything and hear well. I thought that this is just fine. We could just observe everything and take it all in and only take part in what we wanted. We knew most of the songs, so I sang strongly, as I loved to sing.

Later that evening, something wonderful happened. I found that when the song started, I would be singing the words, but later in the song, I couldn't see the words, and it all came out gibberish. Wow! I must have just received the gift of "singing in tongues!" I would be singing on key, but it all came out, with no words that I knew. From then on, when I would be alone, I would start a song and expect that soon it would turn into tongues, and it did! It was a long time before I discussed this with anyone else. I never thought I would receive tongues, because I was a little doubtful and slightly afraid of it, but now I knew how wonderful it was. I knew this was authentic.

Later, when I would be driving the car pool to Brother Rice, I could hardly wait until I would be alone in the car on the way back when I could pray and sing in tongues while singing the familiar charismatic songs. Also, it was something that I used during the start of my private prayer times and found it to be very comforting and inspiring. I felt that it was real and that the Holy Spirit was praying with me for what I needed, but I didn't think I could pray in tongues by just talking!

After that first night, we wanted to sit on the main floor and not miss a thing! Each session, we ended up sitting closer, until we were almost in the front. It was all so interesting and informative.

The conference was marvelous, very well attended, and the speakers were truly wonderful. Mother Angelica was young then, already talking about her first experience of being on TV. She said that she was planning a TV station entirely dedicated to Catholic programming. She was humorous and had a down-to-earth way of speaking; we were all charmed by her. She really got into our pockets, as we generously contributed to every collection that was taken up for this purpose of establishing a Catholic TV station. It did happen and this station is now known as EWTN (Eternal Word Television Network) and has a world-wide reach.

Father Francis McNutt had a strong gift of healing and was a very interesting speaker. They all were! That was the beginning of our exposure to Father Mike Scanlon. After that, we attended all of the conferences that we could at Steubenville and made many trips to the summer tent programs there. We were so inspired with the great teaching and information that we received at every conference. When we drove home from that first conference, everyone in our car talked and talked about all the many things we had learned; we were so inspired by it all.

Later at one of our core meetings, Sister Lucille told us about Sister Cyprian, a retired nun living at the mother house in Monroe, Michigan. She had been in the Charismatic Renewal for years and was a personal friend of Father Degrandis, who had a healing ministry. She had told Sister Lucille that she was going to arrange for Father DeGrandis to come to us and do some teachings and workshops for us, and she did. The next time he came to our area, she arranged for him to come speak and said that we should invite him to stay at our house. He would like that.

Indeed, he was our house guest at that time, and continued to come to us about three or four more times over the years. Sometime later, he told us that this would have to be his last time to come to us, but he would send his (biological) sister to us and he did. She had been divorced and had a real ministry for divorced people. She was an excellent speaker and we enjoyed having her, too. He had a huge, worldwide ministry, and was traveling all over the world giving teachings and retreats to priests, so he had a very busy schedule. He had written and continued to write many books about the gifts of the Holy Spirit. It was truly life changing and a blessing to us all.

I can't begin to tell you all the things that happened in those days that he was with us, but I would like to relate some of the highlights of that first, special time. For his first visit, we had prepared in advance of his coming by scheduling and advertising the several evenings to be held in St. Walter's Chapel, where he would hold healing Masses and teachings. The first meeting was very well attended, but the next night there was an over-flow crowd with many people standing.

On Saturday afternoon, the first day that he was with us, he had asked me to invite members of our prayer group to come to our home for a get acquainted workshop about the gifts of the Holy Spirit. He explained about the experience of resting in the Holy Spirit. We had seen this from afar at the Michigan Charismatic Conference, but had not experienced it personally, nor understood how it worked. There, in our living room, it became very real and authentic to all of us. It was not something to be afraid of. When the Holy Spirit comes to you in power, it is such an overwhelming experience that your knees become weak and you just fall but never hurt yourself and do not lose consciousness. You hear and know what is going on around you, but you are completely unable to move. Your eyes are closed and all you can do is receive His power and healing.

This was demonstrated to the group, when Father said, "Here, I will show you. Jane, come and stand here."

I did and he said, "Now look." And he reached out to me to pray over me and tapped my forehead and down I went. I could hear him talking to the others. "Did you see that? I did not touch her or push her. I only prayed for her and she went down."

I don't know how long I was "out", but when I tried to move, I couldn't, and I knew that the Holy Spirit was still working within me. It was a wonderful, powerful experience.

He went on to explain that, in preparation for all the meetings at the St. Walter's Chapel, we should arrange for "catchers" to be present, so that when he prayed with people, there would be someone to carefully guide the people to go down slowly and comfortably. We were instructed to allow each person plenty of time to "rest in the Spirit", but when they were ready to get up, someone should be there to assist them.

We had prepared for his coming but had not arranged for this, so it was a very good thing that we could now get prepared. There were meetings on Saturday night, Sunday night and Monday night, with each one better attended than the previous night.

That afternoon at our house, he asked if all of us had received the gift of tongues. Some had and some hadn't. I was doubtful, as I felt I could not "speak" in tongues, only "sing" in tongues. Those that had not received this gift, he asked to stand and form a circle. Then we started to pray, and when he came to me, he said, "Oh, you already have the gift of tongues. You have had it for a long time. Go sit down." Then he talked individually with each one and prayed with them. Before long everyone was praying in tongues. Also, he explained more about the gift of prophecy, which was very helpful. It was really confirming for all of us; it was a very fruitful and blessed time.

His teachings and meetings were a great blessing for our prayer group. Now the attendance at our prayer meetings had increased tremendously. In the following year, we needed to teach the Life in the Spirit Seminars four or five times a year, as the attendance at our prayer meetings grew from about forty or fifty to sometimes over a hundred. At that time, Father Esper arranged for us to hold our prayer meetings in the chapel, as we really needed that much space. We served coffee and cookies in the choir rehearsal room after our meetings, so that there would be a time for fellowship. Also, this was the time for people to be prayed with privately for their individual intentions in the chapel.

Much later when the new convent was built and additions were built to the school, our prayer meetings were moved to the Father Esper Room, which was large enough to accommodate our needs, and the kitchen, which was attached, made it possible for us to serve our coffee and cookies from that space.

In August, the same year as of the conference in Muskegon, Michigan, there was a Charismatic Conference scheduled at Notre Dame. Jack had already graduated from there, but we were very familiar with the University and had a great desire to go. The boys were old enough for us to leave for a few days and take care of each other. School had not started yet, so we made plans to go, and Sister Lucille decided to go with us, too. Our main concern was that John's dad was not well at all. He had been failing gradually throughout that year. The Nuns assured us that it was alright for us to be gone for a few days, so we visited him the day we left, and Jack and Jim planned to visit him on Sunday, so everything was arranged.

The conference opened on Friday evening in that lovely stadium. What a wonderful place to celebrate this occasion! It was a powerful beginning to our weekend. Saturday, during the day, we attended the meetings and workshops that we selected and we looked forward to the Saturday night large assembly of everyone scheduled for that evening. It began with music, singing and praise, followed by opening prayers and announcements. Then, another song was announced, when someone interrupted, by coming to the podium with a note. Before that announcement was read, the leader asked everyone to stand, and he proceeded to read the announcement.

We were startled when our names were read. We were asked to go to the main office to receive a very important phone call, and everyone was asked to pray for us as we left the stadium. Sister Lucille went with us, as we were in a daze, as we made our way down the many steps to the main level. It seemed we floated down the steps, surrounded by the sound of the prayers of this huge assembly.

When we got to the phone, it was Jim that spoke to us. He told us that he had received word that Granddad had passed away! We were in shock but began to recover and started to think about how we were to handle this unexpected turn of events. We placed our faith in God and trusted Him to guide us and help us decide what we should do next.

The Nuns at Lourdes were wonderful and many of the arrangements were already underway. The entrance forms had requested tentative, future funeral plans, which called for the funeral in Danville, and they had been setting the wheels in motion. Following many phone calls back and forth, everything fell into place. Janet was to drive down to our house in the morning. Then the children would all drive down to Danville together. We were nearly half way to Danville, as we were in South Bend, Indiana. We would start driving the rest of the way to Danville in the morning. Sister Lucille assured us that she could find a ride back with Sister Cyprian, so everything was planned.

Thanks to all those powerful prayers, we felt comforted and calm through it all. I have thought about those prayers that escorted us as we were leaving the stadium many times since. I am sure that those prayers were with Dad, too, as he left this earth. I'm sure he benefited from this prayer escort, also.

When we arrived in Danville, we went directly to the funeral home. Dad had arrived before us. We had talked briefly to the funeral home the night before. Now all we had to do was complete the plans for the funeral and interment in the cemetery next to John's Mother.

The funeral was lovely and was very well attended with many of their old friends present. It was a beautiful send off, and it was so fortunate that all our children could be with us. It was a blessing that it all happened before school started. We stayed an extra day to see the farm and take care of any loose ends there and caravaned home together.

Many things happened the first year of the prayer group. There had been two conferences, Father DeGrandis's visit with us, and Dad passing. But it all added up to a big growth spurt in all of us. Following our contact with Father Bob DeGrandis, I was more confident to speak in tongues and to speak out the words of prophecy that I received at the prayer meetings. I want to share some of those prophecies with you.

I continued to first experience a picture and then the explanation, as I had with the radish. But now it all took place very rapidly. It takes longer to tell it than it took to experience it.

One night at prayer group while I was in deep prayer, I saw a giraffe come striding into my view.

"What is this?" I asked Him in prayer.

"What are you seeing?" He asked me.

"A giraffe!" I said.

"Yes! I want to talk to you about this. I want my people to be just like giraffes! What can you tell me about giraffes?"

"Well," I answered, "probably the most important feature about giraffes is that they have very long necks."

"Yes!" He said. "I want my people to be willing to stick their necks out for me. What else?"

"Well, compared with the rest of him, he has a very small head."

"Yes! I want my people to have small heads, not swollen with pride, but humble in spirit. What else do you see?"

"I have always wondered about those knobs on the top of their heads. Are they horns that didn't develop, and what are they for?"

"Yes! They are like antennas, which are tuned only to my voice. I want my people to hold their heads up high, high above the noise and distractions of the world about them, and listen only to Me. What else do you see?"

"He has very large ears, compared to his head." I said.

"Yes! The better to hear My voice. Anything else?"

"Well, he has a small, insignificant body, but very long legs, and strong ones, as I have heard that they can run very fast."

"Yes! I want my people to be less concerned about their bodies. And their looks, and listen only to Me and run quickly to do My Will!"

After receiving this prophecy, I knew that this was for the whole group, so after our quiet prayer time, I shared this with the group. Eventually I felt secure enough to speak out the words of prophecy that I received more quickly, as I felt confident that I was hearing His words.

Another time, I saw a cocklebur. As a farm girl, I certainly recognized this. So I asked Him about it, and He said, "Look closely at the bur." And I did, and I saw that suddenly all the prickly spines dropped from the bur and it was docile! Then He said, "Tonight I am going to be healing relationships, in families, between friends, between husbands and wives, all relationships. Tell them this and asked them to pray for this and expect healing in these areas for themselves." So I did. Later it was reported at our prayer group meetings that, indeed, He had healed many relationships of the members that were in attendance that evening.

I now realized that the Holy Spirit had given to me the gift for teaching. I continued to do much of the teachings at our prayer meetings and for the Life in the Spirit Seminars during the following years with the help of the many books that we bought at the book table of every conference we attended. All of this helped to add members to the group, and together we grew in the Holy Spirit.

At one point when I had just finished teaching a Life in the Spirit Seminar, I received a phone call from a couple that wanted very much to receive this teaching and as soon as possible. They had heard about it at a youth conference that they had attended, and felt that this was something they definitely wanted. We had not planned to have another one until about three months later. I told them I would get back to them.

When I prayed about it, I sensed that this was something that should be done, so I brought it up at a next core group meeting. As we discussed this, it was mentioned that a young man had started coming to the prayer group after the last seminar had begun. He had expressed an interest in attending this seminar, but it was too late for him to join this group. So it was decided that I should promptly teach another seminar in our home for these three people.

In retrospect, this seminar turned out to be a very fruitful and powerful one. Perhaps this was because of the informal way that we met, which helped them feel at ease. They were able to ask a question when it occurred to them in that informal home situation. We were glad that an exception had been made to do this at that time. Those three people became long time members of the prayer group and a blessing to all of us.

The Prayer Group continued to grow and thrive. Our membership was averaging fifty to sixty or more each night. We were blessed that Father Esper was so supportive of our group. Now, more than 35 years later, The Light of God Prayer Group continues to meet in the Father Esper Room every Monday night.

More Trips

●──●

In the fall of 1979, John and I began thinking about making another trip to Europe. We talked about the many places in the world that we would like to explore. It was then that I told Johnnie about the stories I had heard regarding Oberammergau. This is the name of a small village in Southern Germany. During the time of the great plague that covered so much of Europe in the early years of the seventeenth century, the people of this village joined together to pray that the Lord would protect them from this terrible plague. If He did this and none of the people of this village died or became ill with this plague, they promised to perform a passion play about the sacrifices that Jesus had made when He died on the cross for our sins and would continue to perform this passion play every ten years until the end of the world.

Obviously the Lord answered their prayers, because when this terrible plague was over, not one person that lived in this village had contracted this disease. They stared to plan for their first passion play. It was performed in 1632 and every ten years following until after the end of the performances in 1692. At that time they decided to continue performing this play, but from then on, it would be performed on the 0 years. As a result, beginning in 1700, it was performed that year and every year since then on the 0 years. If we wanted to go, we should go now or wait ten more years. It would be presented in 1980, and I very much wanted to see it. We had not traveled in Germany, so it would be new territory to explore, and in the process, we could see this passion play.

Johnnie had never heard this story, but he agreed that this would be a wonderful time to see it. So I contacted our travel agent, and we learned there were trips that would be going there, however the tickets would have to be purchased soon in order to get the better seats. We were required to make hotel reservations in that village at the time we purchased the tickets. It was an all-day performance starting at 9:00 a.m. in the morning and ending at 5:00 p.m. with an intermission for lunch. The play dates began at Easter time and ended in the fall. There were packages with escorted tours, but John and I thought we would enjoy it more if we flew into Germany, rented a car and drove about to explore this country, and then stopped in to visit Oberammergau and take in the passion play. We would need to purchase the tickets well in advance.

We looked over our calendars and made tentative plans to go in the fall of 1980 after Joey would be back at Dayton University.

We began to explore this idea and thought it would be fun to go with another couple. We talked about it with some of our good friends. June and Bob were the ones that decided to go with us, and they did. We had lots of fun getting together, pouring over maps, and deciding where we wanted to go and what we wanted to visit. We booked our tickets for The Passion Play for Sunday, Sept. 14th. We scheduled our flight to Frankfort on September 6th. We would drive about to see the "Mad King Ludwig's Castles" and other points of interest and then arrive in time to explore this village and see the Passion play. After that we would make our way back to Frankfort to fly home on September 20th.

It would be great to have a little time off as our family life, our busy social life, the prayer group, my work at Birthright, and the classes I continued to take at Oakland University made our life very busy but rewarding. Eventually I had obtained enough university credits to receive my BS&A degree, a dream that I had long desired but had wondered if it would ever become possible.

We did go on that trip to Germany in 1980 and it was a wonderful. The passion play was fabulous. The script and the music and songs had developed over the years and now were put together in a very polished and professional performance. We purchased an English Guide to this play, as everything was presented in German.

The stage of the play was all out doors. The seats for the audience were under roof with no obstruction between the audience and the stage. When the performance was about to begin, a hand reached out from between the curtains and released a white dove symbolizing the Holy Spirit, which flew up in the sky. Then the music and singing began, and the curtains opened on the scene with Jesus riding on a donkey, as people spread olive branches in his path as He made His way to Jerusalem.

The play progressed from there to portray all the events leading up to Easter Sunday and beyond. Each event was shown and then the event that echoed or predicted this event in the Old Testament is played, as well. Of course we knew the plot of the play, but this back and forth between the Old Testament and the New, might have been confusing without an English translation to consult. The German voices were strong and beautiful. The guide book revealed that everyone who was part of the cast was required to be born in this village.

Our tickets were for a Sunday performance; we had planned to attend an early Mass at this village church. The night before, it was revealed to me that the Lord would give us a wonderful, surprise gift at that Sunday Mass. When we arrived we saw a beautiful, baroque church, so beautiful and complete with lovely statutes and lovely sculptures throughout the church. The interior of the church was mostly white, and it complemented the works of art. We were in awe of it, but the best was yet to come. The choir was wonderful! We theorized that the choir would also be singing at the passion play, and they were warming up their voices at Mass. We were doubly blessed to have visited this lovely church in addition to the passion play. The entire experience was a great blessing, as it revealed the commitment, talents and deep faith of the people in this village.

We so enjoyed our visit there and seeing this small village located in the mountainous area of southern Germany. The villagers painted scenes of this area on the outside of their houses. Sometimes they included paintings of people, which added to the uniqueness and quaintness of the area. Also, the village is famous for the talented wood carvers that live there. We knew that the large crucifix that hangs in the main altar of St. Hugo's Church was carved here, as well as the two, life-sized angels that guard the Eucharist reservation area. Also all of the carved Stations of the Cross in this church were carved there. These people were talented artistically, as well as musically. Wood carving shops were open for business and displayed samples of the unique carvings. We brought home a few small pieces (mostly of small angels) that I treasure and have hanging in my dining room. We talked enthusiastically about returning again in 1990 to Oberammergau.

When we left this village, we had some extra time but thought we had covered the part of Germany that we most wanted to visit, so June suggested that we try to visit Florence, Italy, which was not far but through the mountains. None of us had been there, but all of us agreed it was a good idea, so we decided to take the train from a point just north of the border between Germany into Florence, Italy. We left our rental car at the hotel for three days until we would return.

We took the late night train and arrived early the next morning at the train station located near the center of the City of Florence. The first thing we bought was a City Guide Book to get our bearings. There was a lovely hotel just a short distance from the train station, so we booked our rooms and arranged to leave our small bags there for safe keeping until later when our rooms would be ready. Then we were free to explore the city.

What fun we had. There are so many museums to explore, all within walking distance. Michelangelo's statue of David is there with many pieces of sculpture, as well as many famous paintings. What a treat. Scattered throughout the city are cafes and restaurants, so we found many places to enjoy and explore. In one museum we found many ancient scrolls all hand done by monks of scripture passages, beautifully embellished with colorful ink drawings, all displayed under glass. Such treasures! We spent two delightful days poking about and making discoveries with a visit to the Cathedral and Bell Tower.

Sometimes John and Bob rebelled from the cultural overload and took time out to enjoy the local wines and wait for us at an outdoor cafe. We all had a wonderful time. Our return train ride, which was in the daytime, took us to Venice. We had a short stop there, so we had a quick view of the canals and the City of Venice.

When we returned to Germany, we picked up our car and had plenty of time to drive back to Frankfort for our return trip to Detroit, loaded down with little bits of treasure and souvenirs from our travels and marvelous memories of all the places we visited. Now it was time to return to our busy world, refreshed and renewed.

The prayer group was developing very well. It was such a blessing to be involved. Through my good friend, Helen, who played the organ at church, we learned about Hank, who played the guitar very well, and his wife Kathy sang, so they became our music ministry. Their presence and their music greatly enriched the prayer meetings for many years to come.

It was not all smooth sailing. Indeed we had problems that surfaced, and it all had to be prayed about and addressed, but there was help available to us from other groups in the area. It was a wonderful time of spiritual growth for us all. The many visits from Father DeGrandis, the annual conferences, and trips to Steubenville really helped us as we continued in leadership.

Mother, now in her 80's, was still living in her big house in Dixon, Illinois. But following a car accident, she decided that her driving days were over. She had sold her car and now relied on cabs for trips to the stores and friends to help her go about, attending meetings, and church services. But trips to the farm were more difficult to arrange. I visited her as often as I could. Finally, I suggested that she have me manage the farm business for her. John had managed the Danville farm very well from Michigan. We visited this farm three or four times each year and we were in close communications with the farmer who farmed it, so I thought that I would be able to do the same for my mother with help from John, of course. It would also include visits to mother as well as the farm.

At this time she wanted to change the tenant farmer, as she was dissatisfied with the way things were being handled. Eventually, she agreed to have me take over this responsibility. I began planning and putting things into motion for the next year. I had John to rely upon for advice, so it worked out well. It gave me a good reason to go over four times a year to visit the farm, do the farm business, and keep up with how Mother was doing. Now she spent her Christmas holidays with us, flying over, which was more comfortable for her.

Our family was maturing and becoming independent. Jack and Jim had graduated from their respective universities. Both were working in the Detroit area and had their own apartments. Jack was pursuing a Master's Degree in Business and Accounting at the University of Detroit in the evening. Janet was now divorced and working happily at the Marina. She had recently purchased a house over-looking Portage Lake. Joe had two more years to go at the University of Dayton and expected to graduate in 1982. John and I went about our usual busy schedules without having to work around the children's schedule, except in the summer time when they all returned for a time. The lake was always a big draw for all of us, as we all enjoyed swimming and boating.

During the last decade it was our habit to take winter vacations in the islands, as the weather there was predictably nice and sunny. We would spend a week or five days on a different island in the Caribbean each year, flying down and relaxing in the beautiful weather. We played with the idea of buying a vacation place somewhere there, but because of the volatility of the governments in these areas, we were not seriously considering it. Now with John having four weeks of vacation each year, we decided to begin exploring Florida as a possible vacation site. This year we wanted to begin a serious search for a winter vacation site, and perhaps, as a retirement location in the future. We decided to book a flight sometime in January of 1981 to the Miami area, rent a car and look things over for two weeks before flying back from Tampa.

We had friends in various areas, so we began our search on the east coast but didn't quite find what we had visualized. We decided to explore the Gulf Coast, and were delighted to discover Sanibel, and Captiva where The South Seas Plantation is located, which seemed just right for us. After working with a sales agent, we purchased a time-share condo there for the first two weeks of November. It was just a short walk to the ocean from the condo and included golf privileges on a nine holes golf course. Also he showed us property on Fort Myers Beach. This condo was a time-share, also, and was in the process of being built. After much thought and prayer, we decided to purchase a condo on the top floor of this building, which had a great view of the gulf, for the first two weeks of March. It all seemed just right for us and we could continue to explore when we returned. Eventually, we might decide to invest in a year round home somewhere in this area. We had decided to stop for a short visit with my cousins who had established themselves in Clearwater, before we flew back to Michigan from Tampa.

The prayer group was a major focus of our lives. That kept us in touch with Steubenville and the wonderful summer programs, which were held each summer under the large tent set up on campus. We had great admiration for Father Michael Scanlon and planned to attend as many Steubenville events as we could.

We were delighted to receive information about the upcoming Steubenville Pilgrimage and Tour that was been planned for July, 1982. The theme was to follow the footsteps of Jesus and the Missionary Journeys of St. Paul. In this process, we would be visiting the very places we had dreamed about visiting. We would visit both the Holy Lands and Rome, and a cruise on the Mediterranean, ending in Athens, all in sixteen days!

After much prayer and careful planning, we concluded that it seemed to be His plan, and it was all doable. Joe's graduation from the University of Dayton was scheduled for the last weekend in April, 1982, and the All Michigan Charismatic Conference was scheduled for Lansing on the second weekend in August, so the July date for the trip would work out fine for us. We happily signed up for this wonderful trip, which would be our first escorted trip out of the country.

We flew to New York, and while we were waiting to board our overseas flight, we met Pat and Maggie, who became our good friends on this trip. Any time there was a little lull, we got together with them and played bridge, which helped get us through several little snags along the way.

Our flight from New York took us directly to Rome where we were escorted about to see all the major sites we had longed to see and had heard about over the years: The Vatican, St. Peter's Cathedral, the Sistine Chapel, and the wonderful painting on the ceiling, the ruins of the ancient Arena, the modern city of Rome, the Spanish Steps, and all the major points of interest. We traveled to the village where St. Francis of Assisi and St. Theresa had lived. We visited the lovely small chapel in which St. Francis and his followers prayed. It was designed to serve about fifteen to eighteen monks. It was all very impressive.

This tour group was a very large group consisting of about 500 people or more traveling in five large buses. There were seven Priests accompanying us on our trip, so each day we celebrated Mass somewhere along the way. In addition, most evenings after dinner there would be a prayer meeting held in the conference room of our hotels. This meeting included a Bible study that reminded us of the Bible events that occurred on the sites we would be seeing the next day. This helped us stay rooted in the historical and biblical significant of each place we visited.

From Rome we were to fly to Egypt. We were following where Jesus and St. Paul went, and of course, where Jesus fled with his parents to Egypt to avoid the King's mandate to kill all the children of a certain age, hoping this would include the newborn "King of the Jews". Our flight to Egypt from Rome included a stop-over, and the group had to split up and take separate flights, in order to reach our destination. We were stranded in the middle of the night somewhere en-route. So the four of us, Maggie, Pat, John and I, decided to play bridge. This facility was a very plain, metal fabricated building, but it did include a little snack bar. So Johnnie placed a couple of bills on the table and said, "Whoever is dummy next can go and get some sodas for us."

Immediately two armed guarded arrived and instructed us, "Play cards, okay, but no money on the table!"

This was a sharp reminder to us that we were very far from home, and we had better pay attention to our surroundings.

Much later we arrived in Cairo and were taken to a very lovely, modern hotel. There were many people milling about at 3:00 a.m., wearing the local costumes. It was quite a scene for us, not something we had seen before. The next day our group reassembled, and we were taken about to see the many wonderful places, such as the pyramids and the fantastic Egyptian Museums in this area. John and I had gone to Toronto to view the King Tutu's traveling exhibit when it was there a few years before this trip. But it was just a tiny display compared to this huge exhibit in Cairo. We were even given a ride on a camel, which was a swaying ride compared to the gait of a horse.

Later we were treated to boat rides in small row boats on the Nile River. We sang, "Michael row your boat ashore, Alleluia," with much exuberance! Our singing echoed up and down the river. There were about twenty or more small boats, scattered along that section carrying members from our Pilgrimage.

From there, we were told at our evening Bible study that we would be traveling in buses across the desert as we entered Jerusalem. We were to keep in mind the Israelites wandering in the desert for forty years in search of the Promise Land.

Usually we recited the rosary each day, and this would be a fairly long bus ride with all the members of that group participating. After the rosary, we settled in to enjoy the scenery. There was not much to see except endless desert with a small oasis here and there or the broken remains of tanks left behind after some previous modern day war in the area. I know I dozed a little and took this time to rest, reflect and pray.

Suddenly, I couldn't believe what I was seeing! There was a huge ship, and it was traveling perpendicular to our path just ahead of us! *It must be a mirage*, I thought. About that time, our guide announced that we were approaching the Suez Canal. That explained it! We would be crossing it on barges, which would be there waiting to ferry us across. It was quite a project to load and unload our buses onto the barges and ferry us across, taking one bus at a time. All of us remained seated on our buses as we traveled cross the canal. There was quite a sharp incline that led down from the desert to the edge of the water and then up again on the other side. It took awhile, but it was very interesting to be there and observe this canal, which we had heard so much about.

Later, as we approached Israel, you could see the evidence of the settlements made by the Israelis. The green plants and houses were a sharp contrast to the endless desert we had just crossed. At last we had arrived in the Holy Lands, the place of Jesus' birth and the site of so much history from Biblical times. We had five days to explore the region. During that time, we visited Bethlehem, Jerusalem, and the Dead Sea, the site of the recently discovered ancient scrolls, which had been stored in pottery in the caves there. We walked the path that Jesus walked to his crucifixion. There were so many Bible events mentioned in the scriptures that are located in this area.

At one point we visited the grove of olive trees where Jesus prayed the night before his crucifixion. It is thought that some of these trees were living during that time in history. The guide told us that the gate in the wall of Jerusalem above this area is called the Beautiful Gate. It is sealed and he told us that it would not be opened until the Second Coming of Jesus.

We were ushered into a very lovely cathedral. We would celebrate Mass here shortly. Coming in from the bright, July sunlight, I was temporarily blinded and could barely see inside. There were folding chairs set up for this large gathering of over 500 people. Before Mass began, there were some announcements. It was announced that some of the tile floor was the original tile. The places where it was covered with glass was the original floor and the uncovered area was the newer, replacement tile, which matched beautifully.

In due time Mass began, and, after receiving the Eucharist, I returned to my chair. I bowed my head and completed my prayers of thanksgiving for the privilege of been able to go on this wonderful trip and see all these fabulous places that we had longed to visit. When I opened my eyes I saw a beautiful sight reflected in the glass over the tile by my feet. It was then that I heard Him say, *It is time that you wear my cross, and this is the cross that I want you to wear.*

I began to study the image that I saw in this glass, so that the memory would be fully etched in my mind. As soon as Mass was over, I whipped out my Instamatic Camera and took a flash picture of this, but as soon as I did this, I realized that I would only have a very nice picture of the tile and not the reflected image I was seeing. John whispered, "What are you doing?"

But I said, "I'll tell you later. I'll meet you on the bus. I have to do something first." And I slipped out to go in search of the image that I had seen reflected in the glass. Soon I found it in the sky light, which was located above the altar. The cross was pictured there and this was the cross that I had seen. So I took a picture of the cross, but by now, I felt sure that I would remember exactly how it looked. It was a cross with both the vertical and horizontal beams the same length. The cross was encircled with a lovely curved circle with lines radiating from the cross. It reminded me of the way the Eucharist is sometimes displayed for adoration.

When I returned and boarded our bus, I told Johnnie what I had heard the Lord say, and I sketched a picture of what I saw. From then on, whenever we had free time, we looked in jewelry stores to see if we could find this cross. As it turned out, it was not difficult to find jewelry stores, because the next day we entered our cruise ship and stopped at the Greek Islands along the way, following the footsteps of St. Paul's missionary journeys. There were jewelry stores everywhere! As well as visiting these very old and lovely islands, we stopped at each village and had time for shopping along the way. We shared our project with Pat and Maggie, so they helped in the search. Everywhere they said the same thing. "The cross you describe is called the Crusaders Cross with the bars that are even or the same length, vertically and horizontally, but I have never seen it outlined in the way that your sketch indicates."

We saw many lovely gold items, so we ended up buying things for our family and friends, as gold was relatively inexpensive at this time. In one shop John spotted a very nice solid, masculine-looking Crusader's Cross. He bought it for himself, put it on and wore it from then on. I had extra gold chains with me, so we put his cross on one of my heavier chains. He really enjoyed wearing his keepsake from the Holy Lands and wore it continually for the rest of his life. But it still remained a mystery to me as to where I would ever find the one I had been shown.

We enjoyed this segment of the trip and viewed so many places which are mentioned in the Scriptures, especially in the letters from Paul to the people in these locations. We visited the Island of Patmos where Saint John spent his last days and where he wrote the Book of Revelations.

Eventually, we made our way to Athens, which would be our last stop before flying back to the States in a few more days. Poor "Mama Myers" as we affectionately called her was having such a time herding this very large group of tourists about these areas. She was the representative from the travel agency, and it was her responsibility to see that we all got to the right places and hotels on time. When we arrived in Athens, she discovered that the Hotel that had been reserved for all of us was full! It seemed that there had been a political uprising in the home areas of the occupants. They had flown there with their families to be safe from the war-like conditions in their home villages, and they refused to release their rooms. So "Mama Myers" had to find other hotels for all of us! This gave us extra shopping time to investigate Athens, while she worked feverishly to find hotel space for this very large tour group.

John, Pat, Maggie and I stopped at a fruit market; where we purchased some lovely, juicy peaches. We sat down to enjoy this fruit, while deciding where to go first. We had a guide book for this area and had been told where to meet our buses at a designated time.

While the others chatted, I silently prayed earnestly, asking The Father to help me find the cross I had seen. It seemed like He was smiling, and He responded, *I thought you'd never ask! Don't be anxious about this. I will be with you to guide you.*

I was so thankful! I had been worried about it and couldn't understand why we had been unsuccessful in finding this item. So I relaxed, prayed for "Mama Myers", and we continued on our walk about Athens.

Mama Myers had received her own miracle, as she found hotel rooms for all of us. She had to split up the group between five different hotels. She explained that these hotels were very good hotels but not the excellent one that would have housed us all. We didn't care, as it had been a wonderful trip and our hotel was very nice indeed. Later that day when we were all safely situated in our hotel rooms after having dinner there, I prayed again before falling asleep. I knew that we had only one day left before we were scheduled to fly home, so I assured God that if I didn't find the cross I was looking for, I would not ignore His wishes. I would find someone in the States to design and make the cross I had seen. I fell asleep peacefully, knowing that it was all in His hands.

The next morning, we met Pat in the hall on our way to breakfast. She was very excited, as she told me that she thought she had found what I had been looking for. Yes! It was displayed in the window of the gift shop in our hotel! The gift shop didn't open until 9:00 a.m., so I made sure I was there when it opened. I asked to see the cross that was in the window. After examining it closely, I asked more about it. I was certain it was exactly as I had seen it. He assured me that it was made of very fine gold, and on the cross was a tiny jewel where His body would ordinarily be. I was thrilled to find it and asked if he had additional ones like it. I thought I would like to buy one for our daughter. He checked and said no, he didn't have another one like it, and in fact, he didn't remember ever seeing one like this before. I silently prayed a prayer of thanksgiving and timidly asked the price. I knew I would buy it, no matter what the price!

It was very reasonably priced, and I delightedly completed my purchase. Wow! I have recalled this incident many times during my life. I felt in my heart that we were sent to this particular hotel purposely by the Lord, so that we would find this very item! I put it on the chain I was wearing and since then, I have only taken it off to be cleaned or during doctor visits. It was all such a remarkable experience. I thanked and thanked Him! I realized once again that all we need to do is place our needs in His hands and ask that His will be done, not ours. Nothing is impossible with Him!

We returned home that day, filled with marvelous memories of this most wonderful trip to Rome, Egypt, the Holy Lands, the cruise of the Greek Islands, and finally Athens. It was all wonderfully complete with Mass every day and Bible teachings each night and the miracles that had occurred. This was our first escorted trip, and we decided that it was really the best and greatest way to travel. After this we took many other trips, but nothing could ever top this one!

Our Growing Family

W̶e returned home filled with lovely memories of our trip and full of enthusiasm to resume our life, picking up the life threads of our friends and family. Our family seemed poised to take a leap forward by growing in numbers. Our family had remained a family of six, John and I and our four children for the last twenty years or so, but now that Joe had graduated from the University of Dayton and was engaged to marry Linda in June of next year, a growth cycle had begun that would end up more than doubling the size of our family in the next ten years.

Joe had been searching for a position in the Detroit area since his graduation in May but had recently expanded his search and found just what he had been looking for in the Cincinnati area with the help of the University of Dayton's placement office. It fit not only his work goals, but its location promised to be very acceptable to Linda, her family and ours. Linda had one more year at the University of Dayton, and following her graduation, they were planning to be married the next June. Linda's Mother and Dad lived in Louisville, Kentucky, so Cincinnati would be even closer to them than it was to ours in the Detroit area. Also during Linda's senior year, Joe would only be about forty-five miles away, so he could comfortably attend functions at the university and still see Linda. His job was to start very soon, so our first project was to help him get settled in an apartment in Cincinnati and pull together a suitable set of basic furniture.

We played catch up for the first few weeks after we returned home. John had lots of things waiting for him at his office and, as I was still President at Birthright, there were many things that needed my attention there. Of course we couldn't wait to go to the Prayer Group and find out how things were going in our absence. In addition, there were many phone calls to our children and our friends. Jack had completed his Master's Degree from the University of Detroit some time ago and was now working and living in the Chicago area. Janet was happily employed at the Marina in Onekama and Jim had returned from Philadelphia and was working in the Detroit Area and settled in a condo in Troy. So it was just John and I living in the lake house on Hammond Lake, but it did not seem too big for us, as we entertained frequently, the children came home for weekends or, in Jim's case, stopped by for Sunday dinner or a swim in the lake in the summer.

I was driving home from the Birthright office one afternoon and praying about the needs of our office when I heard Him say, *It is time for you to train a replacement for yourself and for you to resign as president of Birthright.*

I was stunned and asked Him if I had done something wrong or had failed in some way. He simply answered that no, He was pleased with my work there. He had other plans for me.

I wondered what that could be, but I felt sure that He would tell me when the time was right, so I began to think about whom to suggest as my replacement. In a way it would be freeing, as I did have many other responsibilities. It was soon time to make a trip to Dixon and check up on the farm business and visit with Mother. After that trip, we would need to check on the Danville farm, also.

We were enjoying our two time share condos in Florida. Soon it would be time to book our flight to enjoy our two weeks of R&R in November. We were feeling right at home down there and regularly attending a prayer meeting in the area, which we enjoyed very much. We were getting acquainted with some people in this area, as we came down in November and March. Sometimes we invited another couple or members of our family to join us for one of those weeks, either at the Captiva condo in November or one of the weeks in March at Fort Myers Beach, but we usually reserved the first week for just the two of us. This was our time to just relax, read books, and talk out what each of us was thinking about and what we really wanted to be doing for the rest of our lives.

At that time in our lives, retirement seemed a long way off. John enjoyed his work very much and thought it might be possible for him to continue in this position until he was seventy, so the idea of retirement seemed a long way off in the future. However, neither of us could imagine retiring and coming down for just a couple of weeks here or there as our ultimate plan. For one thing, these two condos were much too touristy. Each time we came down there were different people in the building and, only occasionally did we recognize some family that we had met the previous year. It was not conducive to making friends. When we retired, we wanted to have one place that we would call our own and return to the same place each year for the whole season, put down roots, and have a place to play golf. However, retirement was a long way in the future, we thought. There is no hurry, but we did like the climate in Florida.

Joe and Linda's wedding was coming up next year, and I wanted to be available to do all the right things in my role as Mother of the Groom. Soon, I found that my responsibilities as Mother of the Groom were much less extensive than Mother of the Bride. It was pretty simple really, show up for showers, pick out a dress for the wedding that was dignified, not too showy, and smile a lot. The old adage that Mothers of the groom should wear beige, smile a lot and not talk too much was a simple outline for my duties. Great! I could sit back and enjoy the show.

I found the right dress and I couldn't think of anything else that I needed to do for the upcoming wedding. So, we were off to Florida, and the first two weeks in March to get some R&R and a little suntan. Our good friends, Helen and Ben, would join us for the second week to visit us on the beach.

When we visited our Florida prayer group, as usual, it was a very full house. One of the leaders asked us if we could serve as a prayer team that evening, as there were lots of people requesting private prayers. Of course we said yes. They knew we were leaders in Michigan and were familiar with serving in this way.

Indeed the prayer lines were long. We did remember one young man who came to our line for prayers. When we asked him what he would like the Lord to do for him, he replied that he was considering a job as greens keeper at a new country club community called The Forest. He wanted to ask the Lord if he should take this position and if it would grow into a stable, country club community. Recently he had taken a similar position in another club, but it had gone into bankruptcy, and he didn't want to go through that experience again.

We proceeded to pray for him for this intention. We knew that you never give someone specific advice following a prayer session like this, but when we finished, we hugged him, and told him that we were sure that the Lord would make it clear to him just what He wanted him to do about this. On the way home John and I talked about this. I said that I got such a powerful, positive experience concerning the Forest Country Club that I felt certain it would turn out to be a wonderful club. John said that he felt the same way. We both thought perhaps we should look into this club, but we didn't know where it was located. The young man had said it was on Route 41.

The following week Helen and Ben were with us. It was lovely beach weather, so the first few days we just enjoyed the beach and going out for dinner. Helen asked if we could visit Naples, as they had heard good things about this area. We all agreed that if we had a rainy day we would all go to Naples.

Sure enough, one morning it was pouring down rain when we woke up, and it looked like an all-day rain, so after breakfast we were off to Naples for a day of adventure and exploring. When we were on Route 41, I suddenly pointed to a sign which said, "The Forest Country Club: Villas and Condos available now, soon to be a 36 holes Golf Course". Helen and Ben were agreeable to exploring, so we decided to go in and look around.

We found the sales office just a short way from the front gate, so we went in. They had a large map of the area displayed under a glass top table showing the 27 holes that were already completed, the various condos that had been built and the ones that were available, as well as home sites, and the final, projected 9 holes of golf to be completed later, as well as the completed club house. They had brochures of various homes and condos. We all decided it would be fun to be shown around, so we actually went through some of the condos and the finished club house. Of course it was much too rainy to see much of the course, but we left loaded down with several brochures and lots of information about the club. John and I could hardly conceal our enthusiasm about this area.

We continued on our trip to Naples, shopped, found a great place for lunch and shopped some more as we visited the area, and eventually found our way back to our beach condo. Helen and Ben were scheduled to return to Michigan on Thursday, as she was the organist for St. Hugo's and had responsibilities for the coming weekend.

After they left, John and I sat down and prayed about the Forest Country Club. We had several more days before we needed to return on

Sunday. We both liked what we had seen, and we decided to go back and look it over more thoroughly, maybe play the course and investigate if it would be right for us. Previously, we had looked carefully at two other country club areas, but neither one had seemed right to us. We went back to The Forest and looked carefully at all the available condos. After much prayer and careful consideration, we decided to buy the model, as it was available at a very good price and was fully furnished. We felt certain that this was what God was calling us to do. We planned to put the condo on the rental market until sometime in the future when we might retire. We decided to try to sell our time share on Captiva, as we felt that our Forest condo would probably not be rented in November. We could plan to come down sometime in the fall when it was not rented but to keep the beach time share for now, as March would be a prime month for our condo to be rented. We signed the initial papers with final settlement scheduled for May. We laughed about the fact that we would soon own fifty-six weeks in Florida!

When the Lord is in charge, things work out very nicely. We moved some money around and were prepared for final settlement when we were notified that we had a buyer for the Captiva Time Share. That closed rather quickly. We decided to fly down for a few days in early May, sign the papers for the Forest Condo in person, and stay a few days in our new condo, making sure that everything was in order while playing a little golf. We might decide to add a few items, as we wanted it to be comfortable for prospective rental guests. It all worked out and we spent our thirty-third wedding anniversary in our new condo at the Forest Country Club.

Joe and Linda's June wedding turned out to be just lovely! All of our children were there and my mother, too, plus two of my favorite cousins and lots of our close friends from Michigan. It was wonderful! We had never been to Louisville before, but their hospitality and wedding plans turned out to be just great. The wedding took place in their home parish church with Mass and all the trimmings. The reception was at their country club. We were so happy with the way things were and felt very welcome and joyful. We felt so confident that these two young people would be very happy together.

The morning after the wedding, our family gathered around the hotel pool to catch up with all the news from everyone before, one by one, it was time for all of us to go our separate ways. In our conversations with

Jack, we heard that he was dating a new girlfriend, Karen, and we could tell that Jack seemed happier than we had seen him for a long time.

Yes! He was the next one to be married. Shortly after that, they both came over for a visit, and I could see how much in love they were. They were engaged shortly afterwards and began making wedding plans for May, 1984. These plans were soon set in place. As I had been on this route less than a year before, I sat back and waited to be told about the plans. We got ready for the second wedding in less than a year. It was all so happy and wonderful. Jack had been living in a house he had purchased in Elmhurst, Illinois, so this was where they would start married life. Their wedding was held in Karen's home parish in the small town of Woodstock, west of Chicago, where her widowed Mother lived. It was a lovely occasion with all our family present, along with a couple of my cousins and Mother, and some good friends from Bloomfield.

At Birthright, I had resigned as President and I had helped walk my replacement through the all the procedures, promising her that I would be available if she had questions or needed help in the future. Things were up and running very well at the office. A friend of mine had recruited me to be on the Christian Service Commission for St. Hugo's, of which she was Chairperson. So I was as busy as ever with bridge clubs, serving on the board of directors of Hammond Lake Homeowners Association, and our growing prayer group each week with our annual Mass and Picnic on our deck at the our house in August. Also, I was serving one day a week at St. Joe's Hospital, distributing the Eucharist to patients that requested it.

One day out of the blue, I received a phone call from the central office of Birthright of the State of Michigan. I was asked to Chair the up-coming International Convention of Birthright, which was to be held in Michigan sometime in the summer of next year. Well, well, well, so that was why He wanted me to clear the way by resigning the Birthright Presidency. I asked a lot of questions, specifically about my job responsibilities for the project. It seemed that my role was to develop the program, select speakers and set up the advance promotion for this three day convention, as well as to select a hotel in the Detroit area that had facilities to host such a conference. So I agreed to take on this project.

I knew of a brand new hotel west of the city near Eight Mile and I-275 that had just opened. So I checked this one out first. Bingo! It had all the right facilities, large ballroom, restaurants, and lots of fresh, new hotel rooms so that I could block off the number of hotel rooms that would be needed for this event. Now we could set the wheel in motion to begin to advertise the dates and hotel location. It would be convenient to the Detroit Metro Airport, as the hotel was only about twenty minutes away from the airport.

The Michigan Central office of Birthright worked very closely with me in establishing the program, speakers and workshops for this convention. It was really a very exciting time, planning for this large, international convention with representatives coming from many countries in Europe, Africa, and South America, as well as from other parts of our country. It was amazing for me to see this project take form and grow, to blossom into a full blown convention, in just a little over fourteen months.

At this time other exciting things were happening in our family. Our first grandchild, Meredith, was born to Jack and Karen, in April of 1985, just a few months before the start of the July Birthright Convention. It happened that John had a business meeting in Chicago a few days after Meredith was born, so he was able to stop by and see her, before I could arrange a visit. Karen's Mother was there to help her when she came home from the hospital, so the baby was a few weeks old before we arranged to go over for my first visit. A few weeks later was the baptism, so my mother, John and I and most of our children were present for that event. What a joy!

However, it was during this time that I began to see emerging problems with my mother's health. She had become much more frail. She had a very bad cough and the doctors could find no medication that seemed to help. I began to wonder if she could continue to live alone much longer. We had a couple of long talks about this. Mother was reluctant to give up her home in Dixon. I repeatedly invited her to come and live with us. We had plenty of room in our house on Hammond Lake, but she knew so many people in Dixon. She did not want to move so far away from her friends and her home. She agreed that the best solution when the time came was to live with us. It would be more preferable than a nursing home or living way out in California with Anne. We left it that whenever she was ready, she would let me know and we would work out all the details.

During the three days of the convention, I served as Hostess and Master of Ceremonies of this event. In the end, I felt that everything had gone very well, and it was all well worth the hours of advance planning.

During the convention there were many valuable opportunities to share experiences for solving problems that frequently arise in our offices. I got together with some of the other officers from various offices in the Detroit area to discuss our common problems. From this experience the idea occurred to many of us that we shouldn't wait for another convention to get together for these valuable discussions. We could be meeting on a regular basis. The idea grew and emerged to form a local coalition of the offices in the Detroit area to meet on a regular basis.

I volunteered to develop this idea and select a meeting place that would be centrally located and available for our meetings. Later, it all came together when we began to meet in Detroit at the Archdiocese building. They kindly allowed us to reserve a meeting room there the next year, for the four or five times we would need it. We held our first meeting there in January of 1987. I was elected president of our group and served for a two year period. We felt it was very helpful to share our problems and our successes, which benefited the growth of all of our offices.

But immediately following the convention there were several events that occurred which made huge changes in our personal lives. That Saturday night we had gone out to play bridge with our couple's bridge club. On the way to bridge club, John asked me to review some of the bridge conventions that we had always used, like the number of points it takes to open in one no trump and the various number of points needed for certain responses.

Without thinking, I said, "Why John, you know all that stuff! It's what we have always used."

Well, that was the *wrong thing* to say to him. He got very upset and said that it was easy for me to remember all that stuff, as I played a lot more bridge than he did.

Later, when I had time to pray, I realized that some serious changes were taking place in John. Several things came to mind that substantiated this. John told me that there were some big changes in the wind for General Motors. They had decided to eliminate the Fisher Body Division, and that engineering group would be absorbed by the other various divisions of the company, like Cadillac, and Buick. This was going to seriously affect John's business, because much of his sales had come from Fisher Body. It seemed to me that Cooper would be fair and make the proper adjustments for the division of the business. But that part was not what most concerned

John. He was worried that he would not be able to adjust to the process of meeting new engineers and developing new contacts for the business. This was really at the root of his concern. It seemed that his mind was not as flexible as it had been. I puzzled about it all. Later I prayed for wisdom, as to how to deal with all of this. Suddenly the thought occurred to me that he was developing Alzheimer's! I thought, *Oh, no! That can't be!*

But could it be? After all, both his mother and father had this terrible ailment. Then they had called it hardening of the arteries. Just recently I had read an article about it in the Reader's Digest. I got right up and looked for that issue. I immediately decided to change my plans for the day and went right to the library to research the recent information that had been written about this disease. I checked out a book that described the early symptoms of this condition. Also, it indicated that there was some evidence of a hereditary connection. I kept this book in a place that John was not likely to find it. I read it carefully and wondered about the ramifications. But, as time went on, I dismissed this idea, and things settled back to normal. I thought John is all right. He is his usual self. There is nothing to worry about.

In the summer of 1986 following the convention, I came back to the house after an afternoon of golf to find a phone message from Mother. She had called saying, "Call me, as soon as you can."

I called her immediately. Mother said she had been to see the doctor that day, and he said she had shingles. She was miserable! The doctor said that it was not easily cured. She said, "This is it! I can't stay here alone any longer!"

I told her I would catch an evening flight and be over that very night. But in talking it through with her, she indicated that she did not feel able to fly. She wanted me to drive over the next day in my car. There were things she wanted to bring with her in the car, and it would be much easier for her to travel in this way. That was what I did.

I flew around the house, canceled my appointments for the next few days, made an appointment for her with my doctor for the day after we would return, prepared a room for her and emptied out that closet, so she would have plenty of space, and tried to think of what more I would do to help make her comfortable. I did a load of laundry, prepared dinner, and packed my suitcase so I could leave early the next day.

It is about 400 mile trip to Dixon, but, by leaving early in the morning, I was there by the middle of the afternoon. She had many miserable blisters and was so relieved that I was there. I could see that it would have been very difficult for her to get dressed and go by plane. This way, she could wear a loose dress and with pillows and a light blanket, I could make her comfortable to ride in the car. We talked about the things she wanted to take with her, so I began loading the car. There were precious keepsakes that she wanted to take with her, so we packed those things first. We decided it would be easier just to take all of her clothes with us and sort things out when we got back to Michigan. It was quite a project to close up her house, empty the refrigerator and do all the things necessary to leave the house for an indefinite period of time. During that evening and the next day, we had a chance to talk things through, and discuss all of her concerns.

The next day after we returned to Michigan, we kept the appointment I had made for her with my doctor. He confirmed that she did, indeed, have shingles, and there was a shot available that seemed to help. He said that in six weeks or so she might be completely over it if this shot had been given in time. Without it, she may have shingles that would come and go for the rest of her life. Frequently this condition is triggered by stress or anxiety but is caused by the Chicken Pox virus. She had the shot and we hoped and prayed that soon Mother would feel much better. Her days of living alone were over, and it was time for her to be with us. After all, she was eighty-nine years old.

Mother slept and slept for the next few days. She was so relieved to be there with us and knew that whatever happened, we would work things out. Mother told me that she had been worried about how she would be able to entertain Lura, my cousin from California, because she no longer had a car. She wanted to plan meals, but it seemed overwhelming to her. She wanted to take Lura out to the farm and maybe take her to dinner, but how would it all work out? Lura was scheduled to come in August for a two week visit.

Later, when I could see that she was improving rapidly and really feeling much better, I called Lura and told her the change of plans and invited her to come to Michigan instead of Dixon for her scheduled visit with Mother.

It all worked out very nicely. The first week of her visit, we had a great time talking over old times and catching up with all of the latest family news. I needed to go back to Dixon and wind up some business details there and put her house on the market, but I did not want to leave Mother alone. I discussed it with Lura and we decided that now would be a good time for me to do those things. Lura and Mother could have visiting time with just the two of them. I prepared some meals for them and put them in the freezer and stocked the refrigerator.

During the second week of Lura's visit, I went over to Dixon, met with a Realtor, put her house on the market, and began to deal with the contents of her house. There were many keepsakes and pieces of furniture that we wanted to keep in the family. Jack came out while I was there and took some of these things back with him. Linda took some vacation time and came up to Dixon to help me. She was a wonderful help, and we had a great time visiting while we worked. She told me all about her job as Public Relations Representative of a hospital in Cincinnati. She had hoped to have a baby by now but was optimistic that it would happen soon.

She chose some of the furniture and things that they would like, including some of the many books which were in Mother's extensive library. Mother had suggested that we give a lot of her books to the library, so I arranged for that. Joe came up for the weekend with a van, and they were able to take some furniture back with them. So in a week's time, the basement was cleared out and the most precious items placed among the family. I brought some things back with me.

It had worked out to be a great blessing that Lura had come for that extended visit. Lura and Mother enjoyed their time together on the lake, and John was there evenings to take them out or pick up things from the store. Mother did not want to be in Dixon to see her home dismantled. Much later that year when the house was sold, the transaction was handled by telephone and by mail, so Mother didn't need to go back for that. I planned to continue to handle the farm business. At times when John and I were scheduling a trip to see the farms, Jim or Janet would come and stay with Mother during the time we were gone.

It was an adjustment for all of us. Mother was healing quickly. By the end of the initial six weeks, Mother was completely well and over the effects of shingles. I was concerned about her eye sight, but Mother said she knew that she had cataracts. She did not want to have anything done about it. She was afraid of this procedure, as one of her friends had a very bad experience.

I took her regularly to a nearby Lutheran Church and she was beginning to feel at home there. I checked around about social activities that she might enjoy at the local Senior Citizens groups, but nothing seemed to click with her. For the most part she seemed to feel contented at our home and enjoyed the lake and the changing scene out there. In nice weather she loved to go out in the paddle boat with me and travel around the lake. There were lots of things going on at our house, but Mother became used to it all. She took a nap every afternoon and went to bed early. Soon she was feeling better than she had in years.

But John continued to have some problems at work, and I saw signs that he might be forgetting things. I tried to erase the worry that it might be the beginning of Alzheimer's. But I did see that things were changing for him. In my daily prayer times, I prayed specifically about this. I put it all in His hands and asked for His guidance and wisdom.

In that fall of 1986, another baby was expected in Jack and Karen's family. Karen had asked me to be there, to take care of Meredith when the new baby arrived. I had agreed to do this. Now with Mother so much better, it all looked possible. Mother could stay alone during the day time, and John would be there in the evenings. I planned to leave easy fix dinners in the freezer. John could pick up things from the store, if needed. Things were all in place for this event.

I drove over to Barrington in late October and was there for a few days getting re-acquainted with Meredith and the family routine before Molly Ann arrived. What a joy! I felt blessed to be there for this wonderful event. When Mother and baby were safely home from the hospital and things settled down, I returned home to Hammond Lake.

Next we planned to go to Florida for two weeks in November, and Mother planned to go with us. We were looking forward to showing her around The Forest and our new condo there. After that, our Christmas plans would be fast upon us. Mother would be celebrating her 90th Birthday on December 24th, and Molly Ann would be baptized at St. Hugo's Church on December 26th, all upcoming special events. All of our children and grandchildren would be with us for these celebrations and this wonderful time of the year.

As I was preparing for Thanksgiving, the concern about Mother's eye sight came back to me. I decided to call a Doctor who was a specialist in the removal of cataracts. I explained her situation, and after our phone conversation, I decided to make an appointment for Mother to see him. I told Mother that he was a specialist in this field and maybe he could give her new glasses which would improve her vision enough so that she could see to read again.

I drove her to the appointment, but while she was actually seeing the doctor, I went to the nearby grocery store and bought all the things I needed for our Thanksgiving dinner. Then I went back to the office and waited until she came out from her appointment.

When she came out, she was glowing! I was surprised to see how happy she was! She said that the doctor told her that she was a very good candidate for this type of surgery, and she decided to have it done! The only question was when. We scheduled an appointment for the middle of December and another one later in January for the second eye to be done, as they never do both eyes at once. Mother's surgery was a success, and it was wonderful to have her eye sight return. She was fitted with new reading glasses in late February. Then she could enjoy reading again and it made watching TV much more enjoyable.

In March of 1987, Mother flew down to Florida with us, but since she had visited our beach time-share condo several years before, she decided to visit the cousins in Clearwater near Tampa during that time. It gave us a little break so we could do our own thing, just the two of us, and Mother would have a great visit with the cousins.

We knew that our condo was rented for a nine month period. A couple had sold their home up north and wanted a place to stay while they watched their new home in the Forest being built. Of course, we were delighted to have it rented for that length of time. The rental agency told us that the rent should be reduced, due to long-term rental and the savings of not having the condo cleaned. It had to be cleaned after each rental period.

As this rental period continued, I became uneasy. Suppose these were big party people. There might be wine stains on the carpeting or furniture. What if they were smokers and there were burned holes in the furniture. After all, everything was brand new in the condo, and it was a special, future home for us. It is amazing how your imagination can cause uneasiness to increase. We discussed making up an excuse to check the condo while we were in Florida. While we were in town, we called and made an appointment at their convenience to check the condo.

When we arrived and met this couple, all our doubts and concerns vanished. They were lovely people and everything was in wonderful condition. We asked if there was anything that we could do to make their stay more pleasant. She said that she wanted my advice about the potted tree that was on the screened-in porch. She said she had been watering it every three days and it did not seem to fade, but she wondered if she should be doing anything else for it.

I hated to tell her that it was a silk tree and nothing was needed, but I did. We all had a good laugh about it. We knew that we would enjoy knowing them better when we retired and would be neighbors. Much later, we did become good friends and enjoyed many a golf game and bridge game with them.

Later that year, two things happened that really changed things for us. Mother had an episode of scrambled speech. It happened at the lunch table. I had returned home from the grocery store and was fixing lunch when Mother came to the table. She tried to tell me something, but it just came out as gibberish! I thought she was trying to tell me that there was a phone message for me. No, she shook her head. I tried to guess what she wanted to tell me, but she was becoming more and more agitated, so I gave her a piece of paper, so she could write what she wanted to say, but that, too, came out as a scramble of mixed letters that made no sense. She looked so puzzled. I was frightened but tried to remain calm.

"It will be alright; just take it easy and relax." I said. "Here, have a drink of water, and don't try to talk now. Oh, I have to go to the bathroom. I'll be back in a minute." With that, I excused myself from the table and slipped out to call the doctor from our bedroom phone. He said it was probably just a TIA, and if things didn't improve in an hour or so, to bring her right in. He suggested that I make an appointment to see him for a checkup next week. I returned to the table and chatted on about what I had gotten at the grocery store and told her not to talk for awhile, and things will be alright. Sure enough things returned to normal after awhile.

Later, when we went in for the check-up, he told us that everything seemed just fine. Privately, he told me not to leave her alone for more than an hour or so at a time, as it could advance into a full blown stroke. I asked if a TIA, meant a "temporary interruption in an artery". He laughed and said that was not exactly the definition of a TIA, but it was a pretty good description of what had happened. He reassured me not to worry, that Mother was in very good health for her age. But it continued to worry me, even though things seemed to return to normal. And I did change my schedule.

The second thing that happened was that John's little episodes of forgetting things were occurring more frequently. I really didn't know what to do about it. The things I had read stated that there was no medication that had proved to be effective to cure or lessen the progression of Alzheimer's, if that is what he had. Also, there was no definitive test that would indicate whether or not the patient had this dreadful disease. In my reading, I did come across an article that stated that, if someone retired before the age of 65, it would lengthen that person's life, in direct proportion to the number of months he retired before 65.

After thinking about it, I decided to discuss this with John. Perhaps, if early retirement was beneficial, it would be helpful in reducing the symptoms of Alzheimer's. Also, if he retired soon, maybe there would be no embarrassing incidents of his forgetting important things at work. I decided to talk to John about this latest study. I did not want to tell him that I suspected Alzheimer's. But maybe he would welcome the idea of early retirement.

So, I suggested that he read that article, as it had occurred to me that perhaps we should retire much sooner than we had planned. We had a wonderful retirement fund, thanks to Cooper's matching funds and the fact that we had always put in the maximum amount. Also, the mortgage on our home on Hammond Lake had been paid years ago. We only had a small amount of indebtedness on our Florida condo, which we could rapidly pay off. So, why not take early retirement and have that many more years together to enjoy it?

John liked the idea, as he was finding his job more stressful than it had been. Also, now we could envision what retirement life would be like, since we had purchased our condo at The Forest. We could divide our time between our home on Hammond Lake and our condo in Florida, and we could play golf the year around. Now, with our Forest condo, we wouldn't need the Time Share condo on the Beach. If we could sell that condo promptly, that sum would more than pay off the mortgage on the Forest

Condo. John thought this was a good idea! John made an appointment to see our financial advisor about the tax consequences.

Our advisor said that John's pension would be available after he had worked for Cooper for twenty years, and that had already occurred. His Social Security could be started any time after the age of sixty, with proportional deductions for every year short of the age of sixty-five. I could begin social security whenever I wished after sixty. Therefore, if we wanted to retire soon, it would be wise to wait until the first of the year of 1989, as then all our reduced income would all occur in the same calendar year. The best time to apply for Social Security was shortly after his birthday in April of that year. Did we really want to retire in 1989? That was the question. We would have to consider this carefully.

Now in 1988, we began to seriously consider retirement. When Mother became aware of the conversation, she asked how this would affect her. I said she could come along with us and enjoy it, too. We were thinking of spending part of the year in Florida, and the larger part each year in Michigan on Hammond Lake. Several days later, she said she had been thinking it over, and she did not like Florida. She thought she would like to stay here in Michigan while we were gone.

We discussed how this could be arranged. Perhaps we could hire someone to stay with her while we were gone. She didn't like that idea, either. What she really wanted was to go back to Dixon, as she missed her friends. She said people she met here were very nice, but they were mostly my friends, and she missed all her old friends and the familiar places she had always known.

I asked her if there was a place in Dixon that provided assistant living, and she told me about Heritage Square, where many of her friends had lived. It was an assistant living facility that had a range of care levels, from relatively independent living to a full scale, skilled nursing center. But she didn't think that she could afford it, as she thought it was probably quite expensive, and they might have a long waiting list. We had plenty of time to consider how everything would work out, as potential retirement was more than a year away.

It was time for me to go to Dixon to check up on the farm, so I said that I would check out Heritage Square while I was over there. When I investigated the property, I was impressed with all that they had to offer. It would be wonderful for her. It was a lovely facility, well planned and located in a very nice area. They had lots of activities, so that she could be as active as she wanted to be. I thought she would probably know many of the people there, as I recognized some of the names of current residents. I asked about the waiting list. The director stated that because Mother had lived so many years in Dixon, she would receive preferential treatment. Perhaps there would be a vacancy soon, and it could be Mother's, if she wanted it. So I placed her name on the list.

When I returned, I told Mother all about Heritage Square. The cost was reasonable and well within her price range. She was so pleased. So, it all worked out well. A few months later, Mother was informed that now an apartment was available.

As we talked about it, Mother asked, "Now, when I enter, the deposit that I will make, will it go for the next month's rent?"

I answered "Yes, that's right."

"Now, as I understand it," she said, "When I receive my pension check and Social Security, that money was payment for the month that we just had. Is that right?"

I nodded, "Yes, that's right."

"Well," she said, as she thought it over, "The only way to have it all come out even is to just die on the last day of the month. And I am going to make sure that it is a long one!" We both laughed about that!

After talking it over, she decided that this was really what she wanted, so we began making plans for her to move. It was July of 1988 when she actually entered Heritage Square. She was so excited and happy to be going back to Dixon where she had lived for most of her life. She quickly adjusted to her new situation. She had a lovely apartment on the first floor with a little sitting room and her own bedroom and bath. It was a short walk to the dining room, but that walk would be beneficial for her. She could go over there at any time and be in the common living room and visit with other residents when they gathered there before meals. We arranged to bring over the bookcase and secretary that she had used for years and a chair that she enjoyed. The rest of the furnishings were in place and very nice, including a small TV set. We arranged a physical with a local doctor in Dixon, so all things were falling into place.

We planned to come over often to visit her and take her out to see the farm and the spring or whereever she wanted to go. The move to Heritage Square had gone very smoothly. Mother had lived with us about two years.

It was an interval in which Mother had gotten completely over shingles, had cataract surgery on both of her eyes, and had enjoyed several trips to Florida, where she visited with cousins and stayed at our condo.

When we returned home, the house seemed very empty without her. But it was freeing, because now I could turn my attention to some of the projects I had pending. We could begin to make definite plans for our retirement, which would start in January, 1989. We needed to decide what changes to make in regard to the organizations in which we currently had leadership roles. It was clear that we needed to resign as Leaders of the Light of God Prayer Group, in which we had been active for nearly twenty years. We announced our retirement plans at the next Core Group Meeting. Plans were made to have an election in the fall for new leaders to replace us.

John had completed his term of President of the Detroit Rubber Group and was now in an advisory position. I had finished my term as president of the Hammond Lake Home Owners Association but now was Chairperson of the Christian Service Commission of St. Hugo's. I had added several projects that were under this group's direction, such as a Bereavement Support Group for our parish and the SOS Project.

SOS was the South Oakland Shelters group that had been formed a few years before. This organization served the homeless in this part of our county by providing shelter for those in need. It was facilitated by support from churches and organizations in the area, which provided a place to stay and meals for one week each year. This was the second year that our parish had hosted this group. When we started, the summer weeks had been taken, so we were scheduled for the week between Christmas and New Year. The school was not in session then, and we could use the Father Esper Room and the gym. We served the meals in the Father Esper Room, which also served as a living room and place to meet and talk. Since there was a full kitchen attached to this room and bathrooms in the hallway adjacent to the Father Esper room and gym, it served very well as a shelter for one week. The men's dormitory was in the gym and, if there were women and children, they slept in the teacher's lounge, which was also in this area. The homeless people came to the SOS office in Royal Oak, about fifteen miles from our parish. There, they received help to find employment, counseling, and direction. During the day the host group would deliver them back to the office each morning and pick them up there at five o'clock each night when they were transported out to the host church of the week. SOS provided folding cots, pillows, and blankets and basic needs. The host group provided breakfast and dinner in their facility and sent them out each day with a bag lunch. The host group provided transportation to and from the office of SOS to the host church for the evening.

The first year we formed the necessary committees. There was a set up group on Saturday when the cots and materials were delivered and a tear down group, including laundry for sheets, for the following Saturday. There were committees to provide breakfast, dinner and bag lunches each day, car pools morning and evening, and night couples to stay over-night as hospitality people. They stayed awake all night, in case there was something needed at that time. The first year, people in our parish were hesitant, but the second year it was much easier to recruit people to do the various jobs. They could see first hand the needs of these people and felt they actually participated in meeting some of these needs. Many of the people volunteered to serve in the same capacity, as they had the previous year, so it was much easier to pull it all together.

I decided to continue to serve out my term as Chairperson of Christian Service, as it would end in June. We planned to return to Hammond Lake for the Christmas holiday season, at least for the next few years, so I would be available to chair the SOS next year.

One thing that we both wanted to do was start traveling to foreign countries. We began telling our friends that we had definitely decided to retire next January in 1989. Christmas was only a few more months away, so there were holiday plans to be made.

We decided to do something very different for Christmas, 1988. We made plans for a trip to Dixon to celebrate Mother's birthday. Jack and Karen would be spending Christmas in their home this year, as a new baby was expected in early January. We announced to Joe and Linda, Janet and Jim, that they all needed to be on hand on December 23, as a special, surprise Christmas present would be delivered early on December 24, and everyone should be there to receive it.

The present was a chartered plane from the Pontiac Airport, which was fairly close to our home, to take us all (Joe, Linda, Janet, Jim and John and me) to Illinois. The first stop was at an airport near Jack and Karen. They and the two girls would meet us there. We were only on the ground for about a half hour, just long enough to give hugs and kisses all the way around, as well as to deliver our Christmas presents to them. It was great fun to see them and the two little girls, Meredith and Molly.

Then it was on to the Dixon Airport, where we were met by my cousin, Nickie, and her husband, George, who had driven out from Chicago to Dixon for the day. A birthday party had been arranged for Mother, so we all had lunch together, delivered birthday and Christmas presents, and had a wonderful time visiting Mother in her new home at Heritage Square. Then it was back to the airport for our flight back to Pontiac and home by early evening to get ready to celebrate Christmas the next day.

Retirement Begins

When we actually retired on January 1, 1989, we were as busy as ever. SOS Week was scheduled for the first week in January. John's retirement party would be held on January 5th. Now we were beginning to feel that our retirement was real. It was a change of pace and lots more time together. Nice! We liked it so far. After the end of SOS Week, we were delighted to hear that John Kevin had arrived right on schedule, and Mother and baby were just fine! As soon as it could be arranged, we flew over to Chicago to visit Jack and Karen and their lovely growing family. Then we drove out to Dixon to visit Mother and show her pictures of the new baby. Our condo in Florida was rented until the first of March so we had plenty of time.

In the previous months as we talked about our upcoming retirement with our friends, the idea had developed that we should take a trip somewhere special to begin this time of our life. It would have to be after SOS was completed and the baby had arrived. We wanted a destination that would have nice weather, yet somewhere different and special. After pouring over brochures and choices, we decided on a trip to Africa, starting on January 27th. Our friends Chuck and Phyllis decided to join us. We were looking forward to this trip, as it would be a very different country. It included camping at two animal preserves in Kenya, fully escorted, of course.

It turned out to be a wonderful experience for all of us! The weather was mild, as we were not far from the equator. Kenya has a variety of landscapes from mountains to flatlands, from modern cities to primitive areas that were without electricity and modern conveniences. Our trip began by flying to New York and boarding an overnight flight to Frankfurt, where we connected with another plane that would take us to Nairobi,

Kenya. We had been en-route for quite a long time, so we were really tired when we arrived.

Our guides met us at the airport and helped us cope with the luggage and gave us the information we would need until we met again before dinner at our orientation meeting. Taxis took us to a lovely, very modern hotel, and the rest of the day we were free to do our own thing, rest, shop, or explore this area and were given suggestions about things to do. We decided to check out our rooms, rest for a while, and set a time to meet later to have a light meal and then begin our exploration of this bustling city. The next two days were spent visiting points of interest in the city, and we were told stories about the history, all very interesting.

Following Nairobi, we were driven to our first camping experience in this fascinating country. We were delighted with the animal preserves and the camping experiences there. There was no electricity, but it was very civilized. The tents were established on concrete slabs. Each unit included a small sitting area and a bedroom with a modern bathroom, including hot and cold running water. The beds were enclosed with mosquito netting, which added a feeling of elegance to the tent. We found it very comfortable and pleasant.

Each morning a native would come by our tent to wake us and bring us hot tea and biscuits. We had been told that we should drink our tea and dress quickly, as soon we would be escorted to the parking area where the Land Rovers would be waiting for us. Then, as soon as it was light, we would start out on our first trip of the day to view the animals as they were waking up and view their kills from the previous night. Each Land Rover could hold four to six people. As soon as one car was filled, it would start out on that day's adventure, so that there were never large groups of cars traveling together. They were careful not to disturb or frighten the animals.

It was wonderful to see all these animals in their native habitat. There were lions, leopards, some deer-like animals, elephants, hippopotamus, hyenas, giraffes and many more. The birds were beautiful and there were many kinds that I had never seen before. It was indeed a wonderland of natural beauty. Our guide was well acquainted with the whole area and very knowledgeable. He kept up a running conversation with us and was happy to answer all of our questions.

Each day was a different experience, as we never knew what we would encounter. One day we came upon a new-born baby elephant surrounded by several adult elephants. They were on hand to protect and take care of the baby. There was a river nearby, so they helped the baby experience his first bath in the river. Another time an ostrich surrounded by about twenty-five or so young baby chicks appeared in our path.

I asked, "How could one lady ostrich lay that many eggs and have them all hatch at the same time?"

Our guide answered, "That's an interesting story. Usually four or five hen ostriches get together and build a common nest, in which they all lay their eggs. Then they each take their turns sitting on the nest. Whichever ostrich is sitting on the nest when the eggs start to hatch becomes their mother. She takes full responsibility for all of them until they are grown, and the other hens are free to go about as they please with no responsibilities. Quite an interesting arrangement, don't you think?"

Another time, we came across a large group of hippos bathing in the river. What a fun time they were having! Our guide cautioned us that we should never get between a hippo on land when he was headed for the water. They can be quite vicious in certain circumstances. They were all in the water at that time, so he decided that it was safe for us to get out and walk around a little so we could enjoy this sight. Each day brought new surprises.

After a couple of hours of viewing the wild life, we were taken back to the dining hall for a substantial breakfast that included hot and cold cereal, bacon and eggs, fresh strawberries, muffins, juice and hot coffee. Then we were free to do as we liked. Lunch would be available at noon, and about 4:00 p.m. we would meet again for another drive through the area to view what was happening in the wild life department. There was a lovely swimming pool available for our use, and we did enjoy that. Sometimes we would sit on chairs outside our tents and just talk or play cards. There were lots of monkeys in the tall trees outside our tents, and they were very entertaining to watch. Or we would take a rest or read a book. It was all very relaxing.

Eventually all our questions were answered. We learned that the hot water in our bathrooms was heated by the sun in large, elevated tanks, and the gravity helped make the water flow around where it was needed. It must have been pumped up there with hand pumps. All our food was cooked over wood fires outside the kitchen. We marveled at how well it was all accomplished. The meals were wonderful with lots of fresh vegetables and fruit, all locally grown. Everything about the camp was maintained extremely well. When we went from the dining hall back to our tents after the evening meal, we were escorted by a guard, who carried a very large spear and a torch to light our way, as it was dark by then. Really, I don't think there was any great danger from wild animals, but they were very careful about keeping us safe. They seemed to have plenty of workers.

When it was time to leave this camp, we were directed to go to the landing strip and board a small plane that would take us to the next camp. While we were waiting to take off, a large group of fifteen or twenty giraffes arrived and looked with interest at our plane. They were occupying the air strip and it seemed that they were in no hurry to leave. Eventually, a land Rover arrived and drove slowly up and down the air strip a couple of times to clear the runway. Then we could take off.

The next camp was very similar to the first one in regard to the accommodations, food and activities, except this camp was located along a river bank. Just across the river was a native village and sometimes we could see the families and their children, who would swim or fish in the river. It was interesting to watch these activities.

This area was much more flat than the other camp. We were told that here there was a site where we could take a hot air balloon ride, if we wanted to. We had never done this before, so we decided it sounded like fun. On the morning we were scheduled for this ride, we went very early in the morning, instead of our normal morning Land Rover ride. We were driven to the take-off site where there were three or four large, colorful balloons waiting for us. We were helped aboard. There was room for four people and the pilot in the large wicker basket. When we were all situated, there was a loud whoosh as the blast of hot air filled the balloon, and we rose up in the air. After that first blast, it was very quiet up there. We floated through the sky as the sun was rising and could view all the activities below us.

We saw the animals below us as they were beginning their day. There were herds of elephants and giraffes. Later we saw lions and hyenas with their kills, feeding their families. It was so quiet and peaceful up there. The animals seemed to be completely unaware of our presence. What fun that was. We flew over a village of native people as they went about their morning routines, all very interesting.

After a couple of hours up there, it was time to return to earth. It was interesting to see how the pilot controlled our descent by repeated, slow releases of the air in the balloon to allow us to slowly float back to land. The Land Rovers were there to take us to the campsite where a lovely breakfast had been prepared for us. There were picnic tables there in an open, flat field. We were served a champagne breakfast with all the trimmings to celebrate our very pleasant flight, high above the earth.

This site must have been very close to the equator. Next we were taken to a place that was right on the line of the equator. This was demonstrated by showing us that on the north side of the equator, water flows down the drain in a counter-clock wise movement and on the south side of the equator, water flows down the drain clock-wise, We found this very fascinating. This was the first time that we were in the southern hemisphere.

After our time in the wilds, we were taken to a very lovely resort, which has been a favorite destination for Hollywood stars for some time. There was a swimming pool, golf course, and a great hotel with all the amenities. Our rooms included a fireplace. It gets rather cool in the evenings. As we dressed for dinner each night, there would be a knock on the door. It would be an attendant, who would light our fireplace. When we returned from dinner the fire would be burning brightly and the room would be warm and cozy all evening. The dining room was nicely decorated and welcoming and the food was excellent.

After a day of checking things out and enjoying a restful time by the pool, John and I decided to play golf the next day, so we investigated this plan at the pro-shop. Phyllis and Chuck decided not to play.

Of course we didn't have our clubs with us but could rent some at the pro-shop. We scheduled a tee time for the next morning. After breakfast we returned to prepare to play golf. We decided to buy a couple of sleeves of golf balls, but when we found out that the balls were five dollars a piece, we decided to limit our purchase to four balls, two a piece. We decided we would be careful not to lose them! They gave us each a bag, just a small Sunday bag, as there were no caddies available. The clubs consisted of one wood, two or three irons and a putter. Oh, well, it would be easier to carry, so off we went.

It was cool when we teed off at 8:30. We were both wearing slacks and sweaters, but it was a bright, sunny day. The first couple of holes went well, but we were surprised at the condition of the golf course. It was not much better than a cow pasture. The greens were hardly groomed at all. This was not what we were used to. We got the feeling that, at any time, a group of elephants could come strolling by. What an adventure!

On the first hole we realized we had forgotten to get tees. Oh well, we found a broken tee, so we used it. Later we found a tee and were very careful not to lose it. We decided that whoever broke it would be penalized two strokes. We were having a fine time on this beautiful day in Africa.

On about the fourth or fifth hole as I was preparing to make my third shot, I felt something and looked down at my sneakers. They were black with small black ants, and they were climbing up inside my slacks, biting me on the way up! I stopped right there, stepped behind a tree and stripped off my slacks. I didn't care who saw me, as I had a one track mind. My legs inside of my white slacks were covered with ants, and they were biting me! John came over to see what was happening, and we both burst out laughing, as we slapped and brushed my legs and slacks to get rid of them.

Once I got rid of them and I put my slacks back on, I was okay, so we continued our round. After that we both were very careful not to step on any other ant hills. The views from the golf course were beautiful. It was the only time I ever saw Calla Lilies growing in the wild. What fun we had.

That night at dinner we reported my encounter with the ants to our guide. He looked at me in shock and said, "Obviously they were not the poisonous variety, or we would be visiting you in the local hospital now."

Our last few days in Africa flew by and soon it was time to prepare for our return flight, but what an adventure we had. It was a very different trip out of the country than we had ever experienced. During our trip we had become acquainted with another couple from Montana. They shared that their next trip was going to be to China. Wow! What a great idea. We decided to keep in touch with them and perhaps we could join them. We weren't back in the States yet, and here we were already thinking about the next trip. Retirement is going to be great fun.

We returned on February 12. We had been gone a little over two weeks, but we had seen so much of the world. It was great to be back to our world and to be catching up with our friends and family. Before long it would be time for us to leave for Florida.

We spent the month of March in Florida getting settled in our condo. We planned to cease renting it now that we would be spending time in it ourselves during the winter months. We became better acquainted with the Forest members and began to develop a circle of friends to join us for golf, bridge and dinners at the club. It was a friendly club and in a short period of time we knew the regulars and welcomed the new members as they joined. The club was growing rapidly, and new homes and condos were being built in order to keep up with the new membership. It was great to feel a part of this, as we had joined in the early stages of the development. This year we planned to return to Michigan in early April, as we wanted to be present for Kevin's baptism in April in Barrington.

We enjoyed our drive North, seeing the summer-like vegetation turn colors, heralding an early spring, by the time we arrived in Illinois. We made a brief visit to both farms and stopped to see Mother at Heritage Square before arriving in Barrington for Kevin's baptism. Then we went on to Hammond Lake to settle in for the summer, which soon was filled with activities at Stonycroft, and St. Hugo's. The Prayer Group continued to grow and was a vital part of our lives. As usual, the Rummage Sale was held in June at St. Hugo's. I had continuing responsibilities at Birthright and the Altar Guild.

In the later part of June, we made a trip around to check on the farms and to see the crops coming up. At Dixon we took Mother out to her farm and the spring. It was wonderful to see how nicely the Franklin Creek Project had developed. In 1970 Mother had agreed to release about 90 acres of woodland that she owned, which included the spring, for the purpose of developing this park. Currently the park contained more than 500 acres of woodland along the Franklin Creek. About four miles of hiking trails and six miles of equestrian trails had been developed.

It is such a blessing for our family, because now there is a walkway about a half mile long, which extends from the parking lot near Sunday's Bridge all the way to the spring. It is constructed of concrete and is wide enough to accommodate a wheelchair. A picnic site had been built near Franklin Creek and the spring, which included picnic tables, grills and seating. We enjoyed our visit to the spring and were so pleased that Mother had been able to see all the changes that had been made. It is comforting to know that this beautiful area has been preserved for future generations.

Later as I reflected about seeing the spring again, memories of the good times flooded back to me. In this world where everything is constantly changing, it was nice that this remained unchanged. Radio has progressed to TV and from black and white to color. We have grown up and changed, as our children and grandchildren continued to, as well. Clothes, styles and our way of life have changed over the years. Trees and flowers grow and change according to the seasons, and new ones take the place of old trees.

Yet, this spring has remained unchanged. It still pours out pure, clear water from the same places as I remembered, and the large flat table rocks remain in the middle of the spring, as well as the other two rocks at the edge of the spring. It is the same temperature winter and summer. It may seem different to us because the temperature in the air changes, but it is still fifty degrees and pours out a continuous amount of pure, clear water as it did when we lived on the farm all those years ago.

The only other thing that I know of that does not change is God. He loves us with an everlasting love. His forgiveness is readily available to all. He is always there for us, regardless of what we do. He waits for us to return to Him and always welcomes us back when we do return to Him. And like the spring water, He is pure and refreshing. He wants to restore us to His family and welcomes us to His kingdom, when we truly repent. We can't possibly imagine what He has in store for us. As scripture says, "Eye has not seen, nor ear has not heard, what wonderful things He has prepared for us."

But, I digress! In August all of our children and grandchildren gathered at Hammond Lake to enjoy swimming and boating before fall began. What fun! Joe and Linda had wonderful news to reveal. They are expecting their first child in early January. We were excited.

Our fall was a busy time. In September we attended the All Michigan Charismatic Renewal Conference in Lansing. This was an inspiring time of prayer and meditation. The speakers were great and we enjoyed the workshops and meditations.

We drove to Florida in October. It was our plan to drive down when the weather would be comfortable. We would enjoy a little golf and sun before flying back to Michigan for the holidays. We would fly back in

January, avoiding any difficult driving conditions. I was still chairman of SOS. All the chairmen for the various committees had been recruited, so things were in place for this event.

SOS began on the last Saturday in December for one week. Things were going smoothly with everyone doing their job. One day after being at SOS during the breakfast time, I went on to Birthright to be at the office until 3:00 p.m. I was at home when Joe called to tell me the wonderful news. Baby Jennifer had arrived at about 4:00 p.m. and all was well. We were so happy and joyful. Oh, how I wished that I could run down and visit them and welcome little Jennifer. As I thought it over, I thought, *Well, why not?*

I called the airlines to check out possibilities. There was a flight that left Detroit at 9:30 a.m., arriving in Cincinnati at 10:30 a.m., with a return flight at 3:30 p.m., arriving in Detroit at 4:40 p.m. I was due at SOS at 6:30 p.m., so it would work out just fine. I talked it over with John. He had other plans for that day, but he encouraged me to go. We would go to SOS together that evening, and I could tell him all about it on the way. So I booked it!

The next day I went to SOS for the breakfast period as usual and then left for the airport. The flight was on time, and Joe was there to meet my flight. We went directly to the hospital. I stopped briefly at the hospital gift shop and bought the cutest teddy bear that they had. It was such a thrill to see that both mother and baby Jenny were well and happy. Linda was so joyful. Jenny was a chubby little girl with a mass of black hair. I remembered that my mother had told me that I had hair like that when I was born. I wondered if her hair would all fall out and would come in blonde, too. Sure enough it eventually did. Later, Linda's mother and father arrived, and we all had a great visit together.

My return flight was just as prompt, so I was able to go to SOS as planned. In thinking about it, I was so thankful that all the pieces had fallen in place so well. Linda's mother would be with Linda when she and baby Jenny returned home. I did not want to intrude on that special time, so my hospital visit was perfect. John and I would plan a visit for a later time.

It turned out that Joe, Linda and Jennifer flew down to Florida to spend a week with us in February. This was John's first visit with Jenny.

We all had a grand time. The weather was perfect, and it was restful and pleasant for all of us.

We had been retired now for over a year, and John seemed to be doing just fine. I wondered if it was because he had less stress now than when he was working. Maybe I had just imagined it. But, oops! Right after I had this thought, it all happened again. John had been working on our income taxes. I had submitted all my paper work of our charitable donations and the farm bills and files. It had been spread out on our dining room table for a couple of weeks. Every night he would spend three or four hours on it. When I asked him about it, he was abrupt and indicated that it was more complicated this year.

Finally, I said, "Let me help you with it this year. Perhaps now is the time for me to learn how to do this."

He readily agreed. We had a tax attorney do all the final work, but we had to submit our data and fill out the booklet that the attorney sent us each year. As I looked it over, I realized that every evening he had been going over and over that first page, checking the same data. With the two of us working together, we finished it all in two nights. What a relief! I knew then that I needed to get medical help for him if it was available.

I decided that it would be wise for both of us to get physicals and have an Internist in Florida in case we needed it. When I made the appointment, John was playing golf and did not hear what I said. I indicated that I suspected that he had Alzheimer's and asked him to check John for that. I requested that he not worry John about his findings, but I wanted to be informed of his opinion and asked him to call me at home with the results. After our visit, the doctor called me and told that I should not be concerned. John was very healthy and had a strong heart and lung system. That was of some comfort, but I thought that the doctor did not see what I saw, living with John every day. John did have short term memory loss, and I was aware of it.

Well, there was not much I could do about it. All the reading I had done indicated that there was no known cure for this disease, if it was Alzheimer's. I would continue to read and keep up with the Journals of Medicine to see if there had been any progress to report.

We heard from our friends that we had met on our African trip that planned to travel to China. Because of a violent student demonstration at Tienanmen Square, all travel from other countries to China had been canceled until further notice. We began to consider other travel destinations for this year. Perhaps we could visit China at another time.

It was an "0" year and there were trips to Oberammergau. Many people made it a habit to go every ten years. After talking it over, we decided that there were so many other, interesting places to visit, so we continued to research.

In October, we heard that there was a trip to Medjugorija, Yugoslavia being planned for July. It was being conducted by a priest from the Miami area. We looked the information over carefully and decided we should go. We had been hearing about this for a couple of years. There were five young people from that area that had been having recurring apparitions of the Blessed Mother. She had repeatedly urged everyone to continue to pray the rosary. Also, she predicted that there might be terrible suffering and difficulties for the people in that area in the near future. But this could be averted, if enough people prayed for this intention.

It was amazing to us that this had occurred in Yugoslavia, but we soon learned that it was quite a distance from John's father's home town. It was interesting to us, so we did a little research and decided to join this tour. It would be a wonderful time of prayer and we wanted to be there and experience it ourselves. Was it really authentic? A present day apparition was certainly important and worth investigating. When we returned to Michigan, we talked it over with Sister Lucille. She had heard about Medjugorija also and was quite excited about it. We decided to invite her to join us and we would pay her way. We wanted to treat her, as she had been so much help when the prayer group had been established. Perhaps she could find another person to go, too, and be her roommate.

It all came together beautifully. There was a woman in our prayer group that Sister Lucille had been close to, so she chose that one to go with us. We left on July 25th and returned ten days later. What an experience we had!

This trip was very different from any other trip that we had experienced. The small village of Medjugorija, Yugoslavia was located in an area away from other large cities. There were no hotels, and only a few restaurants there before the apparitions began. But amazingly the villagers had been inspired to build a fairly large Catholic Church for this little farming community, long before it had become a tourist attraction. Now this church was the center of activities for this area.

Housing had been arranged for all of us in private homes. It was there that we were graciously welcomed. Evidently, several families got together and opened their largest home for the visitors. This was the guest house that was prepared for us. The members of several homes bunked together and shared the work of preparing meals and serving the foreign visitors. The adjacent villages participated in this housing and meals program, so it had become quite a financial boom to this part of the country. It was quite a project to prepare for the many foreign visitors that flocked to this area.

We found our rooms adequate, clean and inviting. Our hosts and hostesses greeted us warmly. Although they did not speak English, they had learned a few words and phrases to provide answers in regard to our accommodations and needs. This trip was well escorted, and our guides scheduled an orientation meeting for all of us in a central location, for an hour after our arrival.

At that meeting we were told where and when we would be able to meet the young people who had witnessed the apparitions. We were given information about the history of this area, points of interest, times of Masses in the church, and various activities that had been scheduled, followed by a questions and answer period. Now, we were prepared to go about and make a visit to the church and investigate the little central business district of this town.

Our days usually started with Mass at the church. It was amazing to see the variety of nationalities of the many people that filled this church each morning. There were Germans, French, Italians, Irish, Spanish, as well as Americans and Englishmen, and probably other countries represented which we did not recognize, at those morning Masses. Frequently there were priests from various countries that co-celebrated each Mass. It was a very prayerful time for all of us. It was like a retreat, except for the special events.

Several times during the week, we were invited to a private home to hear from one of the young people who had witnessed these apparitions. Everyone from our group had been invited, because we shared the same language. A facilitator would be present to help translate for the young people if they couldn't find the right words in that language. We knew from our previous visit to Yugoslavia that various languages were taught in their schools. We were very impressed with their sincerity, and the fact that, when each one reported their experiences during the apparitions, there were no experiences that were exactly the same. The central message conveyed by Our Blessed Mother was always very much the same. She implored all of us to frequently pray the rosary. Wonderful things had happened as a direct result of these prayers, as attested by these young people. It certainly was a faith builder to hear about their experiences. These apparitions are still occurring today.

Outside the church, we noticed portable confessionals lined up, perhaps as many as eight or more. When a priest was available to hear confessions, he would post a sign on one of the doors to indicate the language in which the sacrament could be heard. Sometime during this visit we all decided to go to confession.

We had been told that several years ago, before all the excitement of the apparitions had occurred, a large cross had been placed on the top of the highest mountain in this area and could be seen for miles. The path up the mountain was a fairly easy climb, but it was suggested that if we wanted to go up, we should arrange for a car to take us to the entrance to shorten our walk for the day. One cool morning we decided that today would be the day, and we made the arrangements.

We were directed to the starting point of the path up the mountain. It was not too difficult at first, but, as we got higher, the path became steeper. There were places along the way to stop and rest on the benches there and enjoy the view. When we reached the top, the view was wonderful. The cross was very impressive and much taller than we thought it would be. There was about a four foot high stone wall that encircled this area. We decided that this would be a great place to say the rosary.

Other groups arrived from time to time, and we had interesting conversations with the other tourists. We were rested then and decided to start back down the path, thinking it would be much easier going down than up. Wrong! We found it a little difficult, as it curved and sometimes went down steeply. We negotiated these curves carefully, as we didn't want to stumble and fall. At this point, Sister Lucille was getting tired. It was then that two young girls came by and, sensing the situation, they took her by her arms, one on each side of her, and they fairly flew down the mountain side. She arrived at the starting point at least twenty or thirty minutes before John and me. We laughed about it, as Sister Lucille's guardian angels had arrived at just the right moment.

One evening, it was announced at dinner that the visionaries had been informed that Our Blessed Lady would make an appearance on the mountain that evening. It was suggested that, if we wanted to go, we should finish our dinner promptly, start out soon, and bring our flash lights. There was a buzz of excitement. All of us decided to go, as they told us that this path was an easy trail.

That evening was warm and it was a pleasant climb up the path that began at the outskirts of the village. We could hear other groups ahead of us and behind us singing hymns or reciting the rosary. There was laughter and a hum of conversation. In the distance we could hear dogs barking and prayers in various languages. Our group began to pray, followed by some charismatic songs. There was a strong feeling of excitement and expectant faith.

We had been climbing for some time when it seemed that we had reached a level area. We paused there and looked at the bright stars and moon above. We began wondering if we would see the Blessed Virgin. A group near us had just started a prayer in German when suddenly everything stopped at once. No one spoke. No one sang. No dogs barked. No children cried. No one coughed. It was like a switch had been turned. It seemed like several minutes passed in complete silence. Then, as promptly as it had started, the quiet time was over. People started to talk and laugh again. The singing started, and we all turned around and trouped back down the mountain.

When we returned to our rooms, we realized that we had been gone more than four hours. It seemed like the climb up and back from the mountain took about thirty minutes. The interlude of complete silence seemed to be about four minutes. I reviewed it all in my mind and thought, "How could it have been four hours or more? How could it have happened like that? Surely there had been thousands of people on the mountain that night. To have everything stop at once and then resume again at the same moment would have been impossible in a crowd like that!"

Yet that is what happened. Clearly something had happened that night on the mountain. When we returned, we got ready for bed and fell asleep promptly. The next morning we woke at the usual time and we realized that we were more alert than usual, rested and felt full of peace and joy. At morning Mass the next day, it was announced that the Blessed Virgin had appeared that night to several of the visionaries, and the message was reported. She had thanked us all for coming and told us to expect that our prayers would be answered. She requested that we continue to pray the rosary.

What had really happened that night? It seemed that a miracle had occurred. Many people had climbed that hill that night in the dark, yet no one fell or got hurt. No one seemed to have been distressed in any way. We all became quiet at exactly the same moment, and when the interval was over, we all realized it, simultaneously, and returned to our rooms. I guess we will never understand these things, but this experience made a huge impression on all of us.

We returned home on August first. It was great to be home again. At the next prayer meeting, all of us shared our experiences of this trip with the group, yet it was still incomprehensible that it all happened the way that it had.

There was lots of catching up to do with our family and friends. Jack and Karen were expecting another baby in late August. When we returned in the early spring, they had told us about it. How exciting! This would be their fourth child. Karen had asked me if I would come to help out when she was in the hospital. I told her that I was very sorry, but I couldn't leave John alone that long, and it might be too much if we both came. They knew that John had been having difficulties.

A few days later, I called her back and suggested that perhaps I could help her in some other way. I would like to invite Meredith and Molly to come over to spend a week or so at our house on Hammond Lake. We could call it "Summer Camp at Grandma's House." That way they would not feel pushed out of the way because of the new baby. Kevin was just over two years old, but still took naps, so perhaps he was too young to come. At that time, Karen had said that she could not part with the girls for that long. Oh, how I wished that I could help in some way.

One day shortly after we returned from our trip, Karen called and said she had decided that having the girls come over was a good idea and asked if Kevin could come, too.

I said yes and that I would be delighted, but I didn't think it was a good idea for Kevin to come, as he might wake up in the night and want his Mother and Dad.

Karen agreed, so it was decided that I would fly over on Saturday when Jack and the girls could meet me at the airport, and after a brief visit, we three would then fly back to Detroit on the next flight. I was familiar with the schedules, as I had sometimes flown over and rented a car to go to Dixon for a visit with my mother. I thought that either John could come with me or he would have a golf game, so he would be okay for those three hours.

Jack, Karen and all their children were there to meet me when I arrived. The girls had never been on an airplane before, so they were very excited about the whole process and couldn't wait to get started. I had a brief visit with everyone, but as soon as the flight was announced, Meredith and Molly wanted to board now! The fun began.

When we returned to Hammond Lake, John and a friend had been watching a football game on TV. He had been so engrossed in watching the game that he hardly realized I had been gone. Meredith and Molly had enjoyed the flight and were delighted to be at Hammond Lake. Of course they wanted to know where they would sleep. It had been a long standing tradition that whenever they came for a visit, there was always a bed gift on each of their beds. Usually it was a little gift, like a small toy or a new tooth brush, but this time I had decided to give each of them their own beach towel, with their name tag sewed on it. They liked that gift.

After they had opened their gifts, they wanted to go down to the beach to check out the lake area. I had planned a picnic supper on the deck, so, while John started the grill, I brought out the other side dishes but kept an eye on the girls.

The days flew by. They were filled with boat rides in the paddle boat or row boat, swimming in the lake, story time in the afternoon, and easy arts and crafts projects. Natalie, the girl that lived two doors down on the beach, was just about the same age as Meredith. Soon, she spotted our visitors and joined in all the activities. Most nights she asked to stay for dinner, which was fine with us. But when her dad came to bring her home each night, there were tears in her eyes because she couldn't stay all night.

The next weekend Joe, Linda, and Jenny came up to see us all and find out how we were getting along. While they were there, we got the news that the baby had arrived, a little girl, and all was well. Of course Meredith wanted to talk with her mother on the phone. Later, she came striding out to the deck and announced proudly, "The baby is Brogan!"

But I had a bad moment because I thought she had said, "The baby is broken!" Oh, the baby's name is Brogan! After that was cleared up, we celebrated the wonderful news.

Monday, I announced that we would all go shopping for a gift for the new baby and perhaps a gift for Kevin, because he hadn't been able to come to Summer Camp. Later, when the time was right, John and I drove the girls back to Barrington and had a brief visit with the new baby, Kevin, and Jack and Karen. Kevin was excited to get a present, too. Then we continued on to visit my mother at Heritage Square and show her pictures of the new baby before returning to Hammond Lake.

A tradition was born. The next summer Meredith and Molly called to ask me when Summer Camp would be and could Kevin come, too? So I had to make hard and fast rules about Camp. We established that you had to be at least three years old and no diapers or bottles were allowed. Yes! Kevin qualified that year, as he had achieved all those goals.

Later at Christmas time, Jenny heard all about Summer Camp with Kevin, Meredith and Molly. She had hopes to qualify for Summer Camp in the coming year. She would be three soon and was working on the other two requirements. Sure enough, she made it to Summer Camp the next year. Then, we decided to have the Dads fly in with their campers, arriving at about the same time. John and I would be there to meet their flights. The dads would have coffee together and then fly back to Cincinnati and Chicago, respectively.

By the year of 1993, two more grandchildren arrived, one in Cincinnati, Lauren, in January, and Colin in Chicago in June during Summer Camp. I hoped that I would be able to continue having Summer Camp until all the grand children had a chance to come, as John's difficulties continued to develop. I quickly remembered the Lord is in charge, and I'll place my trust in Him.

We did go to China the next year, after the First Summer Camp, and we went with the couple we had met on our trip to Kenya. I had read so much about China, and now we would actually see it, and we did! We visited the Great Wall of China, took a three day cruise up the Yangtze River, and five internal flights, within the country of China. The connecting roads were not in good condition, so airplane travel was used. The country is vast with large industrial areas, highly populated cities and varied countrysides with lakes and mountains. We spent three weeks in China and I'm sure that there was much we missed.

We visited the site, which was being excavated to reveal the many terracotta soldiers that had been buried with their ancient king. It had been discovered only a few years before. A museum was being built on that site to house the many treasures being discovered in that area. It seemed that this ancient king was very forward thinking and revolutionary.

The kings before him wanted to have his staff and certain family members buried with him so that they could continue to serve him when he entered the life after death. So he ordered the people to be put to death when he died and their bodies would be buried with him. But this king decided that there would be no need for all these people to die with him. It would be adequate for replicas of these people to be made, and these images should be placed in his tomb when he entered the next life. Each of these terracotta soldiers were images of real people. They were truly works of art, life size, and resembled a specific person. Each had different expressions on their faces. They were in various positions, some standing, others sitting. Also, he had ordered carriages and pieces of equipment to be buried with him in his tomb. They were continuing to discover many other objects while they excavated this site. We found it fascinating!

I was most impressed with the people of China. They are very intelligent, friendly, artistic, and talented people. Our Chinese guides were fluent in English. When we had a chance to try to communicate with the ordinary people who did not speak our language, they were delighted to reach out to us and found ways to tell us things through gestures and smiles. It is a very highly populated country. The big cities have large, triple buses connected to each other with an accordion-type connection so they could negotiate corners. Every bus would be jammed-full of people. The streets were full of bicycles and bicycle drawn carts, which transported all sorts of things. I saw one cart filled with different kinds of fresh vegetables. The vegetables were carefully and artistically arranged, so that they were perfectly balanced. The result was like a traveling piece of art or still life painting.

There were many places to visit: high rise buildings, museums, natural caves and rivers. The hotels where we stayed were very modern and elegant and were used only by tourists from foreign countries. The Chinese people stayed in crowded, more ordinary hotels. I have read that this country is much more advanced now than when we saw it. We saw very few cars then. But now I understand that there are many personal cars in use.

At one point, we were on a tour of public buildings and had a brief cruise on the river. Our American tour and a tour of Japanese people were on the same ship as we viewed this city from the river. I was sitting next to one of the Japanese women. She wanted to try out her English and engaged me in conversation. She spoke very well, was pleasant and friendly. She asked me if we planned to travel in Japan. I said no. That we would stop briefly in Japan, but it was just a stop-over at the airport before our long flight home. We had quite a long trip just seeing China. She was disappointed that we were not visiting her country and encouraged us to visit Japan, describing some of the sites that we might visit. That brief encounter helped me to overcome some of my antagonism and prejudice against the Japanese people for attacking us at the beginning of WWII.

Our time had evaporated and it was almost time to start our trip home. On our return trip, we left Cancun very early in the morning, had a brief stop in Japan and then the long, non-stop flight from there to Detroit. People have asked me how long this return flight took. I really can't say, because we went through so many time zones and kept changing our watches. So I said it was five meals and three full length movies before we arrived in Detroit, very tired but joyful with all the memories of the sights and sounds of China alive in our memories. I knew that I could never take John on such an ambitious trip like that again. But, we were so thankful that it had been such an enjoyable experience for both of us.

Great Sorrows, Great Joys!

●————————————————————————————●

After we returned from China, the second annual Summer Camp was held, and by then Kevin had met all the requirements, so he experienced his first session of Summer Camp. It was fun for all of us!

Later when I visited Mother, I could see that she was frail, more than when I had seen her at the last visit. She was recovering from a broken hip, and it had not healed well. She was still in a wheelchair, and it seemed that it might be with her for the rest of her life. But her spirit and mind continued to be strong.

I had been working on preparing a family history, complete with family trees on both sides of our family. I wanted to check out certain details with Mother while she was still here and herself. She had written some of her family history, but I wanted to clarify some of the facts. I also contacted Rita, John's older cousin, to fill in some of the blanks of the Hanzel side of our family history.

After preparing a complete history, including pictures of many of our ancestors, their stories and family trees, I typed it up on our computer, and prepared five copies, one for each of our children and one for us. I decided to give them their copies as part of their Christmas presents. I was pleasantly surprised to learn that they were all pleased, and all of them were very interested in learning more about their roots.

In fact later when Kevin was in second grade in Catholic School, the Nun that was Kevin's teacher that year said. "Now today, class, we are going to talk about our family and its history. Do any of you know your grandparents?" Then, she went on to talk about family trees.

Kevin waved his hand excitedly. When she called on him, he said, "We have a book about our family tree, and we can trace our line all the way back to Noah!"

"I would really like to see that family tree," she replied.

Kevin said, "I'll bring it in tomorrow."

Sure enough, there was a Noah Chapman, nine or ten generations back in our direct line.

The family tree had been read and was meaningful to our children and grandchildren.

Almost immediately there was a new entry to the family trees as Lauren was born to Joe and Linda in early January, 1993. We were delighted to know that all was well. Now we could begin our drive to Florida, going the long way around. We went first to Dixon to visit with Mother and tell her the news about Lauren then on to Barrington and next to Cincinnati before continuing on to Florida, arriving in late January. Ah! Lots of sunshine, golf and bridge was in our future.

Two months later I got the call I had been dreading! The nurses in Dixon informed us to come as soon as possible, because they could tell that Mother was failing rapidly. We flew up immediately, but she had passed just before we arrived. It was a sad time for all of us. I took comfort in the fact that Mother had lived a very long, eventful, and interesting life. She was ninety-six years old, she had touched many people through her many years of teaching school, and had raised the eight of us, her sister's six children and the two of her own. Her marriage had been happy but relatively short, only about twenty-nine years.

But for me it was the end of that generation. It was all so final. I needed to get started on the plans, and there were decisions to be made immediately. I knew what my mother's wishes were in regard to the final plans and funeral arrangements and the specifics of her will. But it was difficult for me to realize that now I was in charge. Later, all the details needed to be worked out, in regard to settling her estate. But, my recurring thought was, "This is the end of a generation."

Fortunately, Mother and I had spent lots of time together and had many long talks. She told me that she did not expect that Anne or any of the cousins would come to her funeral. Mother thought it would be too difficult for Anne, so I should not insist upon her coming. She cautioned me to not expect any of the cousins to come, either. And she was right about all of it.

Several times I asked John for help with some of the details, but he always answered that he thought I should do just what I thought was best. I prayed about it all.

Later, I realized that John had declined to the point that it was not possible for him to decide any of these things. But, thank God, it all came together beautifully. All of our children came; even Linda was able to come. They made arrangements for Jenny to stay with Linda's sister, but baby Lauren was too young to be without her Mother, so Lauren was the only great grandchild present, as Karen and their children did not come. They were too young to come.

Before we returned to Florida, we went to Heritage Square to thank the staff for all that they had done for Mother and to pick up the final bill and her personal affects.

But the office manager said, "There is no need for you to give us any payment at this time, as the bill would be very small, if any. She died on the last day of March, about 11:00 p.m. so there will be hardly anything at all."

Then, I remembered what Mother had said, "Well, the only thing to do is die on the last day of the month, and I intend to make it a long one! Then everything will come out even." I almost laughed out loud when I realized that this was Mother's final joke for me.

After a brief visit in Barrington to see Jack and Karen and the children, we flew back to Florida to resume our life there. But there was a feeling of deep sadness and loss with me for quite a long time.

We drove back to Hammond Lake in late spring. As we came into Oakland County, Michigan, we could see how dry everything was. So I said to John, "When we arrive at Hammond Lake, I would like you to help me, and we will carry our luggage down to the laundry room. I will sort things out and start doing the laundry. While I am doing that, I would like you to activate our sprinkling system. I am sure our lawn will be very dry."

John had a puzzled look on his face, and he asked, "Do we have a sprinkling system?"

"Yes," I said. "You know, we pump water out of the lake. There are three zones, and we need to get some water on our lawn as soon as possible."

He continued to look puzzled. Then I said, "Don't worry. When we get there, I'll show you where the controls are located. We disconnect them during the winter. The controls are all in the garage."

Well, when we got home, it was obvious that John had no memory of it at all. Fortunately our next door neighbor was home, so he came over and the two of them got it all going, as he had a similar system. So it all worked out this time, but I began to realize that his memory loss was more advanced than I knew.

Later when I had time alone, I prayed about what to do. This time He answered promptly, *Yes. Now is the time to sell this house.*

I was shocked! I loved this home and thought that we would have it for many more years. But I could see that it was too large a place to continue to leave empty for long periods of time. Still I was reluctant to sell it.

Then He told me how much to ask for it and stated a figure. Also, He assured me that He would help me to follow through on all the details. So I followed His advice and started to take action to do so.

In the next few weeks, I contacted three Realtors but, when I told them the price that I expected, they were a little doubtful. However, the third one thought that she might have a buyer that would be interested. So I signed with her.

She called me the next day and made an appointment to show the property. We were settled in by then, so John and I decided to play golf, so that we would not be there when it was shown. In the next several weeks she showed it to the same people several times.

Finally, when she called again to make an appointment to show it to them for the seventh time, I said, "Yes. But for goodness sake! This is the seventh time and the last one! Surely they can decide after seeing it so many times."

I half hoped that they wouldn't buy it, but later the next day, she came back to us with the signed contract for the exact amount that He had told me. So naturally, we signed it. Now we had two months until closing to find our next home.

The next morning I was sick in bed. I felt like I was coming down with a cold. I felt sick at heart. I could not visualize where to go or where to look for our next condo or home. I thought I would just stay home in bed and pray all day about what to do next.

John was helpful and said he would do the errands, as there was banking that needed to be done, as well as things to take to the post office. When he came back, he said, "How do you feel? On my way home I drove by a condo community, and I think it might be just what we are looking for. So, if you are feeling up to it, let's go and have a look."

We went, and I was delighted! There were two lakes in this area and for sale signs on several of condos. It was only about a mile from our present home, and it was in St. Hugo's parish. Later I called our Realtor to make an appointment to see what was available in that area.

We bought a condo and requested a closing as soon as possible, as we wanted to make a few improvements before we moved in. It all turned out very well. I wanted to up-date the kitchen with new cabinets, sink, cook-top stove, ovens and refrigerator. Also, we wanted to re-do the floor in the foyer and kitchen with ceramic floor tiles and replace all of the carpeting.

I took lots of measurements. Only then could I visualize the space. I knew that we had to pare down and dispose of some of our furniture. Jack and Karen and Joe and Linda came over with their vans and took some of the extra furniture. Janet also came down and took a few things back with her. I gave the rest to Goodwill. The redecorating was mostly completed before we moved.

Our condo was a two story, built on the side of a hill. The lower level had sliding glass doors to the patio from the family room, which had a fireplace and a wet bar, complete with a small refrigerator and closet. There were two bedrooms and a bath on that level. Also, the laundry room and furnace room were on that level. Upstairs there was a nice sized living room with dining area, kitchen with eating area, and a half bath. The front door opened into the foyer with access to the kitchen, garage, and living room. The master bedroom, with full bath and large closets, was off the living room. There was a screened porch off the living room, overlooking the back.

There were two lakes, a smaller one in the front of the complex, used for fishing only, and Fox Lake, which was down the hill from our condo. This lake was larger and is the one used for boating and swimming. There was a small sandy beach area with a boat dock. A float, which was out in the lake, was a nice destination for swimmers. Out the front door and just down the street was the club house and swimming pool. I could visualize that this would all be great for Summer Camp. And John and I would enjoy it, too.

We had scheduled Summer Camp for that year in August. This would be the first year for Jennifer. There would be Meredith, Molly, and Kevin from Chicago and Jenny from Cincinnati. That first night when we had our camp meeting on the screened porch, I announced that we now had a camp flag. It would be flown only when camp was in session. I showed it to them. I had made it of three strips of nylon: the top strip was pale blue, the next strip white, and the bottom strip was blue-green. There were four red stars on the flag this year, and, as more campers came, there would a star added for each one.

The rule was that the first camper to come upstairs in the morning, fully dressed, teeth brushed and hair combed and ready for breakfast would have the honor and responsibility to Troop the Colors. This referred to carrying the flag around the inside or the outside, depending on the weather and the desire of the person leading the marching. This would happen after we all were dressed and had breakfast. Everyone else would follow and march behind the flag. Then the flag would be placed in the flag holder outside the front door. After that, we would have our morning camp meeting. Just before our evening camp meeting, that same person would Troop the Colors, and then the flag would be returned to the front hall closet until the next morning.

After camp was over, some of our neighbors asked me, "What kind of flag is that?"

I told them that it was our "Summer Camp Flag."

Our first camp meeting for that year continued. We discussed some of the things we might do, had our night-time prayers, and then it was time for everyone to go to bed.

Our traditions at camp had grown along the way. It seemed that if something was added, they wanted to do that every year afterwards, and it became part of the program.

The next morning after breakfast and Trouping the Colors, we met on the screened porch for our morning Camp Meeting for morning prayers and to decide what we wanted to do that day. They were excited about checking out the swimming pool and the lake. We decided we would go to the pool in the morning and go to the lake in the afternoon. They wanted to know when it would be Pizza Day. The year before, we had made pizza for lunch, and it had been a big hit. I had not started the dough, so if they wanted pizza, I would have to make it the night before and let it rise. They decided we would do that tomorrow.

When we had pizza, they watched me make the dough. Then the next morning I showed them how to work the dough and gave everyone their own piece to work on, pat it out, and add just what they wanted for its topping from the various choices I had available, which included tomato sauce and a large variety of vegetables, cheese, and bits of meat. The only requirement was that they had to eat their own pizza. It was great fun! Kevin asked if it was okay to throw the dough up in the air, and I said it was okay, but if they threw it too high and it stuck on the ceiling, too bad! No pizza for that person. That was the only day during camp that they had soda, but, Coke is so good with pizza, so we had it on that day only.

Sunday, we all went to the Mass, and then went to the pool right after that. When we went to the pool for the first time, I would conduct a swimming test for each camper. If they passed the swimming test, they were allowed to go to the deep end. If not, they were restricted to the shallow end only. Meredith and Molly passed, but Kevin and Jenny needed additional instruction. John liked to be with the children, so he supervised the shallow end, but of course we both watched them carefully.

In the afternoon we went to the lake and checked it out by riding all around the lake in the paddle boat before we went swimming. John sat on a chair in the shade and dozed while we did this. I showed them that there was a golf course at the far end of the Lake. On the hole near the edge of the lake, the golfers had to shoot over that edge of the water. Sometimes, they missed and their ball would end up in the lake. I explained that the course was closed on Mondays, so maybe tomorrow would be a good day to go ball hawking there.

That project turned out to be a big hit. We would bring down a couple of ball retrievers, and go out in the paddle boat. When we spotted a golf ball, they would try to fish out the ball using one of the retrievers. It took lots of concentration and eye–hand coordination to fish them out. They treasured their finds and proudly gave the best ones to their dads. Over the years, they collected an amazing assortment of balls.

In the later afternoon, there was story time, which changed as they changed. At first I showed Shirley Temple movies by showing a part of the movie each day. Later, it became Treasure Chest Time. Before Camp I would stock the old trunk that had belonged to my dad, with items all wrapped up in tissue paper, one for each day of camp. When we came in from swimming, I would announce that Treasure Chest Time would begin in fifteen minutes if everyone was dressed in dry clothes and their swimming suits and towels had been placed on the laundry room rack to dry.

Then we would all gather in the family room around the trunk. I would open it, and they would take turns requesting what item we would open that day. Then I would carefully unwrap it and tell them the story of that item. Sometimes it would be a small item, like a precious wedding gift of mine or my mother's. It might be a quilt, like the hand embroidered crazy quilt made by my great grandmother at the turn of the century from the 1800 to 1900. One year I put in the sword carried by my great grandfather in the Civil War. They had seen his picture in the family history book, but I made sure I had my copy handy to show them the picture again of him in uniform with that sword. I would proceed to tell more about each item and the people who had been a part of it.

One year when all seven were at camp, I placed my wedding dress in the Treasure chest. When they chose that item, I carefully removed the tissue paper and spread it all out on the back of the sofa, with the train spread out behind it. I had our wedding album close by and I showed them the pictures of our wedding, telling them when it was and where and all about it. Then Colin, who was only about three at the time, looked at the pictures of the younger Jane and John, and asked, " Did you guys ever have kids?"

The older ones laughed and said, "Sure. They had Dad, Uncle Jim, Uncle Joe and Aunt Janet."

"Oh," he said. He looked around at all of us and suddenly the relationships of all of us fell into place for him.

Another innovation was "The Skit". After story time I announced that I needed to do some things in the kitchen. But it was time for them to begin working on their skit. The first time, they all asked, what it a skit? I explained that they needed to prepare to do something for entertainment on family night when their parents would be here for dinner. It could be to sing a song, act out a little play, or whatever they decided to do. They had a great time figuring out what they wanted to do each year.

One year John and I had purchased a pair of marionettes in Poland. I showed them how to work the strings. I prepared a blank, three piece folding screen made of cardboard to use as a background. I suggested that they have the stage be up on the bar, and the ones controlling the strings would be standing on chairs, behind the screen, in back of the bar. They had to write the script. When they had decided on the script, I would help them paint the appropriate scenery on the screen. There were lots of giggles and laughter, as they learned how to control the puppets and worked out the dialogue for the play.

One year John and I had attended a Charismatic Conference and had learned a new song, "Shine, Jesus. Shine". They learned it very quickly, so they all sang it together. I had given them each a tiny flashlight for their bed gift that year. I showed them how to use their flashlights, to turn them on and hold them under their chins when they came to the Chorus "Shine, Jesus, Shine!" That year Janet would be coming down to visit on family night and that would be the day of her birthday. So I suggested that they might all want to sing Happy Birthday to Janet at the very end of their skit.

It was then that Jenny, who had been to per-school, announced that she could sing Happy Birthday in French. I said, "Let's hear you." And sure enough she could. We all decided that Jenny would sing it as a solo at the end of the program.

I would give the younger ones a small basket and a pair of scissors with the instructions that they were to cut some lettuces leaves from the plants that were growing at the edge of the patio on the lower level. Each year I would plant leaf lettuce there among the flowers. I might suggest, "Tonight let's have 8 red leaves and 9 green leaves." I had instructed them earlier on just how to cut them so that the plants would not be damaged. While that was happening, the other campers set the table in the dining room, or would carry down the dishes and set the picnic table on the patio. Everyone helped while I was preparing dinner for all of us on Friday afternoon,

The final day of camp was the day their parents arrived, Friday evening. We would be ready for "The Skit", followed by the dinner we had all helped to prepare. Then Camp would officially be over. The rest of the weekend would be family visiting time.

One Sunday when we all went to Mass together, as we stood up to sing a hymn, a golf ball rolled out of Kevin's shorts pocket, and it began to roll all the way down to the foot of the main altar. Followed closely behind was Kevin, who had scrambled out of his seat, pounced on it when it came to rest, and secured it in his hands while he scurried back to all of us with his favorite golf ball.

Fortunately, everyone was standing and singing, so only a few people observed this incident. The golf ball was one of Kevin's finest that he had retrieved from the lake, and he had planned to present it to his Dad but hated to part with it. He decided to wait and give it to him on a very special occasion.

There are many fond memories of Summer Camp for all of us. But, sadly, I had to stop having Summer Camp, as John's condition gradually grew worse over time. I was thankful that we had been able to have all those Summer Camp Sessions, and that eventually all the grandchildren had come for at least one year. Actually, we had Summer Camp for seven years in a row. We had two sessions at Hammond and five sessions at the new condo. It had turned out to be a great site for summer camp. I really missed having it, but I knew it was time to stop, as John needed my full attention by then. After we returned to Florida the year that we sold our house on Hammond Lake, I thought that now we would be going back and forth from our Condo North to Condo South. But it didn't work out that way. Our Florida Condo was on the second floor. There were no elevators, and I began to realize that it was getting more and more difficult for John to go up and down. Also, we didn't have a garage there, only a carport, and it was hard on the car to be left there in the hot summer with inadequate cover. Now I realized that it would be wise to make a change in our plans.

In my private prayer time I began to hear that it was time to buy a house or build a house that had both its own garage and swimming pool but, also, no flight of stairs. I wondered how John would respond to another change, and I wondered how to make this happen.

When it was almost Valentine's Day, I told John, "Wow! Wait until you find out what I am going to give you for Valentine's Day!"

After giving him lots of hints, I finally agreed to tell him what it was. We went for a drive one day and I told him I'd like to drive by and let him see his present. It was an empty lot in the Forest. I told him that we would have lots of fun designing a house, just what we wanted, and that it would all be on one floor, have its own pool and a two car garage. I hadn't really bought that lot. It was a place to start and begin thinking about it all.

He looked puzzled and worried. He said, "I don't think that I am up to working out the plans for a new house and watching it being built. Couldn't we find one that is already built that would be just what we want?"

Then I realized that it would be too much for him, so I agreed to look and try to find something already built that we would both like.

With prayer and His help, I soon found the perfect one! It was in the Forest, on a small lake, less than a mile from our current condo, with a large swimming pool, two car garage and all the things we wanted. John readily agreed and we arranged to buy it.

It turned out to be a great blessing. With our growing family, the children and grandchildren loved coming down for Christmas and/or spring break. It had four bedrooms, two and a half baths, with a large living room, formal dining room, large family room, and a lovely kitchen. The pool was screened in with lots of space around it for outdoor furniture. Actually it was much nicer than what I had envisioned earlier, and it was much easier to just move in and enjoy it. We moved all our condo furniture and, with the few extra pieces that I was able to purchase from the former owner, it was all ready to be enjoyed promptly. We moved in and never regretted the purchase. Over time, I did some re-decorating. It was a very pleasant home for us. That year, we just flipped our living arrangements. Now, we had our condo up North and our big house in Florida, instead of the other way around.

One day, John asked, "Where are we going on our next trip?"

I really had not thought much about it, as it had been such a full year, with Mother's passing and buying and selling condos and houses. Also, I thought that the China trip might have been too much for him, as it had been so special but exhausting. I asked where he wanted to go next, and his response was, "You always plan such great trips, let's look to see what is available."

Eventually, after combing through lots of brochures, we decided on a Baltic Cruise for the next summer. It started out by a flight to Copenhagen, Denmark, where the famous Mermaid is depicted on an island nearby. After a day or so there was time to visit the various points of interest, we boarded our cruise ship and made our way around the Baltic Sea, stopping in Germany, Poland, Estonia, Russia, Finland, Sweden and some of the small islands along the way. It turned out to be just wonderful! It was all very interesting and pleasant. It was easy for us, as we did not have to check in and out of hotels. Most of the time, the ship was our hotel. There were so many highlights for us on this trip, because most of the cities were in countries we had never visited.

In Poland we visited the Marine Stockyard, where recently there had been an up-rising. We visited a department store, but, sadly, it was not very well stocked. Later we visited a cultural center, and a group of citizens in native garb danced the Polish waltzes with great enthusiasm.

Estonia and Russia were wonderful areas to visit. In Estonia we visited a lovely seaside resort area, which had a wonderful view of the Baltic Sea. It was all very interesting, and the people were friendly. Our cruise ship was small enough to go up the river to St. Petersburg, where we were docked for three or four days. That gave us enough time to visit many of the places I had heard about and longed to see. The Hermitage Museum was outstanding! There were many fabulous paintings and pieces of art that I had never actually seen; others I had only seen in photos.

We visited government buildings, summer palaces, parks, and attended a concert in the afternoon in a large concert hall. I had an opportunity to have a conversation with a Russian there and was very interested to hear that person express regret that our two countries had not always been on good terms with each other. It found it fascinating.

Finland and Sweden were both very prosperous when we visited and I enjoyed seeing several very lovely churches in the area. People were well dressed, friendly, and their shops were well stocked with many beautiful things. I decided to buy several pieces of their lovely cut glass, which I still have and enjoy.

We returned to Copenhagen and flew back to the States refreshed and renewed, with lovely memories from this trip. It was a very comfortable way to travel. John got along just fine, too. I thought that perhaps we could continue to travel to places in Europe, if we traveled at a comfortable pace.

About a year later, it was time to start thinking about our next trip. The Assistant Pastor at our parish in Florida, Father Toner, announced he would be conducting a trip to visit many of the important Catholic Shrines in Paris. It would also include visits to Lourdes and Fatima along the way.

Wonderful! I thought. This is for us. I had always wanted to visit Lourdes and Fatima. We had been close to these places at other times, but it had not been on the scheduled tour. They didn't want us to leave their tour to visit other places. So now was our chance. I talked it over with John, and he liked the idea. We both knew Father very well. He celebrated Mass for our prayer group once a month. His presence on the tour was especially appealing, as we had great respect and confidence in him. Mass would be celebrated every day of the trip.

The very next day, I went in and made a deposit, so we were fully booked. I had great hopes and expectant faith that surely on this trip to Lourdes, John would be healed completely from Alzheimer's disease.

About a week later, I received a brochure from University of Steubenville describing their next trip. It was a Pilgrimage to follow the footsteps of Pope John Paul, the Second. He was born in Poland and educated in that country. The trip would visit where he became a Priest, Bishop, Cardinal, and finally Pope. Father Scanlon and several other priests would be with this tour, and Mass would be celebrated every day. Oh, how I wanted to go on this trip, also.

Then, I looked closely at the dates for this trip. It began in Vienna, Austria. The date that they would be arriving there from the States to begin the Pilgrimage was three days after the first trip would end in Paris.

I thought, *Wow! Maybe it would all work out! Perhaps we could just stay in Europe and arrange to meet the other trip in Vienna.*

I went right to the phone and talked first with the travel agent for our first trip. She seemed very certain that this would all be possible. So I called Steubenville to see if I could book that trip without the cost of the trip over but to include the transportation for the return trip with this tour. It was all doable! I talked it over with John. He was all for it. So I booked it all. I thought that this might turn out to be very comfortable for John, as we would have two days in Vienna to rest before the next trip began.

I arranged for us to take the train from Paris to Vienna, instead of flying. I thought how pleasant and restful it would be to ride through Europe and see it all from the train. After investigating this, it was arranged for us to leave about 7:30 a.m. from Paris and arrive in Vienna about 9:00 p.m., but of course we would be going through time zones. We booked an excellent Hotel for the two nights that we would be in Vienna. During those days, we rested, arranged for some laundry to be completed, and visited some of the points of interest in that city. Then on the morning of the third day, we planned to take a taxi to the airport in time to meet the flight that would be coming over from the States.

We would be spending nearly the entire month of May in Europe. And it would be so special to be escorted through these wonderful places that we both wanted to visit.

It turned out to be a wonderful time for us. We flew from New York directly to Portugal. First, we visited some of the interesting places in this area before we traveled on to Fatima. There we heard all the stories of this village and visited the lovely Churches that had been built there. It was a very moving experience to actually be there.

On our bus trip on our way to Lourdes, we stopped at a church, and Mass was celebrated at a church where a famous miracle had occurred. We had heard the story many years before. There was a parish priest that was experiencing some doubt concerning the actual presence of Jesus in the Eucharist. One morning, when he came to that part of the Mass when transfiguration occurs, the Host became an actual, visible piece of flesh! A portion of that Host is still on display there, behind glass. It has remained so, after all these years. We were invited to go to the place, where it was on display. What a moving and interesting experience it was for all of us.

We continued on to Lourdes and learned all about the history of this area. This is where miraculous healings have occurred. We were able to go into the baths there and I was so hopeful that John would receive healing. Many different prayer teams had prayed with John for this intention over the past several years. I had expectant faith that, in time, this prayer would be answered. Maybe now is the time at Lourdes.

This area was very crowded with local people and tourists. We had Mass at the main church, which has beautiful white cathedrals, with two levels, up high on the hill. In 1958 Pope Pius X opened this church which is the second largest in the world at this site; only St. Peter's in Rome can accommodate more people. Later we visited the baths there, which are located in a cave like setting. We were taken about to the various points of interest.

We knew the story about Bernadette, but it became real for us when we visited her home. It was believed that the Blessed Virgin Mary began appearing to Bernadette, who was fourteen at the time, in 1858. These appearances occurred eighteen times, until she revealed the healing powers inspired by the Lord of the spring water that pours from a cave in the area. Bernadette was to make this known to as many people as possible. Thousands of people visiting the area have reported healings.

That evening there was a candle light procession from the baths to the main church. It was a moving experience to see all these people with their family members, some in wheelchairs or others very ill, seeking healing. We learned that on a regular basis, nurses volunteer to be present, in order to assist those that need it. It was all very inspiring and beautiful.

Next it was on to Paris to visit the various shrines there, some of which we were unaware existed. Another wonderful trip! On the last night, there was a final banquet in the hotel. At the close of the evening, we said our goodbyes to everyone because in the morning we planned to leave very early to board the train to Vienna. They would be flying back later that morning to the States.

I really enjoyed our train trip to Vienna. It was a comfortable day, watching the scenes of Europe pass by our window. The dining car was nearby, so we had our meals aboard the train. John dozed and rested, so it was a catch-up day for us both. I had that day to review our first trip and to start planning for all the things we would be experiencing when we arrived in Vienna.

It all came together beautifully. The first day we rested, took a stroll through the shops that were in our area, sorted out our clothes and took things to the laundry and dry cleaners. The second day we decided to take the city tour to acquaint ourselves of its history and visit the major points of interest. We visited the major churches in Vienna and learned so much about this city's history. On the morning of the third day, we had breakfast in the hotel and took a cab to the airport in plenty of time to be on hand to greet the Steubenville Group when they arrived from USA.

There were several buses reserved for this tour. They were easy to identify, as they had the Steubenville Tour signs prominently displayed on their windshields. In due time, we all got together and were on our way.

It was a wonderfully escorted trip, well planned, with Mass celebrated each day. The seven priests aboard rotated the Masses, so we quickly became acquainted with all of them.

From Vienna, we drove on to enter Poland where we began our trip to visit all the major places that Pope John Paul II had lived, was educated, and served as priest. It was most interesting to see the village where he was born. There, the family had lived in a humble apartment on the second floor of the building right next to the church. This was the church in which he was baptized, received his first communion, and where he served as altar boy. There were articles there that had belonged to family displayed in the apartment. In a lighted closet enclosed in glass were the vestments that he had worn when he became Priest, Bishop, Cardinal, and finally, Pope. It was such an impressive sight.

There were many highlights along the way. One day, our first stop was at a concentration camp in Poland, where many, many Jews had suffered and been exterminated in gas chambers. We saw how crowded and ugly their living arrangements were. They were forced to work at various strenuous sites and to sleep in three tiered bunks, which looked very uncomfortable, furnished with no or inadequate bedding. Stories were told about what had taken place there during World War II. The whole experience was overwhelming and literally made me sick to my stomach, as I thought about the awful suffering that had taken place there.

After that, we drove on just a mile or two to visit the Church of the Black Madonna, which was truly a Holy Place. This image of Our Blessed Mother is thought to have been carved from the dining table the Holy family used when Jesus was living at home as a young boy. It is called the Black Madonna, because over the years, that piece of wood has darkened from use and misuse. Here we celebrated Mass with this sculpture visible to us. This was a very special event, because, usually, this carving is not displayed for viewing, except for only a few hours each week. Most of the time, it is retained in this place, invisible, and secured behind sliding panels above the altar to protect and safe-guard it.

The contrast between these two places is enormous; one place is filled with the horrors of the concentration camp with suffering and evil, and the other one is a precious, special shrine, filled with peace, and holiness. Yet they are only few miles apart.

I have many wonderful memories of this very special trip. John held up very well during this month long trip. There were times during the long bus trips when he would ask, "Why are we taking a bus through Indiana? To go and see the farm?" But I think that when he dozed and then woke up, he didn't remember where we were and was confused. Parts of the landscape did remind me of Indiana, so I could see why he might have thought that. I was concerned that John might get separated from me and the tour, and since he did not speak the language, it might be very frightening and tragic. So I was very careful that this did not happen.

In Poland, we did visit the church where Sister Faustina had her vision of the Merciful Jesus with healing rays of light radiating from His Person. It was a very special visit, because we learned more about her life and visited where she had lived and worked.

Coming back into Austria, we visited the overseas campus of the University of Steubenville, which is a beautiful place. It was on this trip somewhere in Poland that we purchased the marionettes that we used for skits during summer camp.

When we returned to Vienna, the tour included a one day city tour to view the important churches and sites in that area. Since we had done that trip prior to joining this tour, we decided to take the train to Graz, Austria, instead. I remembered that John's dad had spoken highly of Graz. He had told me many times that if we ever traveled to this area, we should be sure to go to Graz and see the glockenspiel, which is in this town's square. This was where he was sent as a very young boy of about thirteen years old to work as an apprentice in shoemaking.

The travel agent had purchased a month long Euro-pass for trains for us, so we inquired and found that we could use these passes for the train to Graz and back with plenty of time for lunch and a walk around that area, so we decided do this instead. It was a great thrill to see this area. Yes, the glockenspiel still does its thing every hour, and at noon every day. It is really a dramatic event. Really, it is quite a special performance. We could appreciate how entertaining it must have been for John's dad. This was a special highlight for us.

We had a pleasant flight home, weren't too tired, and I loved all the wonderful experiences we had on these two trips. After we arrived safely back in Bloomfield, I thanked God for all the blessings we had traveling through all of these countries, but I decided that this would have to be our last trip to a foreign country. Given John's health, it was too risky to attempt it again.

Following this trip, I decided to look into the possibility of treatment for John at Mayo Clinic in Jacksonville, Florida. It is about a four hour drive from Fort Myers to Jacksonville. We drove up on Sunday, taking it leisurely, by stopping frequently, once for lunch and later for a little refreshment. We had reservations at the hotel, which was just across the street from the clinic. His appointment was for 8:00 a.m. on Monday.

When we checked in at the clinic, we found that he was scheduled for x-rays, and following that, there was an appointment for additional tests and examinations. Then, at the conclusion, there was an appointment with the Head of Neurology Department. He told us that the x-rays showed definite damage to his brain, typical of Alzheimer's. I reported that both his mother and father had the same type of disorder. He agreed that there was strong evidence that this condition is hereditary.

Unfortunately, he had no medication to recommend for treatment. There was a new medication that had just come out that was somewhat effective in the early stages, but he really didn't think it would help John, as he was in middle stages at this point in time. If we wanted to try it, he would write a prescription for it. Since there was nothing else, we decided to give it a try. John could not tolerate it, so we had to discontinue its use.

The doctor did suggest that we call the Fort Myers office of Medical Study, as he thought that soon trials would begin on a new medication. Sadly, there were no other suggestions for treatment at the time.

We did participate in several studies in the next couple of years, but they were "blind studies", which means that we were never told if he was receiving the real meds or the placebo. John did not show any improvement when he took part in these studies. But we felt that at least we were helping the research in a small way by his participation.

In early spring of the next year when we returned to Michigan, I realized we had arrived in time for me to attend an Altar Guild Board meeting. It was fun to see many of my old friends and get caught up on the news. During the committee reports, the President announced that the Chairman for the Rummage Sale had resigned. She was concerned that the construction for the enlargement of the gym would not be done in time for this event. Without the gym, she could not envision how there would be enough space to conduct the sale. After much discussion, it seemed that the board might decide to discontinue this event permanently.

It was then that I spoke up and stated that I hoped this would not happen. This event is such a worthwhile project, and it is a blessing in at least three ways. One, it provides a great source of income for our charitable projects. Two, it makes it possible for families in need, to clothe their entire families for very little money. Three, this project provides a real opportunity for fellowship, because when you work that hard, side-by-side with other members of the parish in a sort span of time, you really get to know each other in a very special way. Surely, it may be possible to open additional classrooms or hallways to provide the needed space. Or if the construction is not completed in time, perhaps the date could be moved closer to the end of the summer.

It was decided that the President would try to find a new chairman for this event, but it was only two months before the scheduled date. Later, during coffee, the President took me aside and asked if I would be willing to serve as the rummage sale chairman.

My first thought was, *Oh, no! It would require a lot of time away from home. I wondered what John would think*! So I told her I would give it some thought. I would have to see if John would approve of my spending so much time on this project. While I was driving home, I prayed about it, but I felt sure that John would not like this idea.

When I returned, I told John all about it, and he surprised me that he was so supportive of this. He said that he would help me in whatever way that he could, so I called the president back and I agreed to chair this event.

The other chairmen of the various committees of the Rummage Sale were all in place, so I decided on whom to invite to be my co-chairman and called a first meeting of all these chair people. Before the meeting, I made an appointment to meet with the Principal of the School to get an up-date on the construction progress. She thought it might be done in time for the sale. We discussed it, and I suggested that if the gym floor was in place, the final finish of varnish could be done after the sale. There was a tarp to cover the gym floor when it was not in use, so that could be used to protect the floor during the sale. Things had progressed rapidly by the date of our first planning session.

One day when John and I were out shopping, I spotted a sign for a Rummage Sale in another church, which was in progress. We stopped in, hoping to get some new ideas for organizing this event. There I spotted some great shoe racks, which organized the shoes very well in three tiered racks, which took up less space and would be easy to take apart and store. John thought it would be easy to make some for our sale, so we looked at them carefully and later bought the materials. John completed them, six racks in all, in time for our sale.

The week of the sale arrived. John and I went together every day. John really enjoyed it, because he had a great time working with the other members of our parish. The sale turned out very well. All the extra space in the gym was a big help, and John's shoe racks worked out great. In the end, the sale set a new record high of well over twenty thousand dollars.

On the final day of the sale, it was open for only a half day. Everything was marked down drastically. Closing time was at noon when everything would be packed up and social service agencies would be there to take all of the leftovers.

At about 11:00 a.m. on that last day, I strolled up and down the gym between all those racks and silently prayed and thanked God for all His help during this project. When I paused, I heard him say, *Do you see that rack of coats over there?* As I nodded, He continued, *I want you to go over there and examine them thoroughly.*

I was surprised, as I did not need a new raincoat and neither did my daughter. But I walked over. Then He said, *"See that coat?"* I knew which one He had identified, and He said, *"Look in the pockets of that one."*

It really was a lovely coat. I took it off the rack and in one of the pockets I found a Fisher Theatre ticket stub and a twenty dollar bill. In the other pocket I found a very nice pair of hardly ever worn long, black leather gloves. I was stunned. All week long we had drilled all the workers to carefully empty all the pockets of clothing and all the contents of the purses.

Well, I knew what to do with the twenty dollars; I put it in the till, but I didn't know what to do with the leather gloves. It was much too late to put them out for sale. I didn't need them, as I had a new pair. Then He said, *Give them to your co-chairman.* So I did, and she was delighted, and they fit her "like a glove!"

I have thought about this incident many times and played it over in my mind and marveled that He took such great care of everything, even down to this tiny detail. Truly He knows everything! As it says in scripture, "On my own intelligence I will not rely, but I will trust only in the power of God, and His infinite knowledge and mercy!"

Later, John asked where we were going on our next trip. Then I said that I thought perhaps it was time for us to see some of the areas of our own country, which we had never visited. Later, we decided on a trip to visit many of our National Parks in the west. It started with a flight to Albuquerque, New Mexico, and would progress by bus to many of these National Parks, visiting the Grand Canyon, Bryce Canyon National Park, Yellowstone, and coming a little east to Mount Rushmore to see the carvings of US presidents depicted on the mountains, and ending in Denver. We would fly home from there.

It was a great trip, and it was so fortunate that we ended in Denver, because Bob, John's best friend growing up, who had been our best man at our wedding, lived there. We had arranged in advance to have dinner with Bob and his wife in the hotel. We had not seen them for many years, so that was a special visit.

The next year we went to Hawaii, and the following year, we went to Alaska. After that it was obvious that our traveling days were over. I was so thankful that we had been able to go on all those wonderful trips. John seemed to have enjoyed it all and we did not have any serious difficulties along the way.

But there were many signs this disease was continuing to destroy brain cells. There came a time when he couldn't find his car after playing golf. A friend of his drove him home. John and I drove back to the club parking lot in my car. We drove up and down until we found it. John was able to drive home by following me, but I knew that it was time to sell his car. What a wrench in our plans that was, and I had to tell John that I would be glad to drive him wherever he wanted to go from now on.

It was at that point that I started telling some of our close friends that John had Alzheimer's, which surprised them, as they had not noticed. He could always make some funny remark, so his illness was not so obvious. I wanted them to know that I was aware of it, so if they guessed it, they were assured that we were doing all that we could for him.

Shortly after that, one night, I knew that John had gotten up to go to the bathroom, but I suddenly realized that he had been in the bathroom a long time, so I got up to see if he was alright. He wasn't there! Just then I heard him coming in the front door. I asked him where he had been, and he said, "You know, that newspaper still isn't here!" It was only about 12:30 a.m.

The next few days I got busy and had a security system installed in our house and faithfully activated it when we went to bed and sometimes when I would be involved with something, so that he could be prevented from straying away and getting lost.

I came to realize that I should not leave him home alone any longer. I arranged to have someone come in to stay with him while I played golf or when I had to do other errands. I told John that we needed a helper now. It was a difficult time for both of us.

Later, he told me that he no longer wanted to play golf, as he did not enjoy it. I couldn't believe it and thought maybe he just needed a golf lesson to improve his game. So one Sunday I suggested we go out and just play nine holes. Then I realized he had no idea where the hole was, what club to use, or where his ball was after he hit it. I had to agree with him that it was time for him to give up golf.

He began to realize that he had problems. Every morning when we woke up, I would go out to the kitchen in my robe and start the coffee while John was in the shower. He would come out crying, every morning, saying he no longer could do things, and he was no longer a good husband for me.

I tried to think of what to say, to comfort him. I said, "Well, John, lots of people have prayed for you and still are praying for this. I'm sure things will be better soon." That did not help at all. Another morning I said, "You know, we went to Mayo Clinic, and, hopefully, they will soon call us to tell us that there is a new medication that will help you." That didn't comfort him. When the same thing happened yet another morning, I was stumped. I said, "John, I know that you can't help this. You know that both your Mother and your Father had the same thing, so you probably inherited it. It is not your fault."

Then his eyes widened, and he said, "That's right!" He turned this new thought over in his mind. He straightened up his shoulders and continued, "Well, if my dad could take it, I can take it, too!"

He never complained after that. It was amazing that he seemed to remember that fact and it helped him. I learned in situations where I felt helpless that I needed to keep trying, to find the right thing to say. The worst thing you can do is criticize a loved one suffering from memory loss, because they truly can't help it!

Later I heard about an adult daycare center. They were open five days a week, Monday through Friday from 8:00 a.m. until 6:00 p.m. The charge was the same daily rate, regardless of how long they were there, or you could sign up for the weekly rate and take them every day for those five days. During that time they were safe, entertained, and served a light lunch at noon.

After I had investigated this, I decided to try it. I told John that I had found a new Social Club for him to join, now that he wasn't playing golf. If he liked it, he could join, if not, we would make other plans.

Well, he liked it, so at first he went about three days a week, and it was evident that he enjoyed this, so he starting going for the five days. This worked for us for quite a long period of time. When we returned to Michigan for the summer, I located a similar adult day care center and arranged for him to attend. It brightened up many days for him.

I could see that there were changes, and it was becoming more and more difficult to go back and forth. I prayed about this and He confirmed it. Now was the time to make a change in our living arrangements. I decided to talk this over with John.

I began by saying to him, "It is getting more and more difficult for me to go back and forth. I have to close up one home and then open up the other one when we get there. I think it is time to pare down to one place and live in it all of the time. Where do you want it to be? Do you want Michigan full time or Florida full time?"

John answered promptly, "Why, I want to be in Florida!"

That summer we made our last trip to Michigan together. We sold our condo promptly, and I began planning what to take to Florida and what to do with all of the other furniture. At the end of summer we settled into our Florida home as our one and only home.

Our children and grandchildren traveled to visit us as often as they could. It was comfortable and big enough, so we had great times there. I continued to pray about the situation and asked Him to guide me every step of the way. I was hoping that John would suddenly receive a complete healing, but it was not happening.

After we settled in, I said to John, "We always said that when we decided to stop going back and forth, we would get a dog. Do you think that would be a good idea now?"

John thought about it and then he replied, "Yes! That would be great! I would like that."

So I started thinking about what breed would be best for us. I talked it over with a veterinarian. He suggested that I watch the newspaper for a dog that was two or three years old. That way, we would avoid all those puppy stages when they chew on everything or have accidents. In regard to breeds, he recommended poodles, as they are not likely to cause allergy problems and do not shed. He said he would call me if he heard of any such dog.

A few weeks later I saw an ad in the newspaper, so I went to investigate. Bingo. It was a three year old male, apricot toy poodle, about eight pounds, and very sweet tempered. The owner had been raising poodles and had two white females. She had a new job and would be traveling more, so she decided to stop raising poodles for a time and wanted to sell Toby.

I thought it over and went back the next day with John and brought Toby home with us. I told her I would take him to a vet the next day for a check-up. If he was not healthy, I would bring him right back. She agreed. And it turned out he was a wonderful, healthy dog and a good fit for us. We did have him neutered, as the vet recommended. He was a joy for us right from the start and lived to be nearly eighteen years old.

Toby sensed that John was the one who needed him most, so almost immediately, he was John's dog. They spent many hours together with John cuddling him on his lap. It was good to get out, and Toby liked to go for his walks. John and I with Toby on the leash enjoyed our little walk times. He was good company and continued to bring joy to both of us.

Big Changes Are Coming

L ater we made a second trip to Mayo to see if there were new medications or if there were new suggestions. After the tests were completed, we spent two hours with the Head of Neurology. He told us that there were no new meds he knew about that would help us. However, he stated that, in his opinion, in about ten years it would be possible to test the entire population and determine who was at risk for Alzheimer's and that there would be ways to prevent it from developing. He said that it was now possible to determine who was at risk. But it would be too upsetting for people to know that they were at risk without providing a solution to this problem. He advised us to return to Fort Myers and seek additional help as needed with a local neurologist there. It was just too difficult for us to make this trip again to Jacksonville. That was that! We both had tears in our eyes when we left.

Shortly after that visit, the staff at the day care center told me that John was too advanced and that he needed more care than they could give him. He no longer qualified for that level of care. I thought it over and prayed for direction and guidance. I did not want John to go into a nursing home. I wanted to care for him at home as long as possible. I looked into all possible alternatives.

I interviewed a company that supplied registered nurses for care in the home, so after considering all that was available, I decided that this would be best for both of us. At first, I employed nurses several times a week for a day, but soon it expanded to two shifts a day, every day. By this time, it took both of us to help him in and out of the shower each day.

Eventually, John had to be in a wheelchair, as walking was too risky and difficult. Then I rented a hospital bed, as he spent longer amounts of time there. It had side rails and I felt that he was safe from rolling out of bed at night. We had a large bedroom, so there was plenty of room for his bed in our bedroom. Once he was safely established in bed for the night, I could watch over him until the morning nurse arrived at seven.

By then, John had difficulty swallowing, so I pureed his food in the blender. I needed to help him, as it was too hard for him to feed himself, to hold the spoon, or a cup or glass.

The nurses were great, and we got along okay. I took some time to get out, and I did play some golf and bridge, but I carried a cell phone, so that I could return quickly if something was needed. Amazingly, John's spirits were very good. He never complained and slept well, so we got along okay.

Two years had gone by since we had last visited the Mayo Clinic. Then one day out of the blue, one of the nurses took me aside. She said, "We have been talking it over, and, if you want to continue to take care of him at home, it will be necessary for two nurses to be on every shift, and we think that soon, we will require two nurses to be present during the night-shift, as well, because of safety concerns."

I must have looked shocked and discouraged.

She continued, "We do not really recommend this as the best solution. We have been talking it over, and we think he would benefit from being in a nursing home, as he needs to be socialized. We advise you to look into a good nursing home. And don't make the mistake of asking for an Alzheimer's Care Unit, because, at this time, he needs skilled care nursing, as this is his level of care now. We don't think that it would be best for him to have a private room, as he would not be able to ring a bell. In a double room, for example, the nurses would be in that room twice as often. Perhaps his roommate would ring for him if he was having difficulty.

I was stunned and said, "I will have to think about all of this."

"Yes, of course. We have established our schedule for this month, so you have a little time to decide what you want to do," she responded.

John was asleep at that time, so I excused myself and went into the office to pray and consider all she said and perhaps make some phone calls. I realized that it was very difficult for one person to help him in and out of bed or in and out of his wheelchair, but usually I was there and helped. I helped the nurse to get him in and out of the shower. This request was not unreasonable, but still it came as a shock. To continue to have him at home with two extra people coming here all the time would be a terrific intrusion. Also, the cost would be huge!

I started to pray about all of it. I wondered what the cost of nursing home care was currently. I thought that I would check about this, so I called the nursing homes that I had previously checked and liked. When I explained my needs, they all said that they had no empty beds for a man at this time. So I looked in the phone book. I called every nursing home in the area, and it was the same story in all of them. Then I began calling in Cape Coral and finally in Naples. There seemed to be no empty beds anywhere near us. A feeling of panic was taking over me. I needed to start dinner for the nurse, John and me.

"Okay," I said to the Lord. "I will get back to you soon about this."

The day nurse and I got John up from his nap and she left. We had a wonderful nurse, a man from Jamaica who was strong and caring. He came every morning and evening for about three or four hours each visit to help us through the evening and morning routines. He usually came about five or six in the evening, had dinner with us, and then he would prepare John for bed for the night, leaving about 9:00 o'clock.

After he left that evening, I settled myself in my prayer chair in the living room and began to pray. I apologized to Him for running ahead of Him by calling all those nursing homes. Now, humbly I came to Him to seek His will. What decision should I make in this regard? Should I continue to care for John at home, or should I look for care for John in some facility, but where would this be? I wanted Him to tell me what plans to make. What was best for John? What was His will in regard to all of this?

I decided I would pray all night, if necessary, because I wanted to do only what He wanted me to do. I prayed and prayed. I thanked Him for all His help. I prayed the rosary, read scripture, and prayed some more.

I checked on John, and he was sleeping peacefully. I returned to my prayer chair and continued to pray again. I had confidence that He would show me what to do in this regard. I read again that passage from Matthew 7:11: "Ask and you will receive, seek and you will find." I continued to pray and pray. I prayed another rosary, read scripture, and prayed....

About four o'clock in the morning, I woke with a start as a cool breeze floated through the room. *Oh! I must have fallen asleep.* I thought. *Did someone open an outside door? What is happening?*

Then I heard His voice, *Don't be afraid. I am here with you. I have heard your prayers. You can go to bed now. It has all been taken care.*

"But what am I to do?" I replied.

"*You can go to bed now. It has all been taken care of,*" He repeated.

"But that is not an answer." I replied. "What am I to do about this?"

"*You can go to bed now. It has all been taken care of.*" He repeated, speaking more slowly, kindly, and clearly.

"Oh! I am sorry!' I responded. "I thank you....Yes, I will go to bed now. I place my trust in You. Thank You."

I got ready for bed, checked on John, and fell asleep promptly.

I woke at the usual time, rested and refreshed. I hopped out of bed and got dressed before the nurse arrived at 7:00 a.m. as usual. We went through our normal morning routine of getting John through the shower, dressed and back in the wheelchair. He shaved John while I dashed to the kitchen to make the coffee and prepare our breakfasts.

While we were eating breakfast about 8:30, the phone rang. It was the office manager from one of the nursing homes, which I had talked with, the night before.

She said, "I wanted to call you first. We had a death last night, about 4:00 a.m. in the morning. This will free up a male bed. It can be yours, if you still want it. We have others on the waiting list, so, you are under no obligation to take it if you have made other arrangements. But I remembered you, and your need seemed to be urgent."

I said a silent prayer of thanksgiving, and replied, "Thank you! Yes, I still want this. What do I do? Come in and fill out forms? When are you available?"

She said, "I will be here until five, so come when it is convenient for you."

I was so relieved! Now I knew that this was what I was supposed to do. He had answered my prayers!

Once when I shared this story of how God provides, someone asked, "And what about the guy in bed who died?"

I said, "I don't really know, but perhaps he had been knocking at the Pearly Gates for months seeking to enter."

When the day nurse arrived, I left to go to the nursing home. I filled out all the forms. They told me that the two bedroom would be ready in about three days, as they needed to deep clean this area and the personal items from the previous patient had to be removed. Also, we would need to have John get a chest x-ray to make sure that he did not have TB. This was to comply with state laws. We set the day for his admittance. A transport vehicle was arranged to transport him, first from our house to the x-ray appointment and then on to the nursing home. I would follow this vehicle, so that I would be with John through this entire process. I could no longer take John in my car, as it was too difficult for me to get him in and out of the car, alone.

I informed the Home Nurse Agency that I had made these plans, and when the final day would be in this regard. During the next couple of days, I did not tell John in advance, because he would not be able to remember, or, if he did, it might confuse or worry him.

So on that morning when John would be admitted, we had finished our morning routine of showering and breakfast. Then I explained to John that today, I had arranged for him, to try out a new facility to take care of him. We would give it a five day trial period. If he really did not like it there, I would make other arrangements. John was satisfied with this, so the vehicle arrived, and off we went.

It all worked out very well. His x-rays were normal, as I was sure they would be. Then we went on to the nursing home, and he was admitted. I had brought the clothes he would need for a few days, and we went about the new facility, getting acquainted with it all. During the next few days, I went to see John every day for lunch and helped by feeding him. Afterwards, I would take him in the wheelchair outside on the patio for a little visit. On about the fourth day, I couldn't wait any longer. I asked John how he liked it there.

He replied, "I…..I am glad…that you…don't have to do it anymore." I was so relieved. That was quite an endorsement. Actually, I could tell that he had adjusted very well to this new situation. Perhaps he really needed to have this facility now at this time in his illness. It was so kind of him to want to save me the effort of taking intimate care of him.

The first few weeks were difficult for me, but soon I was confident that this was the right choice for us. John enjoyed being with the other people. There was lots of activity swirling around him and things to watch or participate in. Several times a month, groups of people would come in to entertain with music or group singing. Sometimes a dance group would arrive and perform a routine with great style in full costumes. Other times, a piano player would arrive and play "Name This Tune" with the group. It was amazing to me that John was able to name most of the songs from the 40's, sometimes before I could think of them. John really enjoyed all of this.

I learned that once a month, a Catholic Mass was celebrated in the auditorium in the afternoon on Sunday. What a blessing that was, as this was familiar and comforting for John. I knew of no other nursing home in the area that did this. Also, he received the Eucharist once a week, usually on Fridays.

In a short period of time I felt confident that this was the right choice for me, as well as John. But our house seemed empty without John, and I missed him terribly. I was so glad that I had Toby. Now he turned to me and became my dog. When I returned home, it was not to an empty house, as Toby was always there to give me a great greeting, and of course, we went for nice long walks together. But it was a huge adjustment for me. When I entered the family room the spot where John and his wheelchair used to be seemed empty without him.

I was a little uncomfortable at night. Of course I still used the security system, but I did check all of the outside doors every night to make sure that they were all locked.

When I swam up and down the pool every day, it was Toby watching me instead of John in his wheelchair. Poodles do not like to go swimming, so that was a good thing. Thank goodness for Toby, as he was a great comfort to me now. He was the reason for me to get up early to take him for his walks, which was also good for me. Toby started to sleep in my room now instead of the laundry room where he had slept before this. I accepted this, because I felt more secure with him there with me. It was better than being all alone in that big, empty room.

Still, it was terribly lonely without John. This was not surprising, because, after all, we had been married for over fifty years. It had been a wonderful, loving fifty years!

I did go and spend some time with John every day. Sometimes I would go in the morning and stay and feed him lunch. Other times I came at lunch time and then took him out on the patio for a visit. Other times if I had appointments, I might go in the later afternoon and stay for dinner before returning home. Toby could be left alone for quite a long interval.

One day the head nurse took me aside and told me that the nurses were concerned about his difficulty in swallowing. The doctor suggested that x-rays could be taken to rule out the possibility that there was some sort of blockage there. She asked me if I would consent for these x-rays to be taken.

I answered, "Yes, I will consent, on one condition. That it will be scheduled at a time when I could go along with him, as I am concerned that John would be anxious about being driven away unless I was with him."

She said, "Of course. Let's go into my office now and schedule it at a time that works for you." And it was all arranged.

When that day came, I arrived in plenty of time and rode with him in the transport vehicle. At the place where the x-rays would be taken, the driver helped John in his wheelchair, down the ramp and helped us go into the waiting room. I would call him when we were ready to return.

When John was settled in a comfortable place, I said, "You stay here. I need to go to the desk and turn in your paper work."

I had my back to John when I said to the desk clerk, "John is here. He may look like he knows what is going on, and he may sound like he knows what is happening, but he has severe, short term memory loss. If you explain a lot of things that will take place, he will be confused and not be of any help to you. Just tell him one thing at a time and he will cooperate with you. Also, when you need him to stand up, he will need help, as he is a dead weight and really can't stand alone. You will need at least one or two strong men to get him up on the table. If not, someone may get hurt."

"Oh, I'm so glad you told me. It will all be taken care of," she said.

Sure enough, later, when we went back to the x-ray room, there were two strong men there to help John.

One of them said, "Now, John, first, we are going to stand you up."

"That's okay," John replied. "I've been stood up before."

They both laughed spontaneously and looked at me as if to say, "There can't be much the matter with this guy!"

John had a way about him. He could always come up with little one-liners, in order to put people at ease with him. Most would never guess he had memory problems.

The x-rays showed no throat problems. Soon, we returned safely back at the nursing home.

Our children and grandchildren came down as often as they could, as I wanted to stay here and see John at least once a day. I did go up for special occasions like graduations. I tried to limit my visits to three days. On the travel day up, I would take Toby to the sitter, stop and see John at the nursing home, and then drive on to the airport and fly up. On the travel day in return, after I arrived, I would go directly to visit John and then pick up Toby and return home. That way, I only missed one day not seeing him.

John had been in the nursing home for about a year and a half when I was returning from such an event. After I was settled comfortably in my seat, I closed my eyes to avoid a lot of casual chit-chat. I decided to first have some prayer time and then doze a little on the trip back, as I was feeling tired from the wonderful visit I had with the family.

Later, while I was resting, I heard him say, *Now it is time for you to sell your home.*

I thought, *What? Really! Well, yes, it is rather large for just Toby and me. But where would I go? I need extra space when the family comes for visits. And we do enjoy the pool.*

It is time to sell your house, He repeated.

Okay, I thought. *You always know what is best. Well, if that is what You want me to do, I will do it. I will get started on this, as soon as possible.*

After I was settled back in my routine, I called several real estate agents. They all told me the same thing. They thought my house would sell well, but I should wait to sign a contract, as during the summer there was not much activity. They all thought it would be better to sign up in early October. My next door neighbor was an agent and she told me the same thing, but in the meantime, she suggested I clean all my closets so that I would be ready to show it in the fall.

After that, during my prayer time, I would hear, *Now I want you to sell your house.*

"Yes." I would say. "I will, but I have decided to wait until fall to put it on the market."

Every day, I would have the same conversation with Him. Finally, I said, "Look. It seems best to me that I should wait until October to do this. But if You think I should do this sooner then just go ahead and do it. I give You full authority."

Two days after that, I go a phone call from my next door neighbor, the real estate agent. She said, "A client is here from up North. What they described as the kind of home they are looking for has all the features your home has. Would you be willing to show it to them?"

"Yes." I told her. "But I haven't cleaned all my closets yet."

"Oh, don't worry about that. Your house is always clean. I want you to take Toby and all his dishes and bedding and go for a drive. I don't know them well, but some people don't like to buy a house where a dog has lived. Would tomorrow morning about 10:00 a.m. be okay," she asked.

"Sure. That will be fine. We will leave before that." And we did.

I had some errands to do, like banking that I could do from the drive-in window, and then we drove up to the post office to mail some letters. About an hour and a half later, I drove by my house, but cars were in the driveway, so we went for a longer drive. I stopped at a drive-in and got a hamburger and shared some of it with Toby. When I came back to the house, the cars were still there, so we went to a park where I could take Toby out for a little walk.

After more than three hours, we returned, and I could see them getting into their cars, so I drove on and circled around a bit more. Then when we returned, they were gone! Hmmm, well, well, well. They must be interested.

Yes they were! And they were the ones that bought our house.

A few days later, the Realtor presented the contract, which was for my asking price.

I said, "This is wonderful, but where am I going to live? I really haven't researched this yet, but I have been thinking about buying in The Fairway Woods Condos."

"I know of just the one. I think you will really like it."

So it all worked out perfectly. Closing was scheduled for two months later in the last week of September. I closed on both properties the same day, one in the morning and the other in the afternoon. I planned to move in the next day.

It was a busy time for me. I arranged for a mover and started packing. I packed the dishes and all the little stuff. Of course I went to see John every day and took Toby for nice long walks.

I told the children what I was doing. Janet and Joe both arranged to come down and help me through the move. It was wonderful to have them here to help me on the actual moving day.

It all worked out very well. Toby didn't seem to mind at all. Surprisingly, I moved all the furniture, except for a few pieces of patio furniture. The window treatments were all in place, and the carpets from the previous owner were fine. I was surprised at how well all our furniture fit in this condo.

This condo was a two story town house. Upstairs were two bedrooms and a full bathroom. Overlooking the two story living room was a sitting room where I placed the leather sofa and side chair, which we had in the family room before. I put the game table up there, also. It was fun to play cards up there or watch TV. I planned to have some book shelves built there with room for a TV on one of the shelves.

Downstairs, there was a small entry way where the front door was. On that level, there was the large, fully appointed kitchen, including an eating area. The room that I used as my office was furnished with my desk, computer, and sofa bed. So it could also serve as another bedroom.

Going straight back was a nice sized dining room and then the large living room with a corner fireplace. It seemed larger than it really was, as it was a two-story room. In the back was a rather small but pleasant screened-in porch. Off the living room was the master bedroom with a very nice walk-in-closet and full bath. There was a half bath off the living room. I knew that Toby and I would be very comfortable here. It wouldn't seem so lonesome, large, and empty, as our house had been. Most of the time, we would function on the first floor. But when the children and grandchildren came, there was plenty of room for them upstairs.

I marveled at how all this had been accomplished in such a short time. Thank you, Lord! It was early October, and the move had been completed. Joe and Janet were wonderful helpers. By the time they went back, everything was in place and working well like the computer and TVs. The pool was the condo pool just a short distance from our house, so Toby was never invited to go, but he didn't mind, as he took a nap while I went.

I realized I would be very well settled by Christmas time. I would have plenty of time to arrange for the bookshelves, to do my cards, and make plans for the family visits. All of the children and grandchildren were planning to come down for a visit at that time. How wonderful it would be. Perhaps I could arrange to rent another condo for one of the families, but it would be great to have them all here for meals and games and party time.

I thought how nice it would be if John could come out for the day on Christmas Day, and we would all be together. I talked it over with the nurses who cared for John. But they definitely thought it would be a mistake to take John out of where he was now, as he had adjusted very well. Also he had never lived in this new place, so it would all be strange and puzzling for him. So I decided not to try it. But I knew that we would all spend time with him at the nursing home. Maybe it would be better to take turns and not overwhelm him with all of us at once.

I had a thought from time to time that if John were suddenly healed, how great it would be! I thought that he would really like it here. There was always hope that this would happen.

The holiday plans all came together very well. The children arranged to come at different times but overlap one day so that everyone was here for a nice visit. For Thanksgiving, Jim came down for his birthday about a week before Thanksgiving. Janet and Jim over lapped a day or two. Jim went back and Janet was here for Thanksgiving Day. It was so nice to see them and they really liked my new place.

Christmas came and went with Joe and Linda and family here, arriving a few days after Christmas. They had spent Christmas day with her family. Jack and his family came, and it was great for everyone to see where I was now and visit with John. Of course, Janet and Jim came at Christmastime, too.

In the New Year, I found myself more active at the club with golf, bridge, and with the prayer group at the church. Of course I still visited John every day and spent several hours with him. He was slipping a little but continued to enjoy the activities at the Nursing Home. They were taking wonderful care of him. When he saw me coming in the door, his face would light up like a Christmas tree, but sometimes the same thing would happen when a favorite nurse would come by. It was nice to know that John still recognized the people that he saw frequently. At least I knew that John was contented there and well cared for, which is so important and comforting.

The days flew by and I was relatively happy and busy. Easter was the second Sunday in April. Janet called and said she would be coming down for Easter and John's 77th birthday! How lovely! We had a grand visit and went to visit John every day. The day Janet returned, we visited him in the morning and then we went out for lunch. I took her to the airport for an afternoon flight back to Michigan. I returned home and decided not to visit John again that day. We had just seen him that morning, and I wanted to do the laundry and get the condo in order, as I had a busy schedule for the next few days.

The next day Toby and I got up early as usual, so I took him for a nice walk. After we had breakfast, I left to go and visit John before I went on to my dentist appointment and to do other errands.

When I arrived at the Nursing Home, I went into the morning room where I would usually find John watching TV with the others, but he wasn't there! I was shocked! I decided to go and see if he was in his room when a staff member stopped me in the hall.

She said that she was on her way to her office to call me. She told me that when the nurses were getting him up that morning, they realized he was feverish and had difficulty breathing. The doctor had been called, and he said that John had pneumonia. Medicine had been prescribed, and he was now resting comfortably while receiving oxygen.

I rushed down to his room to see him. I was shocked. I had seen him yesterday, and now, 24 hours later, he was so ill! He had been well the day before. Now he was breathing unevenly and seemed to be sound asleep.

She suggested we step out in the hall to talk. She went on to say that several other patients had come down with colds. If I wanted him to be hospitalized, he qualified for the transfer.

I asked, "Would they be able to do something more for him than is already being done here?"

"No." She replied. "But Medicare would pay for the hospital bills for his stay, and, if he comes along well, when he returned, Medicare would pay the bills for several weeks while he recovered here. The only difference was that there would be doctors immediately available if he needed them."

I was having trouble deciding what would be best for John. I thought, *In the hospital he would be in a strange room, with nurses he did not know caring for him. When he was awake, maybe he would be upset, not knowing what was happening or where he was. I wouldn't be able to be with him all of the time.*

"Well, you think it over, and come to my office if you want to make a change." And she was gone.

What to do? I went in and sat in the chair near John and prayed. Thoughts were whirling around in my mind. *This is not a financial decision,* I thought. The deciding factor is what is best for John and where he would be the most comfortable and most likely to make a good recovery. I stayed for about an hour and gently talked to John, told him I loved him, and encouraged him to get better and breathe better. He continued to breathe audibly, and the hum of the oxygen was monotonous and made me feel sleepy. He seemed to be comfortable and was not anxious or in pain.

His day nurse came in. She said that she would be keeping a close watch over him. Eventually, I decided to go to my dentist appointment and would return after that to see if there was any change.

After thinking it through, I decided that the best thing for John was for him to stay here, as everything would be familiar to him. I was very concerned, though, as I thought it might go either way. When I returned home, I called all the children to let them know that John had taken a turn for the worse. Janet wanted to fly right back down, but I said it would be better for her to stay where she was but to get caught up on all the paper work at the office. I would call her if there was any major change.

During that day and the next, I decided to try to keep to my regular schedule. I planned to go down two or three times a day to spend an hour or two at a time with John. I could leave Toby for a four hour period with no problems. It seemed that every time I was there, John was sleeping. I talked to his nurse about his condition, and she said that the doctor checked on him daily. It could go either way. I was very worried and concerned. I prayed and prayed and put it all in His hands.

I did go to the club that day, as there was a special luncheon for our bridge group. I told them about this new development with John.

Later one of my very close friends took me aside, and said, "Look, if you get the call in the middle of the night, please call me, and I'll come and be with you to drive you there. I don't want you to drive down there in the middle of the night under these circumstances. For that matter, call me on my cell phone, and I will be there for you, day or night."

I thanked her, but I thought that it was not going to be necessary. John will get better. He has a strong heart and lungs. The doctors always told me this. Then she asked me to promise her that I would call her, so I agreed.

I went to see John again that afternoon and his night nurse, dropped by to talk with me. I had never met her before. She said that she was in the building and wanted to tell me that she would be on duty that evening, and that it was not necessary for me to stay all night. She had been caring for him for some time. She said she would call me if there is any change.

Later I left, as I needed to walk Toby. At home, I decided not to go back there again tonight. I would rest and go to see him the first thing in the morning. I felt that he was in good hands. His nurses knew him, and John would recognize them, as he was used to them. Yes, it was best to not disturb him in this situation. He was better off to be right where he was.

That night at 3:00 a.m. in the morning I got "the call". I called my friend and quickly dressed. Toby went back to sleep. By the time I was ready, my friend arrived. We were off. It was so comforting to have her with me. When we got there, John had passed. The nurse told me that they had notified the funeral home and that they would be there shortly. I sat in the chair next to John and patted him. I thought about how peaceful he looked. Oh, how I would miss him. He had been such a great husband and we had such wonderful times together. I prayed silently to please give me the strength to somehow get through this and to do all the things I should because John deserved to have everything done just right.

In due time, the funeral home people came, and they knew just what to do and say. I assured them that I would be in touch with them the next day. Before long we were on our way back home. It was so comforting to have my friend with me that night. I thanked her and in no time, I was in my robe, sitting in my prayer chair in my bedroom.

I was wide awake and decided to use this time to pray and plan what I needed to do when morning dawned. I made a list: called all of the children, called the Church and started the funeral preparations. I made an appointment to see the funeral director and looked at my calendar to see if I needed to cancel any appointments.

As I prayed, I remembered about the night that John and I had talked about our funerals. I was so thankful that we did have that talk. One evening after John and I had definitely decided to take early retirement, I said that it was time for us to talk about what we each wanted when we passed on. Immediately, John stated emphatically, "I never want to talk about that!"

I insisted that I needed to talk about the funeral arrangements because recently a friend of mine had been on a trip overseas with her husband, when he had a sudden, fatal heart attack. But fortunately she knew what her husband's wishes were in this regard. Since we are making plans for our future retirement, this should be discussed as well.

Finally John agreed but insisted that this would be the only time we were ever going to discuss this topic. The discussion started, but after talking about some of these things and possible alternatives, we began to realize how difficult it is to plan, because we did not know when or where we would be or when this might happen. How could we decide where burial would be when we didn't know where we might be living at the time we passed? Also, now the church recognized that cremation was acceptable. Did either of us want that?

Then John turned the question to me and asked, "What do you want? Have you thought about it?"

I said, "Well, what is most important to me is that I want my body to be present for a funeral Mass. I think it is a nice closure for our lives and good for those left behind. And I want and need all those prayers. But after that, I really don't care.

As to the final resting place, I think it should be up to those left behind to decide where this is to be. They may want a place they can visit conveniently. Whether it is at a cemetery or at a columbarium doesn't really matter to me. After all, our bodies are just our shells. I don't care where the burial takes place or if there is cremation where the ashes are placed. But I would like to be placed wherever you are placed because at the Second Coming, when Jesus returns to earth, we will be reunited with our glorified bodies. Then I want to be where you are."

John said, "Yes, I want that, too." So in the end, we decided that whoever was left behind could decide all of the other things but that the most important thing was to have a funeral Mass with the body present.

It was comforting to know that John would be satisfied with whatever we all decided. I started feeling sleepy. I knew that it all was in His hands. He would help us all in the coming days and years.

Suddenly I was wide awake again, because I realized, "John, you have been released from your body and now you are free! How wonderful for you!"

I recalled that feeling from that time I had my "out of this world experience." I could think much more clearly and quickly, and my awareness and knowledge was wonderfully strong and vibrant. Oh, Johnnie, I am so happy for you! Now you have been set free from your body, which no longer functioned properly. Now you are able to think quickly and remember accurately! Oh, Honey, I wish I could be with you, and we could celebrate all of this, together! I will be with you when He tells me it's time. Oh, Honey, how wonderful for you! What marvelous experiences are waiting for you! Your time of difficulty is over! You did get your healing, a complete healing! Congratulations! Know that I love you."

I praised Him and thanked Him for releasing John from the prison of his malfunctioning body.

Shortly, the morning sun was shining in my bedroom window. I made all those calls as soon as it seemed right, according to the time zones. Before the day was over, all my children were with me to help in making the final preparations for John. The wives and grandchildren would come later, after all the plans were made.

Our life together is over for now, I thought. I knew that I would miss him terribly, and there would be difficult times to come. But with His help, everything will work out well! He has promised this, for those who trust in the Lord. And I do place my trust in You, now and for always.

Final Thoughts

I hope you enjoyed "My Story". It truly happened much as I have written it. But I want to clarify a few things. I do not think that I am special in any way, because I heard Him or He talked with me. God has no favorites. He loves us all, and He is available to all of us. And that means everyone! When you really spend time with Him, you really get to know Him.

It is just like that with your friends. When you spend time with them, you really get to know them and all their likes and dislikes. God already knows you. After all, He made all of us. He knows our strengths and weaknesses, talents and shortcomings. But do you know Him? If you want to know Him, you can read about Him in Scripture and take courses in the Bible or Scripture classes. You will make your own discoveries. Spend time with Him in prayer, and you will really get to know Him!

One of my favorite passages is Matthew 7:11. (I love this Scripture, and I believe it is so true! I easily remember the verse because of the number of the chapter and verse: "seven-eleven".) I invite you to read it for yourself, but basically this passage says, "Ask, and you **will** receive, Seek, and you **will** find, Knock and the door **will** be opened for you."

Our Heavenly Father, like most of our earthly fathers, knows what is really best for us. Take the time to get to know Him. When you do, you will be glad to place your trust in Him in all things, everywhere and in every circumstance. And eventually, when we finally get to heaven and spend all eternity with Him, then you will understand Him well! And remember that the Message is Joy. He **will** fill you with His peace and joy.

Oh, what wonders He has waiting for us, "that eye has not seen, nor ear has not heard', Oh, think of all that beauty and wonderful music! GOD BLESS ALL OF YOU!!

Made in the USA
Charleston, SC
19 December 2014